The Cornerstones to Early Literacy

*Childhood experiences that promote learning
in reading, writing, and oral language*

Katherine Luongo-Orlando

Pembroke Publishers Limited

For Issabella and Deanna,
The childhood adventures we shared in literature, language, and play were my best
moments and lessons.

© **2010 Pembroke Publishers**
538 Hood Road
Markham, Ontario, Canada L3R 3K9
www.pembrokepublishers.com

Distributed in the U.S. by Stenhouse Publishers
480 Congress Street
Portland, ME 04101
www.stenhouse.com

We acknowledge the financial support of the Government of Canada through the Book
Publishing Industry Development Program (BPIDP) for our publishing activities.

We acknowledge the assistance of the Government of Ontario through the Ontario
Media Development Corporation's Ontario Book Initiative.

Library and Archives Canada Cataloguing in Publication

Luongo-Orlando, Katherine
    The Cornerstones to Early Literacy : childhood experiences
that promote learning in reading, writing and
oral language / Katherine Luongo-Orlando

Includes index.
ISBN 978-1-55138-257-9

1. Language arts (Elementary). 2 English language—study and teaching
(Elementary). I. Title

LB1576.L858 2010   372.6'044   C2010-939838-2

Editors: Jane McNulty and Paul McNulty
Cover Design: John Zehethofer
Typesetting: Jay Tee Graphics Ltd.

Printed and bound in Canada
9 8 7 6 5 4 3 2 1

FSC
Mixed Sources
Product group from well-managed
forests and other controlled sources
Cert no. SW-COC-002358
www.fsc.org
© 1996 Forest Stewardship Council

Contents

Introduction

Watching children grow, play, and explore the world around them brings joy and insights into how they really learn. Children are marvelous inventors who use imagination and creativity to make up games, create music, craft adventures, and build language. From an early age, youngsters grow to become sophisticated language learners and users who discover their own rules and practices for spoken and written language. The road to reading and writing is marked by many events that enable children to become literate. Literacy develops from simple childhood experiences such as banging on pots and pans, making crayon markings on a page, reciting songs and verses, and climbing onto an adult's lap to listen to a story. This book explores the many pathways to literacy.

Building a strong foundation for literacy learning and language development starts with the play episodes, oral language practices, word play activities, print encounters, reading events, and writing experiences of children in their early years. These events are the cornerstones to literacy upon which this resource is based. The pages ahead are filled with early literacy strategies and language activities for children in the formative years from pre-K through Grade 3. Some of these encounters take learning outside of the home and classroom. This allows youngsters to discover print and use literacy in the play environment, as well as in broader cultural and community contexts. These practices build on the meaningful events that children participate in naturally before they begin formal education.

Literacy before Schooling

Children come into literacy long before schooling begins (Ferreiro and Teberosky, 1982; Y. M. Goodman, 1984, 1986; Teale and Sulzby, 1986; Hall, 1987; Clay, 1991). From an early age, youngsters learn about oral language, reading, writing, and print by actively participating in literacy events in the home and local community (Y.M. Goodman, 1984). Many children can recognize print, recite the alphabet, handle books, use materials to write, and demonstrate other literacy behaviors before being taught. Factors including ethnicity, socio-economic status, religion, home environment, family practices, and individual differences may influence children's early literacy development. Nonetheless, all youngsters become literate by growing up in a literate society (Y.M. Goodman, 1984).

Literacy comes from a child's language encounters and social interactions that first take place in the real-world settings of family life and community living (Y. M. Goodman, 1984; Teale and Sulzby, 1986). Through active participation in real-life activities such as shopping, banking, and cooking, children learn how reading, writing, and oral language (listening, speaking) fit into their world and

---

Building a strong foundation for literacy learning and language development starts with the play episodes, oral language practices, word play activities, print encounters, reading events, and writing experiences of children in their early years.

support daily living. Children's experiences with literacy in the everyday social environment shape their understanding of language and concepts of reading and writing. Within these social contexts, literacy is influenced by cultural factors that are determined by the groups children grow up in (Hall, 1987). Social and cultural events provide rich, authentic, and meaningful experiences for children to learn and use language every day. Acknowledging the importance of these early language experiences will help teachers build on the foundations that children have already established.

Understanding Emergent Literacy—Early Literacy Behaviors

Children's social interactions in family and community settings lay the groundwork for language learning and literacy development. Youngsters find occasions to learn about language every day. The process of learning to read, write, and become literate happens even before children pick up a pencil or book.

Researchers have studied many aspects of early childhood literacy development prior to schooling (Durkin, 1966; Bissex, 1980; Ferreiro and Teberosky, 1982; Y. M. Goodman, 1967, 1984, 1986; Hartse, Woodward, and Burke, 1984; Teale and Sulzby, 1986; Hall, 1987; Clay, 1966, 1991). These works have given us a new perspective for understanding the process of literacy development in early childhood. According to this view, the course of literacy learning has extended to include the years in early childhood where language is just beginning to emerge. The time in a young child's life when literacy starts to develop has become known as the period of *emergent literacy* (Clay, 1966; 1991).

Emergent literacy marks the ongoing developmental process during which young children begin to understand and use language from birth until independence, typically to eight years of age (Burke, 2010). This period stretches into the primary years when conventional reading and writing fall into place. During this time, young children start to explore literacy and experiment with language by engaging actively in the world around them. They begin to demonstrate genuine actions and behaviors that are important signs of literacy development. As young children do so, early reading, writing, speaking, and listening develop consistently alongside one another (Jones and Crabtree, 1999). These are some of the literacy-like behaviors that begin to emerge:

- From a young age, children produce marks on paper in the act of scribbling and drawing that resemble writing (Ferreiro and Teberosky, 1982).
- Youngsters pick up books, turn pages, and pretend to read stories using book language (Doake, 1988).
- Children use reading, writing, and language during play to carry out imaginary social roles and occupations (e.g., mother, server, store clerk, or doctor) (Y. M. Goodman, 1984).
- Youngsters notice signs, labels, and print in the spaces around them (Goodman and Goodman, 1979).
- Children try out invented spelling in the cards, letters, and notes they begin to write (Read, 1975; Bissex, 1980; Martens, 1996).
- Youngsters play with language in traditional songs, playground verses, and nursery rhymes they grow to love.
- Children learn to use words such as *read, write, pencil, story,* and *book* to describe the literacy events they engage in (Y. M. Goodman, 1984).

Young people come to know literacy through meaningful social interactions they have at home and in the community. Children's earliest language lessons begin by watching adults model reading and writing (Teale and Sulzby, 1986). As youngsters participate in life experiences, they start to develop literacy and language practices through their own discoveries and investigations too (Y. M. Goodman, 1984; Teale and Sulzby, 1986). These early rehearsals and reenactments provide vital insight into children's growing literacy knowledge and abilities. Although the language skills that children use in this period may be unconventional by adult standards, the processes and understandings that begin to emerge are important in children's overall literacy development.

The literacy knowledge and reading- and writing-like behaviors that youngsters demonstrate during this time are essential to language learning and contribute significantly to conventional reading and writing later on (McGee and Purcell-Gates, 1997). The insights and practices that children gain from authentic and purposeful hands-on activities with language and literacy in everyday life build the social meanings and cognitive processes necessary to do the academic work of reading and writing in later years (Roskos and Christie, 2001). This view of language learning grows out of an emergent literacy perspective that gives value and legitimacy to the period of early childhood during which literacy development happens before school. Understanding the emergent literacy process invites us into the world of young children and allows us to view and put into context the early attempts they make to construct knowledge and communicate.

Children as Language Learners

Many childhood experiences are at the heart of language learning in the early years of life—talking, playing, bedtime reading, art making, music, print encounters, and more. While these literacy events may guide the way to knowing, youngsters themselves play the key role in their literacy development. Children of all ages have an intrinsic desire to learn, explore, create, discuss, and communicate with others around them (Rinaldi, 1993; Elverenli, 2002). From a young age, children become multi-faceted learners able to develop their own literacy knowledge and skills. They discover many aspects of language (vocabulary, structure, meaning, usage) through various activities and personal interests that inform their understanding of oral language, reading, writing, and overall literacy even before they enter school.

argument

Understanding the process of literacy development means embracing the rich and powerful roles of young children as both teachers and learners who take charge of their own language achievements.

As youngsters participate in the social events around them, they experiment with language in constructive ways that build literacy. Throughout the process, children become their own teachers who manage their learning (Bissex, 1984). As Hall (1987) point outs: "children control and manipulate their literacy learning in much the same way as they control and manipulate all other aspects of learning about the world" (p. 8). Understanding the process of literacy development means embracing the rich and powerful roles of young children as both teachers and learners who take charge of their own language achievements.

As children begin their literacy journey, they learn to make of use of words and bring oral language into play. By the time most youngsters enter school, they have gained control of spoken language in English or their mother tongue (Ferreiro and Teberosky, 1982; Clay, 1991). Although young children may not follow standard rules of grammar and word usage, their growing use of language is delightful and charming to listen to.

Young learners gain access to oral language in many ways. Through social interactions and play engagements, youngsters invent ways to communicate—making up words, trying out new forms, and finding uses for language in their world on their own terms. While engaging in life events, children try to make language match with experiences in their social and physical environment as they interact with people and objects around them (Clay, 1991). Youngsters learn to negotiate and communicate messages every day, testing out their understandings with adults and significant others (Clay, 1991). Amid constant feedback, observation, imitation, and experimentation, young people begin to develop their own models and discover how to learn language (Clay, 1991). These understandings emerge from everyday life lessons that turn babbles into words and phrases.

Children also develop control over the functions and forms of literacy in reading and writing (Y.M. Goodman, 1984). Many young children learn to read environmental print in the world around them without being taught (Goodman and Altwerger, 1981; Hartse, Woodward, and Burke, 1984). By participating in everyday life experiences, youngsters come to notice signs and directions, identify labels, and recognize logos on product packages and storefronts. Children learn intuitively to distinguish between drawing and writing as they begin to tell pictures and words apart. Through various text interactions, youngsters develop reading strategies and ways of responding to print. Children discover how to handle books, when to turn the page, and other concepts of print through pleasurable reading experiences. Youngsters take up practice with writing by using crayons and paintbrushes to produce their first marks on paper. In the pattern of daily living, children may find purposes to write on their own (for play, note/letter/card writing). To produce these early texts, youngsters often use oral language to map their ideas and words onto a page (Hartse, Woodward, and Burke, 1984).

Many events in childhood provide occasions when youngsters can grow in literacy naturally. While experiences and materials are important in building opportunities for learning, children often direct and take ownership of these activities themselves. Youngsters invent their own effective methods and functional strategies when they put literacy to work. As leading players in this constructive process, children form literacy knowledge and skills by actively engaging in the world. They discover how to handle books, make up new words, invent symbols as they learn to write, and find ways to communicate effectively with others (e.g., using gestures and pointing to objects). Learning about language and discovering its uses helps children become "meaning makers" (Wells, 1986).

The Meaning-making Process

Discovering ways to learn about the world and become literate is a complex process that involves children in meaning-making. In the pattern of daily living, youngsters try to make sense of the experiences that surround them. Children's need to make sense of the world gives rise to learning as they seek ways to construct and share understandings with others. Throughout the process, youngsters learn to create meaning and communicate ideas in multi-modal ways using various resources (Kress, 1997). Youngsters draw on language, play, the arts, and other forms of representation to express their growing knowledge. By reflecting, interpreting, and carrying on with life events, children take part spontaneously in meaning-making.

Multi-modal Learning
Children, like adults, use modes of representation—various sign and symbol systems—to show their knowledge and reflect their learning in the world. These modes, or multi-modal ways of making meaning, may include:
- oral language and speech
- writing and printed language
- art and drawings
- moving visual images
- digital media
- music, drama, dance, poetry

From birth, youngsters play an active role in their own learning discovering ways of understanding the world and developing methods for communicating in it (Wells, 1986). Many forms of children's self-expressions and communication systems build on language. Literacy learning itself is a process in "learning how to mean" (Halliday, 1975; Goodman and Goodman, 1979). Children learn how to mean through written and spoken language (Y.M. Goodman, 1984). As youngsters participate in literacy events and socio-cultural experiences involving interactions, they uncover the functions, forms, and purposes of language in practical use. By observing others, and experimenting with language themselves, children discover that oral and written language does make sense. Discovering words and language formats gives children access to literacy. Soon, youngsters come to use reading, writing, speaking, and listening as tools to make meaning. As children learn to read and write, they begin to *make sense out of and through print* (Y.M. Goodman, 1986, p. 5). Youngsters make meaning "out of and through print" by developing strategies and techniques to understand and produce text themselves.

The process of making meaning is important to literacy development and life experience. As children grow in knowledge and potential, they learn to use language and other forms of meaning-making (drawing, painting, sculpting, constructing models, dancing, poetry writing, and music) to build insights into the world around them.

The Framework of this Book

This resource is based on fundamental principles about literacy that support early childhood education and early language development. Central to these beliefs is the image of the young child as a proficient language learner, sophisticated literacy user, and competent meaning maker. In these powerful roles, children come to discover and use literacy within the rich, authentic, and meaningful experiences of everyday living. In the context of social interactions with others, children become active participants in constructing their own knowledge (Vygotsky, 1978). This book derives from an emergent literacy perspective and socio-cultural (Vygotsky, 1978) view that takes into an account the importance of children's experiences with reading, writing, and oral language and interactions with others in their homes and communities in the years before schooling. These socio-cultural practices and emergent literacy experiences are the groundwork for children's learning (Roskos and Christie, 2000).

Many of the oral, print, and reading examples in this book are drawn from what might be described as traditional Western literature sources. We must remember, however, that rich materials abound in the oral history, social customs, and literature of cultures from around the world. Global technology and our increasingly multicultural society invite teachers, family members, and other adult language partners to tap these rich, diverse sources as we build vibrant, authentic, and inclusive programs in emergent literacy.

what it includes

This book builds on the foundations of what children already know by presenting both research and practice to support early literacy development. The chapters are filled with rich language activities that shape the play episodes, oral language practices, word play activities, print encounters, reading events, and writing experiences that are the essential cornerstones to early literacy.

1

Play Experiences

Nothing captures the wonder of childhood more than play. Play grabs hold of the imagination, incites curiosity, awakens the mind, motivates ideas, and engages the senses in delightful ways. The joy, pleasure, and power of play invite children of all ages to join in. For generations, play has been a traditional part of growing up, a way for youngsters to explore and understand the world around them. Children do much of their learning through play. Through the earliest years of play and discovery, youngsters build knowledge and skills that they bring to school (Hughes, 1991, Burke, 2010). Play provides the basis for intellectual growth, creativity, problem solving, and emotional development (Hirsh-Pasek and Golinkoff, 2003). The building blocks for life are found in play activities where children can rehearse roles and social practices needed for the future. Play prepares youngsters for the later years by laying the groundwork for literacy learning.

Play is the starting place of emergent literacy. Play experiences in early childhood provide the meaningful social contexts to introduce children to literacy knowledge and language practices. Many of the early hands-on experiences that happen in play are rooted in everyday social activities where language and literacy are used in daily routines. Play gives children genuine opportunities to use language in literate ways and put literacy to work as they see it practiced around them (Roskos, 1988; Roskos and Christie, 2001, Saracho and Spokek, 2006). Through play, children rehearse the scripts, roles, tools and social actions that are part of being literate. In play, youngsters demonstrate pretend reading and writing and other literacy-like behaviors that valuably contribute to the process of emergent literacy development. From this perspective, play is an important part of the everyday social activities that allow children to learn language and develop literacy in authentic ways.

Children's first engagements with literacy happen naturally during play. As youngsters come upon books and print materials, they may start to turn pages, pick up a pen, make marks on paper, or recognize print while they play. Play provides youngsters with authentic literacy experiences where they can practice reading, writing, and language use for different purposes in the context of the pretend scenarios and imaginary worlds they create. Through play, children become wrapped in narratives as they recreate favorite stories or invent tales of their own that bring meaning to their play. Youngsters learn to use richer language and wider vocabulary in their story-like play scenarios. Play promotes talking that helps children become stronger language users. Children try out the rules of conversation while playing with others. The social interactions that happen during play provide opportunities for children to develop literate and creative ways of thinking (Vygotsky, 1978; Gardner, 1991, 2006). The creative thinking that happens in play marks the start of language learning where children use the same thought processes needed to understand print.

Play grabs hold of the imagination, incites curiosity, awakens the mind, motivates ideas, and engages the senses in delightful ways.

If you have built castles in the air, your work need not be lost; that is where they should be. Now put foundations under them.

—Henry David Thoreau

Play is intrinsic to children. It is what children do naturally as their daily life's work.

Play that is integral to the curriculum serves literacy development strategies and supports learning by building on what children already know and have practiced. Teachers can use the strong foundations by which children learn naturally through play to provide classroom experiences that bridge the gap between home and school. To design programs where children can use play as a source of learning, we must embrace its qualities, value, and forms; understand its connections to literacy, and discover ways to put play into practice in the curriculum. Teachers can use play as an effective pedagogical tool for early learning by setting up time, space, materials, support and, opportunities to enrich the ways by which children learn best. Moments of play are the key to lifelong learning.

The Nature of Child's Play

Watching children play can help us understand how they really learn. Through play, children wonder, explore, imagine, create, interact, and pretend. Play gives youngsters the spirit and freedom to choose their experiences and become who or what they want to be. Suddenly, life is open for discovery inviting children to naturally disappear into the world of play (Elkind, 2006).

Play has many features yet it is not easy to define (Fein, 1985). Through the delightful experience of "kid-watching", we may come to identify and embrace the wonderful qualities that make play a source of pleasure and learning for children. When children set out to play, the purpose is to have fun. Play provides children with entertainment and social activity. Play happens for its own sake. It is not powered by expectations or motives such as developing skills. Imagination is the driving force. As children become inspired with ideas, they step into play willingly on their own. The very nature of play suggests that it be self-initiated, intrinsically motivated, freely chosen and improvised by the child (Johnson, Christie and Yawkey, 1987). Youngsters hardly need instructional guidelines, rules, or restrictions to become actively engaged. Play is intrinsic to children. It is what children do naturally as their daily life's work.

Play holds the promise for learning when it captures the interest of children and leads them to discover, predict, investigate, and build new meanings in areas that motivate them. Play provides children with *ways of knowing* about the world through exploration, testing, imitation, and construction (Sutton-Smith, 1971; Burke, 2010). For the most part, young people learn to invent, construct, inquire, and amuse themselves by playing alone or with other children.

Early childhood play experiences can provide rich social contexts for classroom learning. When planning learning experiences, educators need to take into account the elements that shape play. According to prominent researchers (Garvey, 1977; Rubin et al., 1983; Hirsh-Pasek and Golinkoff, 2003), play must:

- be pleasurable, enjoyable and fun
- have no extrinsic goals or functions
- be spontaneous and voluntary
- involve active engagement
- contain an element of make-believe

Play has the power to inspire curiosity in ways that lead children to use their minds to wonder, their hands to experiment, and their words to share ideas. Early child's play can be constructed under different categories. Many of the terms that define play are used interchangeably. The following table describes the types of play that support literacy learning:

The Benefits of Play

Play experiences in early childhood stimulate intellectual growth, cognitive development, brain activity, and academic achievement. Play transcends the mind in ways that also promote physical, social, and emotional development. Play allows children to:

- generate and work through ideas
- build knowledge
- make inquiries
- take risks
- develop problem solving skills
- acquire and use divergent, higher order, and critical thinking
- design innovative, varied, and multiple solutions
- develop mathematical thinking/reasoning (through manipulating, sorting, classifying, and dividing objects)
- understand scientific concepts (quantity and properties of matter)
- develop literacy
- make connections
- pretend and use their imagination
- develop imaginative thinking
- use creative processes to be inventive and expressive
- create new worlds
- communicate thoughts and ideas
- explore interests
- build attention span
- be spontaneous
- gain confidence for life and for learning
- express power
- grow in competence
- experience success
- develop a sense of well-being
- plan new discoveries
- make sense of the world around them
- build physical skills/abilities through active play
- develop fine and gross motor skills
- gain control over their bodies
- use affective thinking
- experience a range of emotions
- deal with emotional issues (cope with stress, feelings, experiences)
- develop social skills (through interactive play)
- interact and work cooperatively with others
- learn to share, negotiate, and compromise
- develop an awareness of others
- understand other perspectives and opinions
- play out social and cultural roles
- make and revise rules
- regulate their emotions and behaviors
- explore, confront, and deal with change
- understand and respect cultural differences
- form their identity

Play "is the key to nurturing happy, intelligent children" (Hirsh-Pasek and Golinkoff, 2003, p. 215). Research has shown that play promotes healthy child development and is important to human development overall (Hirsh-Pasek and Golinkoff, 2003; Elkind, 2006; Burke, 2010). Play holds the promise of joy for all children. It has the magical power to transform time and place and enrich the quality of life.

Play is essential in the life of a child. Every child should have the right to play.

Categories and Descriptions of Children's Play

Category	Description
Free	In free play, youngsters adopt the lead by inventing, planning, and directing their own activities. Unlike organized games or sports, free play is unstructured and unlimited by rules. Through exploratory free play, children have the luxury of time, space, and opportunity to entertain themselves. Children enjoy creating new environments and situations that open up the world of play. In free play, youngsters develop a sense of power as they take control of the real or imagined places they create.
Solitary Object	Through solitary object play, children explore the properties, relations, and features of toys and interesting items in the world around them as they put their intellectual skills (mathematical and scientific thinking) to early use. For toddlers and preschoolers alike, intellectual development is enhanced through the use of toys, blocks, and other play materials, as well as everyday objects that become theirs to discover through hands-on, concrete play.
Guided	In guided play, parents, teachers, adults, and other more capable and experienced partners work with children to move their play along by challenging and supporting them to go beyond what they can do on their own. In guided play, children learn to perform tasks, solve problems, and accomplish things that they are unable to achieve alone by interacting with more knowledgeable others in a range that Vygotsky (1978) referred to as the "zone of proximal development". In guided play, an adult enters the child's world as a partner or facilitator to expand the play possibilities, not to plan, control or direct them. Working within the zone of proximal development helps children begin to learn through instruction and start to realize their full potential. Sharing play with adults marks the start of children's social play experiences.
Social (Parallel and Cooperative Engagements)	In parallel play, young children play side by side with similar toys or objects that interest them. Youngsters often engage in play activities alongside others without interacting or playing directly with them. Although children appear to be playing independently, they begin to develop a sense of the playmates around by keeping a close eye on each other's behavior. Through parallel play, children start to form the social awareness and early friendships that will change the course of their play. As children get older, they move past parallel play and take up invitations to play directly with others. Social play welcomes children into peer groups and joint spaces where they must learn to communicate and collaborate with others. Playing socially with others requires children to negotiate and compromise with one another as they build understandings of the world around them. The social interactions that happen during play become the source of literacy knowledge (Vygotsky, 1978).
Symbolic	In symbolic play, children use their imagination to transform objects and themselves into a range of creative possibilities—from boats to astronauts. In symbolic play, toys, everyday items, and art materials become something else: a spoon becomes a microphone, a mass of clay is shaped into an animal. Through symbolic play, children learn to manipulate items in their world and use representational media in both art and play to stand for different objects. Treating objects in a symbolic way allows youngsters to build cognitive skills and make meaning. According to Piaget (1962), the ability to think symbolically and use objects to represent something different is the main characteristic of human thought and the basic tenet "from which language, reading, problem solving, and other types of higher-order thinking are made" (Hirsch Pasek and Golinkoff, 2003, p. 18).

Category	Description
Pretend	In pretend play, children become authors of their own play scenarios by reinterpreting experiences—real or imagined—and acting them out with others in elaborate stories or dramatic events. Pretend play is the magical part of childhood that enables youngsters to use the power of make-believe to invent alternative worlds. The playground, home, or classroom becomes a stage where children step into roles, dream up narratives, and carry out adventures. Many types of pretend play are referred to in terms often used interchangeably—socio-dramatic, imaginative, narrative, dramatic, and fantasy.

Real Life Play—Children's engagements in pretend play often build on incidents from everyday life and real-world dilemmas (Saracho, 2002). In a child's early years, reality-based play usually focuses on family-related themes and everyday events such as grocery shopping, ordering restaurant meals, or visiting a doctor's office. As children engage in real-world play, they draw on the social practices and cultural roles they see others using. By observing the social interactions and daily conversations that take place within their culture, young people internalize dialogues and relationships that they can practice during play. Children integrate well-known "scripts" from real-life interactions into their play discourses (Hirsch-Pasek and Golinkoff, 2003).

From play performances such as these, children form the building blocks for life by developing language, communication, problem solving, and critical thinking skills (Burke, 2010). As children explore different play scenarios that mimic daily episodes, they participate in a functional form of play that gives them real-life practice (Smilansky, 1968; Burke, 2010). This type of "practice play" becomes an authentic context for learning new strategies and building literacy as children naturally put literacy props, print materials, literacy-like behavior (pretend reading and writing), and oral language to efficient use.

Socio-dramatic Play—As children play out real-life situations, they participate in a form of socio-dramatic play that allows them to rehearse "ideas about how to act in our world" (Burke, 2010, p. 19). When children take on the role of characters or use toys such as dolls, figures, or puppets to act out stories, they engage in socio-dramatic play. In time, plans, themes, characters, and sequences become more elaborate as children work together to organize and solve problems. To carry out scenes, young people transform objects, switch roles, take on responsibilities, and engage in conversations with others. The symbolic representations and social interactions of this form of creative play allow children to develop cognitive, social, and emotional skills while building literacy (see Understanding the Play-Literacy Connection below).

Fantasy Play— In fantasy play, children create stories, act out scenes, and role play in ways that move them beyond the limits of time and space to become whomever or whatever they choose. In pretending to be someone else, visit a new world, transform objects, re-enact literature, or explore diverse situations, children learn to see beyond the mind's eye, use abstract thought, and stretch their imaginative powers while playing alone or with others. Fantasy play promotes literacy development as children step into the lives of characters, enter fictive worlds, and explore genres in the fairy tales, adventure stories, and other narratives they reinterpret or create themselves.

Narrative Play—Children have a magical ability to create imaginary worlds when they tell a story. Through narration, young people use characters, actions, and settings to create elaborate tales to share with others. As in storytelling, children's play often hangs on a narrative structure built around developing storylines and other elements of fiction. A child who assigns roles while constructing the story is engaged in narrative play (Engel, 2005). Through narrative play, young people use story structures and narrative discourse to shape the play experience. The ability to use language in this way draws out experiences for children to grow in literacy. |

Understanding the Play-Literacy Connection

Play inspires a sense of joy and curiosity that allows children to explore their learning potential. Studies show that children's literacy learning can be promoted through play (Saracho and Spokek, 2006). In the last decade, one of the most heavily researched areas of early literacy is the play-literacy connection (Yaden, Rowe and MacGillivray, 2000). The interaction of play and literacy traces back to developmental theories.

The Theoretical Foundations

Our earliest understandings of play and its role in child development and literacy learning have been shaped by leading theorists Jean Piaget (1962) and Lev S. Vygotsky (1978). Both placed heavy emphasis on the cognitive connections between play and literacy (Roskos and Christie, 2001). According to Piagetian theory, it is the symbolic nature of children's play that closely parallels the symbolic nature of literacy (Saracho, 2002; Saracho and Spodek, 2006). Through symbolic play, children develop the ability to recall information and events, and express what they see and remember by imitating and acting out life experiences. These recollections are at the core of the memory work involved in both play and literacy. In their examination of the play-literacy interface, Roskos and Christie (2001) argue that "in both play and literacy children must recall facts and experiences held in memory to make new meanings in context, whether three-dimensional as in play, or two-dimensional as in text" (p. 73). According to this theory, the connections between literacy and play occur at the representational level. As children's minds stretch to recall facts and past events, they draw on the cognitive work of memory that is at the root of pretend play and the manipulation of secondary symbol systems, such as print (Roskos and Christie, 2001; Saracho and Spodek, 2006).

Each of Piaget (1962) and Vygotsky (1962) observed that in the act of transforming one thing into another, children begin to separate meaning from objects and develop representational and abstract thought. This establishes the foundation for understanding other symbol systems, including written language (Neuman and Roskos, 1992). Children's use of symbolic transformations in play is the precursor to emergent literacy and early language development (Pellegrini, 1985; McCune, 1995; Saracho, 2002).

For Vygotsky, children take their first steps toward oral language and literacy through symbolic play when they naturally learn to use symbols in the drawings, markings, sculpting, painting, and imaginative worlds they create. As youngsters talk about the images represented in their playful work, they begin to translate these symbols into linguistic messages that communicate meaning to others. When sharing their play experiences, children use language as a way of verbally representing the world they see around them. These verbal translations become the basis for oral and print literacy (Burke, 2010).

Understanding the cognitive connections between literacy and play leads to other areas of Vygotsky's work and legacy on play theory. Vygotsky (1978) emphasized the role of adults in children's development along with the importance of children's social interactions during play. Through play, parents, other adult family members, and teachers extend children's learning by helping them accomplish tasks they cannot complete on their own. In the zone of proximal

audience

development, children can reach their full potential by performing at the highest level (Hirsh-Pasek and Golinkoff, 2003; Burke, 2010).

When children enter into play situations, they engage in social actions and verbal exchanges as they plan and role-play with others. In pretend play, youngsters need to coordinate actions and events by working through dialogues and social exchanges together. In the process, they may face conflicts as they try to negotiate scenes and behaviors with peers. To move forward, children may have to adapt their individual thinking and compromise by learning to accept different points of view. Through the process of narration and accommodation, children develop literate ways of thinking and learn to use literacy knowledge, tools, scripts and skills (Roskos and Christie, 2001; Saracho and Spodek, 2006). According to Vygotsky, it is in these social interactions that children become exposed to concepts and situations in which literacy may be embedded (Saracho, 2002).

Vygotsky (1976) believed that negotiations and social adaptations that happen during play help children to become literate by requiring them to shift spheres from engaging in play to talking about play—a stance that Williamson and Silvern (1991) refer to as *metaplay*. Children often may be seen moving in and out of play effortlessly as they briefly suspend playing to plan scenes with others. As youngsters shift from role-playing to talking about play, they gain literacy in their ability to think about and use language. Talking and thinking about language in metaplay relate closely to children's later success in reading and writing.

In his recent work, Howard Gardner (1991, 2006) connects the creative thinking processes inherent in play to the same processes that build literacy. Children practice the skill of symbol manipulation in both. Through play, youngsters learn to use objects, events, and ideas in a representational way. To enter the world of make-believe, children transform reality and manipulate objects and situations by turning them into something else. This kind of creative thinking marks the start of language learning when children encounter and begin to interpret other symbols like print. As Anne Burke (2010) explains, "Words are also symbols. Whether we are adults or children, our thinking skills involve the manipulation of words – and ergo, symbols –as we use words, numbers, images and notations to describe the world around us. The foundations of these manipulations are the real beginnings of literacy." (p. 94)

How Play Serves Literacy

Current research and practices continue to broaden our understanding of the connection between play and literacy. This connection is a growing area of focus for parents, teachers and researchers who take an interest in play as a context for literacy learning and language development.

Play provides a rich means for children to explore many aspects of literacy, including its cultural roles, routines, scripts, and tools (Roskos, 1988). As they play, children step into situations where literacy skills and strategies can be developed and used. Both realistic and imaginative play settings that are enriched with literacy resources and print materials present children with genuine opportunities to use literacy tools and abilities in the authentic ways they see practiced in everyday life. According to Roskos and Christie (2001), play serves literacy by "providing settings that promote literacy activity, skills and strategies" (p. 84).

Play encourages children to "build meanings and develop skills closely associated with reading and writing" (Roskos and Christie, 2001, p. 60). As youngsters interact with others and play props, they demonstrate literate behaviors while carrying out play actions and routines that involve reading and writing for a meaningful purpose such as shopping or banking. During play, children frequently engage in reading and writing activities that form the literacy skills needed for formal reading instruction (Saracho and Spodek, 2006). Through play, children begin to recognize that the symbols and letters that appear on a page become words in print (Burke, 2010) and may discover reasons and tools to write. In literacy-rich play environments, children often pick up the pen to produce recipes, grocery lists, prescriptions and checks of their own. Written materials created during play may be the first texts that children write. These early readings and scribbles can reveal much about children's literacy knowledge and understanding of the forms, purpose, and conventions of written language. Play allows children to act like readers and writers as they put literacy to work (Roskos, 1988).

As children invent stories and texts in their play, they begin to develop the narrative skills that are essential to literacy learning. A child's ability to use narrative is an important emergent literacy skill (Saracho and Spodek, 2006). In pretend play, youngsters rehearse well-known "scripts" from their real-world experiences. These familiar dialogues allow them to build oral language and literacy skills through the social interactions that occur during play.

Pretend play allows children to practice literate behaviors that are precursors to understanding the concept of story and the development of narrative competence (Roskos, 1988; Kim, 1999). Children use play as a form of storytelling that allows them to step into narrative roles. Youngsters incorporate character, setting, plot, and other elements of story grammar in their narrative play. They use a narrative framework to structure and bring meaning to their play (Roskos, 1988). During socio-dramatic, fantasy, and narrative play, children draw on storybook language and narrative discourse to script out their pretend-play episodes. The story-like language of this form of play is linked to reading success (Vedeler, 1997). The imaginative use of language and story schema development that takes place in book-related, narrative play enhances children's literacy learning and reading and writing achievements (Rosko, 1988).

Play gives children a language experience to build connections between oral and written modes of expression (Roskos and Christie, 2001). Play invites children to explore language in interactive ways. Children's delightful use of language in play may draw their attention to the sounds of words that can lead to phonological awareness (Bergen and Mauer, 2000) (see p. 59). As youngsters play with words, they develop their understanding of language sounds through joyful exploration. Playing with sounds promotes an understanding of sound-symbol relationships as children discover the links between sounds, symbols, letters, and words. Play allows young children to learn about the language world (Saracho and Spodek, 2006). When youngsters engage with others in play, they build their social language and interpersonal skills. The nature of play enables youngsters to become actively and genuinely engaged in meaningful discussions. While play-making together, children use talk as a way to structure, guide, and sustain their social interactions. In socio-dramatic play, children adopt different conversation patterns and tones of voice to carry out the scenario. Children use play as a way to rehearse their syntactic abilities through word usage and sentence constructions (Vedeler, 1997). Through the language of play in the world of make-believe, they try out sophisticated vocabulary, advanced expressions, and complex language

literacy-rich play environments

Once there was a unicorn who couldn't find her baby so she asked the butterfly, "Are you my baby?"

"No," said the butterfly.

Then she asked the troll, "Are you my baby?"

"No," said the troll.

Then the mother unicorn asked the owl, "Are you my baby?"

"No," said the owl.

Then the mother unicorn asked the wizard, "Are you my baby?"

"No," said the wizard.

Soon the mother unicorn found her baby near the castle. "Are you my baby?"

"Yes," said the unicorn.

Then the fairies came to visit.

Here a child uses a magnetic play set and story structure based on the popular book *Are You My Mother?* to engage in play.

structures. When we turn our ears to child's play, we often hear youngsters using a larger vocabulary, wider expressions, and longer utterances than they might use in another context (Burke, 2010). Play promotes a level of talking that gives children practice applying language rules.

(5) Playing with language builds a framework on which children can learn to decode words and develop emergent reading skills. During play, children take genuine steps toward reading print. Many daily literacy experiences that require reading are naturally embedded in play routines. When children encounter menus, lists, recipes, manuals, books, and other texts during pretend play, they gain understanding, practice, and skills in the act of reading.

switch

(6) Play invites young readers to step into the pages of a book and grasp the concept of story. Children learn to make sense of books in multi-modal ways by responding to literature through book-related dramatic play (Rowe, 1993). Youngsters use props and toys to bring books and play together as they engage with characters, settings, and themes from literature. When emergent readers take part in book-related play, they begin to develop early reading skills by inter-acting with narrative elements. As children re-enact stories and discuss literature in their play, their attention is drawn to features of texts including story struc-tures, details of plot, and characterization (Rowe, 2000).

(7) Play can provide children with the explicit context to make connections between oral and written language. Children may experiment with writing by drafting texts in different play situations. As children practice printing letters and words, they may use spoken language to map and sound out what they write. Drawing on the experiences that happen in children's play, youngsters and adults can share accounts and stories of pretend-play scenarios in language experience activities. When helping to develop children's accounts of play events through language experience stories, adults may direct youngsters' attention to sight vocabulary, language conventions, print forms, directionality, and other writing features. Creating these texts with children can help beginning readers and writ-ers start to match spoken words with print. As youngsters practice reading their language experience stories, they learn to identify and decode words with greater ease because the content and background of reading material are meaningful and relevant to them. Play experiences such as these help children bridge the gap between oral language and reading and writing. At the same time, they present us with "teachable moments" for meaningful and authentic instruction.

(8) Play provides an opportunity to teach and learn literacy too (Roskos and Cris-tie, 2001). Through play, adults and children can interact in different settings while engaging in a variety of playful experiences. By stepping into children's play, teachers, parents, and other significant others (older siblings, peers) can demonstrate and express literacy to youngsters as they play with them. In play scenarios, adults may engage in literacy activities, use literacy props and tools, model the use of oral language and other literacy behaviors, display literacy skills, and share literacy knowledge.

(9) As youngsters play in print-rich settings and literacy-filled environments, they learn to read words and recognize environmental print (Neuman and Roskos, 1993; Vukelich, 1994). Engaging in book-related play helps children understand literature and grasp the elements of story (Rowe, 1993). Through the language of play, children begin to develop phonological awareness and a growing motiva-tion toward print (Sonnenschein et al, 2000). Youngsters learn about the func-tions, forms, and content of written language within play settings and routines.

Advocating the Value of Play

audience → In an age of hyper-parenting, forced accountability, and standardized testing, play has been abandoned in favor of a rigorous academic agenda that suits parents and stakeholders caught up in the race for excellence. Under these pressures, the notion of play in childhood has become lost. In exchange for play, children are being enrolled in organized activities. Time for play has been replaced with packed schedules and supplemental instructive programs, including tutored lessons and enrichment classes. Free time is a luxury few young people can afford. Boosting children's brainpower in this way can lead to what David Elkind (1981/1988/2001) calls 'the hurried child'. Through studying Elkind's prominent work, we have come to understand the pressures and anxieties that children face in an era of rapid change and overwhelming expectations. The aim to raise smart children in the growing "cult of achievement" has taken away the heart of learning through play (Hirsh-Pasek and Golinkoff, 2003).

Despite an increasing number of studies that show the intricate connections between play and skills development, many parents and educators find it difficult to see how the learning achieved through play is transferable to practical, work-related skills that will lead to successful futures (Burke, 2010). They question and challenge the educational time spent on what they perceive to be frivolous activities. As a consequence, for many children play has been pushed out of the classroom and into the limited spaces of the gymnasium and playground.

Fortunately, these attitudes and practices have started to change as more research advocates play as a form of learning in early childhood. Teachers are beginning to embrace play as a pedagogical tool (Burke, 2010). Understanding the play-literacy connection facilitates us in advocating play as part of the curriculum and countering the challenges of parents, educators, and other stakeholders who may question our programs with demands for accountability and educational purpose. As seen, play is essential to the life a growing child. Play supports early literacy development and language learning. Through play, children can also develop cognitive, social, emotional, and physical skills needed for future success and overall well-being.

Implications for Practice

Building the foundation for literacy through play can be established in both the play environment and through the role of others. In play-literacy research, studies have shown that creating print-enriched play settings that contain literacy-related props, objects, and materials can promote young children's literacy development.

Current academic programs are filled with extensive learning outcomes to be measured, making it challenging for educators to fit play into an already packed agenda. For years, conventional methods of teaching and learning have been used to cover a formalized skilled-based curriculum where innovative instruction is left to the creative thinking of teachers in their lesson design. Today, though, an increasing number of early childhood programs are being enriched by play-based experiences that inspire learning in the classroom. Finding a place for play in the curriculum may seem difficult, but there are ways to make play happen.

Many factors can enhance the nature and quality of children's learning through play. Building the foundation for literacy through play can be established in both the play environment and through the role of others. In play-literacy research, studies have shown that creating print-enriched play settings that contain literacy-related props, objects, and materials can promote young children's literacy development (Christie and Enz, 1992; Hall, 1987; Morrow, 1990; Neuman and Roskos, 1990; Vukelich, 1991; Saracho, 2002). Literacy skills for young children can be developed by embedding a variety of literacy resources—books, signs, writing tools, calendars, paper, posters, menus—in the play environment. In this enhanced environment, children's use of literacy materials and participation in literacy acts were found to increase (Kress, 1997, 2003; Einarsdottir, 2000; Kendrik, 2005). Print and literacy-enriched play settings provide children with both the tools and occasions to practice and develop emergent reading and writing skills. Establishing literacy-enriched play centres where children can interact with adults and peers can also lead to language growth and literacy acquisition (Roskos and Christie, 2001). Research has found that literacy activity during play increases through both adult involvement (Christie and Enz, 1992; Morrow, 1990; Schrader, 1990; Vukelich, 1991) and peer interaction (Neuman and Roskos, 1990). In Vukelich's (1991) study, the combination of a literacy-enriched environment and adult intervention led to significant increases in children's knowledge about the functions of writing.

build a more responsive curriculum

There are many factors for parents, teachers, and other educators to consider in finding a place for play in the curriculum. Building on our understanding of the nature, forms, and benefits of play, along with a strong knowledge of the play-literacy connection, we can begin to plan a play curriculum that supports young children's learning. Embracing the value of play and watching the joy it brings youngsters moves us steps closer to putting play into practice in schools.

Putting Play into Practice and Literacy to Work

When children enter the doors of our classrooms, they carry backpacks of knowledge, skills, and experiences gained through their earliest years of play. Teachers need to connect the fundamental way that children learn with the experiences that children encounter in school. They do so by making play a part of early childhood curriculums and programs. To facilitate play in schools, parents, educators, and other adults can become actively engaged with children during play. Providing time, space, and materials is key to creating an environment that encourages playful learning. Play-based activities that allow children to develop literacy through hands-on experiences create genuine opportunities for both teaching and learning. In the context of play, youngsters can work to develop literacy knowledge and practice-related skills and behaviors.

time space materials

The Supportive Role of Language Partners

Children delight in having adults join in their play by getting down on the floor, sitting at a table, or taking part in a game. When parents, teachers, and other adults become partners in play, children are able to build, pretend, invent, work, and learn with them. Studies have shown that both the level and variety of child's play increases when adults join in (Goodnow and Collins, 1990; Hirsch-Pasek and Golinkoff, 2003). Teachers, parents, and significant others such as grandparents and caregivers play important roles in children's play experiences.

audience

Play Participant

When adults step into children's play as participants, they become directly involved by taking on roles, sharing tasks, or becoming active members of a team. As a play partner, the adult follows the child's lead without assuming control. At times, adults can build on youngster's ideas by making suggestions to extend the play. The teacher or parent can work within the limit of his or her involvement to show how enactments, toys, and literacy materials can be used more widely to explore a range of themes and play possibilities (Christie, 1982; Musthafa, 2001). As a participant and model, the adult works within the children's zone of proximal development to extend the authentic learning that takes place (Vygotsky, 1976, Roskos and Christie, 2001). As children work within their natural learning zone with the help of more experienced and capable adults as play partners, they are able to accomplish tasks and activities they cannot do on their own. Adult-child interactions that take place during play can awaken young minds to wonders and prospects they didn't think possible. Suddenly, the challenge of building a skyscraper looks within reach when a parent's or teacher's hand is there to guide them. More so, the verbal exchanges that take place during role-play are enriched when an adult's voice promotes the storyline and takes the dialogue in a further direction.

Facilitator

Teachers, parents, and other adults can also support child's play as facilitators. An adult facilitator may carry out various roles to introduce and encourage play in the classroom. The facilitator can:

- provide children with play opportunities
- plan field trips or other theme-related activities and experiences as sources of child's play
- set up the play environment
- organize time, space, and materials for play
- be patient and allow time for children's ideas to grow
- allow children to develop storylines and play situations on their own without interrupting
- offer comments and suggestions about themes, topics, roles, or play objects
- value child's play and talk to children about their play experiences
- give children encouragement, support, and praise as they play
- note children's interests and use these to develop play themes
- introduce new play props and scenarios to enrich children's play
- ensure that all children have opportunities to play with others and independently
- teach children to play cooperatively through sharing materials, roles, and space
- help children resolve conflicts in play
- encourage children to explore their feelings during play
- challenge learners to develop and explore other interests and activities through play
- model skills, literate behaviors, and social interactions during play
- observe children's learning and development during play engagements

By providing the framework, support, and conditions that invite children to play, teachers and adults as facilitators can build rich settings to capture young minds and enhance growing imaginations.

The Play Environment

interesting starting point.

A strong literate foundation is formed in homes, schools, and social environments where children are surrounded by resources and experiences that encourage them to interact, discover, and play. Play to a child is like work to an adult. Most days of early childhood are filled with play activities. Young children learn about themselves, others, and the world through play. As youngsters engage in the day-to-day job of playmaking, either alone or with others, they learn to use toys, materials, and words, as tools to make play work. The most prominent setting in a young child's world is the play environment where the child can carry out his or her early life's work. To encourage child's work through play, teachers and parents can use time, space, and materials to build authentic, innovative, and creative play settings for youngsters to explore and grow.

Time

Children need occasions to play at home, in the classroom, at the playground, and in the community. Teachers and adults can encourage child's play by allowing youngsters time to play throughout the day. Scheduling play periods as part of the curriculum gives students blocks of time to explore play options and take their imagination to new limits. Rather than offer play as a reward for finishing work, teachers can allocate longer periods for students to participate in elaborate forms of play alone or with others. Children can practice putting their play time to good use by planning independent or group activities such as art or building projects and organizing role-plays and dramatic re-enactments. Time management and group interactions that take place during these longer play periods can contribute to children's social and cognitive development.

Space

Children need plenty of room to play. Access to open spaces in the classroom, yard, auditorium, library, gymnasium, or other school setting encourages youngsters to explore the active potential of free play, the familiar contexts of real-life play, and the make-believe power of fantasy play.

Teachers can create an inviting environment by setting up dramatic play centres in the classroom. Adults and youngsters can work together to organize the room into thematic play centres and areas to keep toys and materials. These play centres may include:

- Library or reading corner
- Author's table/writing centre
- Alphabet centre
- Restaurant or kitchen
- Home centre
- Gardening centre
- Grocery store/bakery
- Doctor's office, medical clinic, or animal hospital
- Administrative office/workplace
- Bank
- Post office
- Travel agency
- Store
- Play school
- Sand table
- Dress-up and drama centre
- Music/radio/TV station or recording studio
- Block area or construction/building site
- Artist corner
- Easel centre

Children can enjoy a wide range of play experiences when various centres and themes areas are made available at a given time. Teachers and students may decide together which areas they wish to use. If space is limited, play centres can be rotated on a regular basis to accommodate different theme areas. Introducing new play spaces enables youngsters not only to explore familiar settings, but also to work in different play areas throughout the year. A variety of play centres and theme areas can enrich play options by allowing children to take on various roles, rehearse a range of life experiences, and discover a variety of prospects that grow from their creative imaginations.

Children discover learning as they explore the endless possibilities of their play. Through play, youngsters try to understand their world and life experiences. They do this by becoming actively engaged in their surroundings. Therefore, it is important to keep spaces uncluttered so youngsters have safe limits and secure room to play. Encouraging children to make use of bins, shelves, and other storage units gives them practice in classifying and sorting materials.

Children can develop literacy skills in these spaces too. Play centres that build on familiar settings allow youngsters to put literacy to work by acting out literate behaviors in the spaces around them. As youngsters step into roles to rehearse common life experiences in dramatic play scenarios, they may try out reading and writing in the context of their playful actions. In addition, dramatic play centres provide a stage for children to work on social relationships as they interact closely with others in these spaces.

Materials

Children gravitate to play when objects are ready at hand for them to use. To promote child's play, teachers, parents, and other adults can gather resources and supplies to help children create ideas and develop play options. Surrounded by print-rich literacy materials, play props, toys, and art-based tools, children of all ages can discover learning through the innovative possibilities that go hand in hand with play.

Having interesting materials to use in play awakens young minds to multimodal ways of learning (Kress, 1997). As youngsters interact with objects, they draw on different resources and materials to make meaning of their world. At times, children may bring familiar items from their culture (household goods, narratives, religious books, faith items) into their play to use as meaning-making materials (Pahl, 2002: Rowsell, 2006). These cultural resources are important to children's construction of meaning in the way they allow youngsters to make the connections needed to develop literate ways of thinking.

The availability of play materials is important to children's intellectual development as well (Hirsh-Pasek and Golinkoff, 2003). Apart from discovering the properties of materials, the introduction of different play props may provide children with problem-solving opportunities. Resources can inspire curiosity, exploration, and divergent thinking.

> In selecting materials, it is essential to keep in mind that the best tools for learning and play are those that inspire the imagination and leave the power of make-believe and discovery in the hands of the child.

Embedding literacy and print materials into children's play environments allows young language learners to develop and use literacy, as research and practice have shown us. As youngsters take hold of pencils, pen, paper, and other writing tools and a variety of texts in their play, they learn about the features and functions of print and come to understand how literacy fits into their world. When children put reading and writing to practice in the context of play, they develop the emergent literacy skills and behaviors that can help them with conventional tasks and formal language learning.

Teachers can encourage children to make flexible use of materials by having resources that children can access freely and easily. To promote inquiry and literacy development, play items should be open-ended and unstructured. Toys based on action figures or film and cartoon characters, for example, may limit child's play by giving youngsters predetermined storylines and set narratives to work with. Children's ability to use language grows when they engage with toys, props, and play materials creatively to produce (or craft) their own scripts. The best tools for learning and play are those that inspire the imagination and leave the power of make-believe and discovery in the hands of the child.

The play environment is a vital component in the learning process (Burke, 2010). Providing time, space and resources enhances the value of play in children's development. To support their emergent literacy skills, youngsters need experiences to engage in various forms of play as part of the curriculum. Using play as a learning pedagogy allows children to develop language and communication skills, make early marks on paper, practice writing for meaningful purposes, produce texts based on play experiences, recognize print, and begin reading.

Play-Based Literacy Activities

Play-based learning builds on the foundations of what children already know by putting into practice the authentic ways that children learn best. From an early age, youngsters explore language by playing with sounds, letters, words and print in the verses, songs, poems, rhymes, and other high-spirited texts that echo childhood. Prior to formal schooling, these word play events parallel a child's play and other emergent literacy experiences. Creating play-based experiences allows children to learn about language, develop literacy, and acquire other skills, such as numeracy, in authentic contexts that are meaningful to them. Through play-based literacy experiences, students can experiment with how language is used, discover its forms, and learn about its meaning.

Understanding the rich potential that play holds for language learning and literacy building helps teachers better use play as a pedagogical tool. Here are some play-based experiences that may foster language growth and literacy development in classrooms and beyond:

Guided Play

The learning potential of play opens up when adults participate by stepping into role or sitting with youngsters at literacy-play centres. Although youngsters need room to explore the prospects of their own play, at times children benefit from explicit teaching arising from their discoveries. Teachers, parents, and other adults may work closely with children to help them make important language connections. Through guided play, we can support children's emergent literacy development by modeling, scaffolding, and teaching lessons to move youngsters along. As children play with language, teachers can discuss alphabet sounds. When youngsters try out writing, adults can point out letter formations. As young readers step into the pages of a book, teachers can help them make out words or develop early reading strategies. By asking questions, offering suggestions, and observing children's needs, teachers can scaffold learners as they discover language and grow in literacy during play.

Play-based learning builds on the foundations of what children already know by putting into practice the authentic ways that children learn best.

In *Ready to Learn: Using Play to Build Literacy Skills in Young Learners* (Pembroke, 2010), Anne Burke examines the learning potential of play and provides effective strategies for incorporating play as a pedagogical tool in early childhood classrooms, along with ideas for home practice.

Recommended Materials for Play Centres

- Writing tools (pencils, crayons, pens, markers)
- Paper products (lined/graph/blank paper, diaries, journals notepads, notebooks, stationary, letterhead, envelopes, cardstock, mural paper, cardboard)
- Writing/office supplies (staples, stapler, hole puncher, ruler, paper clips)
- Clipboards
- Appointment books
- Assorted blank administrative forms
- Computer, keyboard, scanner, printer (color, black/white)
- Children's literature collections (novels/chapter books, picture books, poetry collections, nursery rhymes, short story anthologies)
- Nonfiction books (on various topics)
- Alphabet books
- Audiobooks
- Audio/visual equipment (e.g., DVD/CD player)
- Magazines (travel, lifestyle, technology, construction, automotive)
- Instruction manuals
- How To books (e.g., craft books, do-it-yourself projects)
- Recipe books (including children's cookbooks)
- Brochures (e.g., travel-related)
- Pamphlets (e.g., children's programs)
- Environmental print (posters, advertisements, display boards)
- Traffic and road signs
- Product packages (food, health, personal care)
- Newspapers and flyers
- Drama and dress-up toys (costumes, masks, make-up, hats, uniforms, scarves, bags, shoes, puppets, puppet theatre, props)
- Play scripts
- Role play badges (doctor, police officer, firefighter, librarian, chef in training, electric worker)
- Musical instruments, CDs, recordings
- Music sheets and books with musical notation
- Chalk/magnetic board and colored chalk/markers
- Letters of the alphabet (puzzle, foam, magnetic, fabric, other)
- Mail tray and mail boxes
- Stamps (date, postage, other)

Pembroke Publishers. © 2010 *The Cornerstones to Early Literacy* by Katherine Luongo-Orlando. ISBN 978-1-55138-257-9

- Blueprints, maps, scaled drawings
- Drafting rulers, T-squares
- Furniture (desks, tables, chairs, rugs, rocking chair, pillows, shelves)
- Play equipment (kitchen set, workbench)
- Fabrics and linens (e.g., table cloths)
- Household goods (tableware, cutlery, cookware, lamps, blankets, baskets, tools)
- Menus
- Price lists
- Cash register, money, banking sets
- Telephones
- Telephone book
- Address books
- Calendar
- Cameras
- Toys (pretend food, dolls, cribs, carriages, medical kits, animals, cars, trucks, vehicles, cooking/baking toys, gardening toys, housekeeping toys, spy toys)
- Blocks, construction sets, building tools
- Puzzles and board games
- Art supplies (paints, canvases, brushes, smocks, containers, sketchbooks, drawing pads, drawing/sketching tools, molding clay/dough, scissors, glue, tape, pastels, a variety of paper)
- Craft materials (beads, buttons, shells, yarn, pipe cleaners, boxes, paper bags)
- Easels
- Water table, sand, bucket, water toys
- Natural resources (rocks, minerals, leaves, soil, seeds)
- Cultural artifacts and family literacy resources (jewelry, family photos/albums, clothing, heirlooms, ethnic games and toys, items of faith)

Pembroke Publishers. © 2010 *The Cornerstones to Early Literacy* by Katherine Luongo-Orlando. ISBN 978-1-55138-257-9

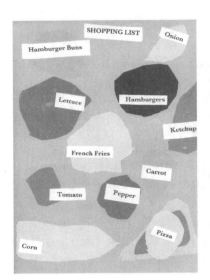

Shopping List

Doctor's Note and Prescription Pad

Reading and Writing at Play Centres

Teachers and students can take full advantage of play's learning potential by promoting and developing literacy at classroom centres. Having a designated time of day for centre play is important to children's literacy development. Youngsters may discover the need for reading and writing while playing at centres based on real-life experiences in authentic settings. Play centres provide children with genuine contexts, materials, and opportunities to practice reading and writing. Centre time allows children to step into familiar experiences and put literacy to work in ways they already know. During pretend play, youngsters spend time visiting doctors' offices, restaurants, or grocery stores, or performing literacy tasks at home such as cooking or reading to younger children. While engaging in real-life play centres, children may need to interpret reading materials such as menus, cookbooks, and children's literature and produce their own texts to use.

Real-life play scenarios allow children to develop emergent writing skills. Youngsters start out pretend writing by making symbols, practicing letter-like formations, rehearsing the alphabet, and attempting invented spellings in order to communicate with others. During "practice play", children make lists, jot down notes, copy messages, compose letters and create other forms of writing. In time, the early marks that start out as scribbles turn into real letters, words and writing.

Through real-life play, children learn how reading and writing fit into the world around them. In "practice play", youngsters step into potential future roles and rehearse the literacy acts and routines they see performed in everyday life.

Creating Texts for Play

Play provides children with occasions and tools to write in many forms and contexts. Learning through play is "enhanced when the idea for writing comes from students' own needs or imaginations" (Schultze, 2008, p. 69). During play, children often face real-world challenges that invite problem solving and organization. Youngsters may enlist materials, tools, and resources in response. When arranging play spaces, children may produce labels and signs to mark supplies and theme areas. Developing charts and lists that sort and keep track of play objects is another way that children can put print materials and writing tools to practical use.

To move their play forward, students can use graphic/visual organizers. During block play, builders may design blueprints, scaled drawings, floor plans, traffic signs, and directions for construction. Young explorers may devise maps and labeled drawings to lead them to real or imaginary treasures. Children may step into the role of instructors and produce schedules, pamphlets, and programs for lessons, practices, or competitions.

Producing charts, maps, lists, diagrams, or other visual formats enables students to move past conventional forms of writing and use symbols, words, and other print features to construct organizers for play. As children move into other forms of play, they may find reason to create new texts for different play purposes.

Imaginative, Fantasy, and Narrative Play

Play invites children to create and enter imaginary worlds beyond the boundaries of everyday life. Through costumes, props, toys, and other play materials, children create fantasy themes to explore in dramatic play scenarios. Youngsters enter make-believe worlds as astronauts, mermaids, pirates, heroes, fairies, and other fictional characters. Children are masters at producing play episodes with story bound settings, adventurous plots, and extensive casts.

Treasure Map

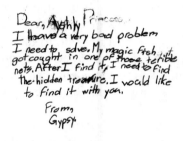

Writing in Role

Imaginative play helps youngsters make important literacy connections. To plan dramatic scenes, children must step in and out of role to negotiate parts, discuss plot outlines, work out actions, organize space, and practice the fantasy episode. As youngsters switch scenes from play-acting to talking about the drama, they practice the skills required for literacy. Children need language experiences where they can enter the stance of metaplay and use communication and negotiation skills while engaging in imaginary scenarios.

Fantasy play can invite youngsters to practice their writing skills too. In the act of role-playing, children might write screenplays and compose related texts to provide both dialogue and artistic direction. As part of the production, students can design posters, tickets, stage plans, and other forms of writing (badges, programs, reviews) required for the performance. At times, children may use a writing-in-role strategy in the context of play to produce letters, diaries, or other texts needed to enact the drama.

Fantasy play also enhances children's reading experiences. Through imaginative play, children may interpret scripts, read letters, diaries, or other texts in role, or invent tales. As they do, youngsters may use book language and a narrative framework to build the storyline. Many imaginary play accounts are based on beloved works of children's literature. As children reconstruct these narratives, they may revisit texts in order to enrich the drama and reinforce their understanding of the story. Through imaginative play, youngsters become skilled at using elements of story to dramatize fantasy episodes. Exploring themes in dramatic play awakens children to rich genres of literature as they create fairy tales, myths, legends, and hero tales of their own.

Language Experience Stories

For many youngsters, finding topics to write about is difficult. Making meaning of texts can be challenging. To help emergent learners, teachers can use the active and joyful experiences of child's play to lead children naturally to reading and writing. To begin, youngsters may share accounts of play episodes they participated in alone or with others in centre play, fantasy play, or book-related play. While listening to stories of children's play, a teacher, parent, or other adult records these experiences using chart paper, a journal notebook, or other written format. Later, the student uses the scribed work as reading material to practice reading independently. In making child's play the subject of these personal narratives, youngsters can contribute to topics, develop the content, and read materials that are meaningful and relevant to them. As teachers produce texts through language experience activities, they can demonstrate links between oral language and print by reviewing sound-symbol relationships in explicit lessons. Creating language experience stories also allows teachers to instruct children on features of writing, including high-frequency words, print concepts (e.g., directionality), grammar, punctuation, and other language conventions, and spelling strategies. (see Chapter 6.) Experiences in child's play may lead to direct opportunities for children to learn about reading and writing through adult guidance and explicit instruction.

Book-related Play

Literature and play work in harmony in a child's world. Reading books is a springboard for child's play because it presents youngsters with play themes, settings, events, and characters to use. At the same time, play provides children with an entryway into books by directing their attention to literature. Providing

Construction Play Stories

Following a book-reading event, my children used a toy building set to construct play props, settings, and characters to retell events from a beloved picture book, *The Magical Garden of Claude Monet* (Laurence Anholt, 2003). In the book, a gardener finds inspiration to paint in the life and work of his beautiful garden. The girls created their own play set consisting of a wishing well, a gate, a wheelbarrow, garden, flowers, plants, trees, a rabbit, and a gardener. The children used these play props to enact their versions of the story.

experiences for youngsters to interact with texts through book-related play is important to literacy building.

Following an experience with literature, youngsters may search for book-related toys and play materials to reenact the story (Rowe, 2000). As children bring together books and related props, they learn to make connections between reading literature and their own life experiences. Youngsters start by locating or creating book-related toys and literature-based play sets (e.g., castle settings) to use as prompts for dramatic play. Later, children can use these materials to recreate story settings, characters, and events. In this way, play makes reading more personally relevant and concrete (Rowe, 2000).

As children produce story reenactments, they use play to respond to books in both an experiential and aesthetic way (Rowe, 2000). Dramatizing scenes from literature allows youngsters to bring stories to life and transform texts. In book-related play, children use story elements, book language, and narrative structures to reenact literature. As children explore their interpretations of stories, they work out details of plot, character, and other narrative aspects. Youngsters may step into role and act out personal reactions and feelings toward a character or event in a book using improvisational drama. Here, children respond to literature by participating in a form of role-playing that combines both actions and dialogue without rehearsal or preparation. Through spontaneous engagements like these, young people have a chance to explore narrative features, grasp story details, and better understand the text.

Stepping into role gives children time and space to explore character studies in the context of play (Rowe, 2000). Youngsters begin to demonstrate specific qualities, examine social roles, or understand personal dilemmas through the pretend characters they portray in dramatic play. When children revisit the lives of favorite characters in play scenarios, they develop relationships and grow to understand the essential role of these characters in the construction of story.

As children act out stories from literature in their play, they may participate in other book-related experiences that develop comprehension and build literacy. Following a reading event, youngsters can use play to talk about books. Through discussion, both children and adults can work out storylines, raise questions, share perspectives, relate personal experiences, discover meanings, and plan play episodes based on literature. As children plan and rehearse scenes in their dramatic play, they negotiate with others about parts, events, and story interpretations by shifting from playing to talking about play. As described earlier, these metacommunications about play underpin children's emergent literacy and interactions with print (Vygotsky, 1978; Williamson and Silvern, 1991; Pelligrini and Galda, 1991, 1993).

Book-related play leads children to a deeper understanding of literature as they uncover genres, themes, and the author's message (Rowe, 2000). Youngsters can use play as a form of personal inquiry to work out issues from literature that they may not understand (Rowe, 2000). Children can use books to explore interests, concerns, and questions they have about human relationships and the world through dramatic play. Reading books helps youngsters invent topics for play that may relate to literature or universal issues they care about (see Critical Literacy Through Play). Play becomes a way to connect books and life experiences.

Media Play

In today's world, children are surrounded by ever-changing media forms. Digital technology, animation, and sound production in films, television, radio, and music create effects that fascinate young people. They enjoy dramatic stage performances enhanced with captivating visual displays and special effects.

These media texts create new potentials for child's play by providing themes, events, characters, and techniques to use as springboards. In media play, children incorporate texts from film, television, and popular culture into their pretend activities. Youngsters use toys, dramatic props, and other play materials to act out characters, scenes, and events they have seen in movies, television programs, and other media formats (e.g., stage plays, musicals, and song performance). Through media play, children draw on the film and television themes, locations, storylines, and roles in films or television episodes to create their own play scenarios.

Playing with media texts can enhance children's reading experiences. Media productions can introduce children to classical literature and children's novels, books, and other publications they may not know. Through popular films based on bestselling children's books and legendary characters—the *Narnia* series, *Harry Potter,* and *Percy Jackson* are examples—young people often are inspired to read literature. To promote literacy, teachers can help children make use of the story frameworks, archetypal characters, and text allusions in their play. Drawing on literary tools found in the media, students can start directing follow-up television episodes or remaking popular films based on these text experiences.

Working with media formats allows students to produce text reconstructions using language, narrative structures, story elements, and popular themes to create their own versions. Through media play, students can make text-to-text connections between movies, television shows, plays, documentaries, musical and dramatic performances, and other media formats that deal with common themes, genres, conflicts, or character portrayals. Children's understanding of text forms, content, and media techniques begins to grow as they make these connections. Text-to-text experiences can promote social awareness, directing children to forms of play that lead to social action and universal change.

Critical Literacy through Play

Children may use toys, play props, costumes, and settings to create elaborate play scenarios that challenge the social order and portray narratives from marginalized points of view.

As youngsters grow more experienced with play, they may construct complex themes and problems to work out with others. As we watch children play, we may notice them taking part in episodes that focus on topics that are sensitive to them, such as relationships or the environment. With heightened social awareness, young people may attempt during play to deal with the impact of critical issues around them. Suddenly, play moves into a space where children can address the emotional problems and social dilemmas of life. Favorite characters, eventful plots, and underlying themes become the feature of continuing sagas that children produce in narrative play. Through these chronicles, youngsters begin to examine social issues such as (poverty, human rights, bias, and gender inequality), challenge stereotypes, deepen their perspectives, and inspire change in the context of play. In time, children may use toys, play props, costumes, and settings to create elaborate play scenarios that challenge the social order and portray narratives from marginalized points of view.

To promote critical literacy during play, teachers can ask students to present alternate versions of fairy tales, nursery rhymes, and other traditional genres. Through close examination, youngsters may uncover the underlying themes and hidden issues in time-honored stories such as *Cinderella, The Old Woman Who Lived in the Shoe,* and *Hansel and Gretel.* Children can use play as a way to deconstruct the text, change the storyline, and develop new adaptations of these age-old stories. Through role-playing, children can explore broader gender experiences that move beyond stereotypes, traditional roles, and socio-cultural expectations. For example, strong feminist tales may emerge in child's play of adventurous characters that overcome the challenges of gendered labels and limited opportunities. As children role-play, they start to explore issues of equality and individual identity that allow them to cross social boundaries and global lines. These critical literacy engagements extend the prospects of child's play to help young people advocate for human rights, redefine social roles, and face the realities of an increasingly-complex world.

As children become more skilled at play, they may create conflicts to solve that parallel global issues such as war, threats to peace, and natural disasters. With adult guidance, youngsters can create fantasy themes around environmental awareness, ecological concerns (e.g., oil spills, forest fires, and endangered animals), or other world issues. In critical literacy play, children learn to focus on specific narrative elements that deal with story problems and character dilemmas to find a solution. They use richer language, elaborate plots, and creative problem solving to look for resolutions. Working out conflicts and dealing with critical issues during play can lead to deeper understandings and moral lessons that may steer young people to community participation or social action. Play motivate young children to make a difference and influence change one act at a time.

* * *

Critical Literacy Play Episode

My daughters acted out a fantasy theme involving mermaids who tried to protect their natural habitat from a band of pirates who were depleting fish while searching for an undersea treasure. Both girls took on the role of strong female leads determined to restore life and order to their ocean home through negotiations with the pirate group. Later, the children continued the saga in other play episodes where the characters had to deal with other ecological issues that affected the waters where they lived (e.g., oil spills, endangered animals).

Play has a transformative quality. Through imagination, youngsters can adjust time and space to become who or what they chose. Becoming skilled at play gives children the insights, knowledge, and critical thinking to challenge and change the growing complexities of our world. From the simple act of playing, young people can build the real-life skills they will need for the future. Play has far-reaching opportunities for lifelong learning that we are only beginning to understand. Realizing the true possibilities that rise from play may inspire us all, as teachers, parents and global educators, to use play's amazing learning potential to build progressive classrooms. These opportunities start by giving children throughout the world the privileged right to play.

The road to becoming literate starts with play. Play marks the beginning of children's early life experiences. Understanding the value of play and its strong connections to literacy changes our view of early childhood programs. This chapter shows us how print materials, literacy props, toys, media texts, children's books, and other resources support literacy learning through play in all its forms.

Children come to know literacy naturally through ordinary experiences that are innately part of growing up. Children's first steps toward using language happen through play. Play invites youngsters into real and imaginary worlds where words and oral language are used in rich, creative, and sophisticated ways. As children enter the social realm of play, they discover ways to communicate effectively with others by becoming stronger language users themselves. Learning to talk and use oral language grow from other opportunities in which children can practice and develop the verbal skills they need to become literate and active members of our social world.

2

Oral Language Opportunities— Children's Talk

Children are born with a natural ability to learn language no matter what community they find themselves in. Even before they enter the world, youngsters are surrounded by language in the voices and dialects they hear. As children listen to the rhythms and patterns of language, they discover and begin to use words, sounds, and structures to communicate. Through daily conversations and social interactions, young people learn the features and uses of oral language in the flow of everyday life. Hearing language empowers children with the tools to master spoken language and be able to talk on their own. Talk builds a strong foundation for literacy learning (Britton, 1992).

The path to literacy is marked with parallel developments in language growth. Children acquire literacy alongside oral language. Oral language plays a significant role in emergent literacy development as the basis for early language acquisition. Through talk, youngsters become language users themselves, experimenting with ways to express thoughts, needs. and feelings in conversation. Soon their babble grows into words that carry meaning and express understandings that make them able to communicate effectively. Children who have access to oral language experiences develop literacy naturally. Daily encounters with spoken language in family, community, and school life foster young children's language development. Through the models and opportunities provided in these settings, youngsters begin to develop oral literacy by using their growing language abilities to talk to others.

To build a solid foundation for literacy learning, children need a strong command of language gained through various emergent literacy experiences (Hirsch-Pasek and Golinkoff, 2003). The development of spoken language in the early childhood years must be a priority in homes and classrooms. After all, children's experiences with oral language and early literacy development are closely linked. To develop a strong hold of language in its many forms, youngsters need to be surrounded by language and practice using it daily.

Oral language is an essential means of communication that is a bridge to teaching and learning. Talk promotes learning, literacy development, and language acquisition. Oral language events help young people build vocabulary, grammar, narrative, and storytelling skills and give them understanding, confidence, and ability to move into reading and writing. Providing children with opportunities to talk adds breadth, depth, and meaning to the knowledge and experiences they gain in life and in school.

The Process of Language Learning

Language learning is a social event that occurs as a natural part of everyday living (Hartse, Woodward and Burke, 1984; Hall, 1987). From an early age, children learn language by participating in daily activities embedded in a variety of social and cultural contexts. As young people experience language in authentic situations such as cooking, dressing, or shopping, they discover how language is used in meaningful and purposeful ways to carry out different social functions (Hall, 1987). Understanding the functions that language serves is an important part of language learning and oral language development (Halliday, 1975). Oral language emerges under supportive conditions that rest on sound principles of language learning. According to Hall (1987), the conditions for learning oral language are the same as the conditions necessary to learn about the world.

Children's early development in oral language starts with holistic experiences at home and in the community. These experiences provide authentic opportunities to engage in conversations and discussions about the social/cultural events and participate in emergent literacy activities. Children play a major role in forming their understandings of oral language and its use (Hall, 1987). In the course of daily living and social interactions, young people become language users themselves, communicating with growing competence. Through everyday language encounters in natural situations, youngsters make sense of their experiences by using language as a resource to express themselves and control aspects of their lives (Wells, 1986; Hall, 1987). Children learn to talk through social interactions and life experiences that are engaging and purposeful to them. As described in the Introduction, the motivation toward language use is to understand and make meaning. Through meaning-making, children acquire other aspects of learning. In a ground-breaking research study of children's early language acquisition, the development of oral language is defined as a process of "learning how to mean" (Halliday, 1973, p. 24). "According to Halliday, it is through learning how to mean that other aspects of language are acquired" (Hall, 1987, p. 12). Hence, the development of oral language is essential to reading, writing, and overall literacy growth.

The Importance of Oral Language to Reading and Writing

The process of language learning is multifaceted and interconnected. Reading, writing, speaking, and listening play equally supportive roles in children's literacy development. As youngsters embark on their literacy journey, they learn to talk while experimenting with reading and writing tasks. To succeed in reading and writing, children need a wide range of experiences with printed and spoken language during the formative years (Palmer and Bayley, 2005). Developing oral language leads to literacy building.

Learning to talk is an important stepping stone to becoming a reader (Baker, 1980: Hirsh-Pasek and Golinkoff, 2003; Palmer and Bayley, 2005). Oral language experiences, like those explored in this chapter, promote the development of reading skills in many ways. By allowing children to share personal experiences through narrative talk or storytelling, young people begin to use decontextualized language and complex sentence structures in ways that shape their own understanding of story and their ability to tell narratives. Through personal recounts, book talks, storytelling, and other oral language events, children learn to use narrative discourse and book language to discuss literature, share personal experiences, and tell fictional stories of their own. Becoming familiar with book language leads to fluent, successful, and enjoyable reading (Doake, 1988).

Building narrative skills gives young people greater access to literature and more resources for making meaning of texts. Oral language experiences help children develop semantics, pragmatics, and other cueing strategies to interpret reading material (see Appendix at p. 156). Youngsters discover language rules and gain prior knowledge through the social interactions, discussions, and daily experiences where oral language is embedded. Later, children use these conventions and draw on their experiences to understand literature. Through talk, readers can decipher print and make sense of what an author's words are trying to convey. The development of children's oral language abilities can foster better reading comprehension (Peterson, 2007).

By helping children to learn to talk and read through holistic, functional, and meaningful learning experiences (e.g., baking, conducting an experiment, completing a class project), we allow children to interact and make sense of the world around them by gaining control of the learning process for themselves (Doake, 1988). According to Doake (1988): "In order to learn to read as fluently and easily as they learn to talk, *children have to establish control over the oral dimensions of written language*" (p. 30). Acquiring an understanding of oral language shares many similarities with building knowledge of written language (Hall, 1987). In fact, children develop oral and written language simultaneously. The use of oral language often supports young people in their writing development. According to Harste, Woodward and Burke (1984), oral language serves an organizational function that directs children's writing. As children produce writing of their own, they use spoken language to guide them. When adults observe and listen as young children write, they often hear youngsters speaking to themselves as they organize ideas. Through talk, children plan what they want to write.

Learning to use and control the oral dimension of language is fundamental to literacy learning in many ways. The process of oral language learning leads to parallel developments in reading and writing by allowing children to grow familiar with the language of books and become authors themselves. Literacy learning is dependent upon mutually supportive language systems. Children learn to make meaning, develop language skills, and acquire literacy by reading, writing, speaking, and listening. Young people accomplished these together as they grow, without having to master one over the other, or develop expertise in any of them first. The conditions needed for children to learn to speak and listen are the same basic conditions needed for them to read and write (Doake, 1988).

Supporting Children's Oral Language Development

To develop oral language and literacy, young people need a supportive language environment where adults and other language partners play an encouraging role in children's literacy learning by nurturing language development and by providing opportunities for children to engage in talk through a variety of oral language activities.

Characteristics of Early Oral Language Development

Children are gifted language learners with an inborn talent to develop language on their own. From an early age, they find patterns in the flow of talk that surrounds them. When children listen to exchanges of conversations, they discover the sounds, words, sentences, and meanings of language. The social interactions that take place during ordinary, daily activities give young people natural opportunities to acquire language. Through everyday encounters with spoken language, youngsters become motivated to talk. As inventive language users, young children learn to produce words, form sentences and craft vocabularies of their own.

As youngsters learn to communicate, they begin to demonstrate early oral language skills in everyday life and social interaction. Despite a wide range of individual differences in early language development, young children experience milestones in language learning at approximately the same time (Hirsh-Pasek and Golinkoff, 2003). When parents, teachers, and other language partners listen to youngsters talk, they may note common traits in children's early attempts to use language to communicate. At first, the rambling and babble of a toddler's delightful chatter mark the child's brief and disjointed efforts to speak in a language code that only parents are able to understand and translate. Through early endeavors like these, youngsters acquire language naturally by putting words to practice. The on-going rehearsals and language exchanges that take place allow children's oral literacy to grow as expected. Soon their word combinations and utterances start to carry a universal message.

As thoughts and language come together (Vygotsky, 1978), young children begin to articulate words, ideas, and emotions more clearly. Children draw on a range of strategies they learn naturally to communicate with meaning and purpose. Initially, youngsters may:

- use gestures to talk
- refer to items in context by pointing to desired objects
- demand objects by using general labels or by creating their own name for items
- invent and use words and language patterns of their own
- produce word combinations that make sense
- string words together into limited sentences
- use sentences that continue to increase in length
- ask questions for purpose, clarity, or interest

As children gain experience with language in social contexts, they become more sophisticated language users and are able to:

- make approximations (of sounds, words, meanings, contexts)
- experiment with words, phrases, and expressions
- use more complex grammar structures and sentences
- deduce their own grammar rules
- make and test predictions of language patterns
- adjust their oral language depending on the social situation or purpose (using pragmatics)

In the pattern of daily living, children learn to master spoken language and understand its meanings as they interact with others. By talking and listening to others, children build the foundation for literacy learning and language development. Through language interactions in social contexts, children gain new vocabulary and information that they themselves can use for different purposes (Hirsh-Pasek and Golinkoff, 2003). By engaging in dialogues at home, at school and in the community, young people become partners in a social dance that teaches them to communicate effectively (Hart and Risley, 1999). As they become literate, youngsters need language experiences that invite them into conversations where they can practice this social dance. Children's willingness to engage in conversations with others is noticeably shaped by the language partners they communicate with. As language partners, parents, teachers, caregivers, and significant others share a common role to engage children in the "communication dance" and keep it going (Hart and Risely, 1999).

The Supportive Role of Language Partners

From an early age, a child is surrounded by language (Hall, 1987). Hearing words, voices, and conversations enables young people to grow as listeners and become language users themselves. Daily routines and activities inspire youngsters to talk. As they participate in everyday life experiences, children learn to use oral language naturally through social interactions with parents, siblings, family members, teachers, caregivers, and other adults and children (Hall, 1987). These language partners have important roles in children's oral language development.

The Supportive Role of Language Partners

Children learn oral language when parents, teachers, and other language partners:
- model/demonstrate language being used appropriately
- participate in conversations that children can follow
- show how to use oral language for different purposes (in various social contexts)
- modify/adjust their speech (change the rate or tone of voice)
- support and encourage children to talk from an early age
- provide culturally appropriate and positive feedback (praise)
- narrate and describe events and activities with growing detail (using a wider vocabulary, paragraphs and more complex structures as children's skills develop)
- talk to children about everyday activities (cooking, shopping)
- use a varied vocabulary
- summarize or paraphrase to clarify meaning
- plan activities that motivate children to speak (drama, role-play)
- play language games, read books, and sing songs that use language in active ways
- engage children in conversations
- talk about themes and topics that interest children
- extend conversations by asking questions
- probe children for answers
- build on what children say
- invite children to share information or describe something new
- encourage children to ask questions
- respond to children's questions with interest and detail
- allow children to invent their own words and correct themselves

As youngsters discover language and its uses, they need to be encouraged to play with language—its sounds, words, structures, and meanings—in purposeful ways. When children learn to talk, they need to experiment, take risks, approximate, make mistakes, and learn to self-correct to learn language most effectively (Doake, 1988). Youngsters' attempts at oral language need to be embraced with a positive attitude of approval, interest, and delight to promote further language use and development.

Family members, teachers, and other language partners can put children on solid footing by supporting their early language learning efforts and encouraging further development. With practice to develop skills and expertise, adults can engage young people in mature dialogues that extend children's conversations to topics about which a wider vocabulary, more complex grammar, and sophisticated language structures are used. Parents, teachers, and other adults can facilitate children's oral language development by providing a stimulating verbal environment both at home and in the classroom.

The Language Environment

The real world provides children with natural conditions for learning to talk (Cambourne, 1988). From a novice age, children are welcomed into a community where language learning takes place in authentic situations. In the flow of everyday living, young people discover language sounds and features for different social functions. As children become language users, the words they put into practice are the groundwork for literacy development.

Language learning begins in natural settings including the home and everyday social environment. In some cultures, many children attend child-care and are involved in preschool programs from an early age. When youngsters enter primary classrooms, they are eager to begin formal schooling. The journey from home to the classroom carries young language learners through environments that are rich with literacy experiences. The verbal environment of the home, school, and local community plays an important part in children's early literacy development because it sets the stage for language learning and later academic success (Hirsh-Pasek and Golinkoff, 2003; Peterson, 2007).

Young children are introduced to the sounds, rhythms, and patterns of language by being immersed in an environment that is surrounded by talk. Parents and teachers promote early literacy and social-emotional development if they create a positive atmosphere where children can participate naturally in rich oral language experiences throughout the day. Building an environment that motivates children to speak and interact with others begins by talking to them about a variety of topics and activities that interest them. Allowing children to sit and work with others in small and large groups enables them to explore, create, and learn through discussion and collaboration. By providing authentic contexts and opportunities for children to talk as part of learning, adults can shape the classroom into a nurturing and stimulating language environment that promotes active listening and speaking.

A solid language environment in the home and classroom exemplifies natural and supportive conditions for language learning. Children are more likely to take risks and express their ideas when they are part of a caring atmosphere where others listen and value what they have to say (Allen et al., 1994).

The classroom and home setting should be:
- nurturing and positive, where listeners are considerate of children by listening carefully and offering smiles, praise, and encouraging feedback
- responsive to children, where adults show an interest in the topics that children discuss
- attentive to the needs, concerns, and likes of children, reflected in appropriate displays, resources, and learning focus
- enriching and enhancing, by building on children's interests, conversations, inquiries
- filled with print, literacy, learning, and art materials to encourage and stimulate language growth and conversation

An environment in which children see, hear, and use language in the flow of classroom life helps young people to develop aural and communication skills naturally. The following classroom resources, materials, and displays promote active listening, productive talk, and dynamic learning:
- Listening/viewing centre with a variety of audio-visual equipment
- Visual displays (posters, environmental print, bulletin boards)
- Classroom library with books and other literacy materials for discussion
- Toys and play centres (home corner, doctor's office, post office, grocery store, restaurant)
- Drama resources (puppets, costumes, props for role play)
- Visual arts materials
- Musical instruments
- Theme and interest areas (for items, books, and other resources such as family artifacts that relate to children's interests and backgrounds)
- Learning centres for inquiry and exploration in subjects such as science and history

A wealth of learning materials and creative resources where children work, play, and learn with others can motivate them to speak and interact in natural, fun, and artistic forms. Literacy materials and learning centres create a stimulating environment in which children discover how to use language as an instrument for learning, literacy development and intellectual growth.

The key to literacy learning and academic success is increasing the amount of language children use in school (Hirsch-Pasek and Golinkoff, 2003). The classroom environment should be rich with opportunities to use language that is purposeful and productive. Every learning experience should be an open invitation to children to express their understandings and thoughts in ways that support language growth. Through a variety of classroom activities that promote talk as a resource for learning, children will learn to understand and experiment with different language styles and uses across the curriculum (Allen et al., 1994). As students make scientific discoveries, visit past cultures, explore math concepts, respond to literature, and engage in visual and performing arts, they use language to make inquires, locate information, explain ideas, make connections, and establish relationships. Classroom events like those explored in the following pages are rich with possibilities for word learning, speech development, and social interaction.

Oral Language Events

For years, reading and writing have been the predominant focus in early childhood literacy programs. However, research and best practices have shown that the foundation of literacy development is rooted in talk (Britton, 1992; Palmer and Bayley, 2005). Parents, teachers, and other educators need to build more opportunities for children to use spoken language to balance reading and writing and succeed in these areas. Talk is fundamental to language acquisition, literacy growth, and learning in general. Children require time and occasions to develop oral language skills through daily life experiences and classroom events that encourage them to talk and learn with others. Activities that engage youngsters in purposeful and productive talk help them discover the many uses of oral language as a resource for learning and a means for communication and social interaction. Surrounding children with oral language activities enables them to build vocabulary, grammatical knowledge, and narrative skills in meaningful and authentic contexts. The goal of these activities should rest on supporting young language learners who are just beginning to experiment with language by helping them build their oral language skills in developmentally appropriate, authentic, and purposeful ways. These experiences should not solely aim to produce expert young users who develop linguistic proficiency or master spoken language by acquiring sophisticated verbal skills at an early age (Hall, 1987).

Word Learning and Vocabulary Development

Learning words marks the earliest stage of language development. When children hear words in real-life, authentic contexts, they are able to acquire language naturally and build vocabulary in meaningful and purposeful ways. From a young age, children understand that words are essential tools for communication that allow them to make meaning. As youngsters explore the use of words and sign symbols to name objects and express themselves, they are building on the language, vocabulary, and meanings they have developed to communicate effectively.

Word learning promotes vocabulary development, an important cornerstone in learning to read. Children who have larger vocabularies are generally betters readers. According to Hirsh-Pasek and Golinkoff (2003), vocabulary is the strongest predictor of reading success and literacy ability. Having a good vocabulary helps children recognize written words and understand print. Building an inventory of words and knowing their associated meanings stretches children's vocabulary to give them a better command of language. "A child who has strong language abilities will have a real advantage when it comes to reading" (Hirsh-Pasek and Golinkoff, 2003 p. 102). Oral language activities represent the best way to inspire word learning and promote vocabulary development.

Talk

Talk sets the stage for language learning. Children need to be surrounded by a surplus of talk to build vocabulary, grammatical knowledge, and language structures. The natural conversations embedded in family, school, and community life offer authentic forums for learning words, grammar rules, and social language functions. The daily routines and shared activities at home and in the classroom allow children and adults to engage in talk that is productive and meaningful.

It is important for parents, teachers and other language partners to talk with children about the experiences they have. Conversations may centre on a range of topics including:

- Past events
- Current events and surroundings
- Future plans
- Relationships
- Emotions
- Life lessons
- Learning experiences
- Explanations (e.g., for how things work)
- New ideas
- Child-centred interests
- Daily routines and activities
- Special events (school celebrations, presentations)

Talking to children facilitates their oral language development by building vocabulary, grammatical knowledge, and better language skills for when children are older (Peterson, 2007). Day-to-day life experiences provide rich potential for language learning in genuine and natural conditions. By using every opportunity to engage children in talk during various activities, language partners help youngsters grow into language users who communicate effectively.

Narrating Activities

Shared activities provide rich opportunities to discover words and language functions through the joy of participation. The child-adult interactions that take place naturally in the context of home and school events shape the conditions for language learning as young people grow. Surrounding children with a flow of language in everyday activities and conversations helps them absorb new vocabulary, language forms, and sentence structures more easily (Palmer and Bayley, 2008).

Opportunities for young people to explore language arise in a variety of ordinary activities such as cooking, shopping, gardening, and household chores. They also arise in educational learning experiences, including lessons, field trips, assemblies, and extra-curricular activities. As children engage in these authentic activities, they build vocabulary, grammatical knowledge, and language structures in a meaningful and purposeful way. Parents, teachers and other language partners provide authentic models and occasions for literacy development and language use when they narrate the activities children are involved in. While working with youngsters individually or a group, adults can explain what they are making or doing throughout a shared event or child-initiated activity. Explanations about indoor and outdoor experiences introduce children to the relevant vocabulary and give them accurate, explicit descriptions to use language effectively on their own. To narrate activities, adults can:

- name objects that may be new or unfamiliar
- repeat the labels and names of tools and materials
- describe procedures (e.g., brushing teeth, conducting a science experiment) by explaining each step in detail
- use precise words and expressive language to explain activities
- use terms and phrases that extend children's vocabularies but are still within reach (understanding)
- explain their own actions or the actions of the children as they are engaged
- provide vivid details that sound interesting and inviting
- allow children to join in by offering their own words, descriptions and explanations

The annotations and running comments of language partners allow young people to bridge oral language with experience. Soon, children are able to make direct, tangible links between words and actions as they participate in concrete learning and everyday hands-on activities and conversations. Adult narrators use contextualized language to frame their experiences. Through the explicit use of language (words, phrases, or ideas) in various situations and environments, children gain the prior knowledge and cueing strategies they need for literacy learning. Teachers and parents facilitate the language learning process by acting as guides to help children build vocabulary, explore language functions, and apply grammar rules in relevant contexts. By creating opportunities for literacy development in daily experiences and interactions, adults can scaffold children's language learning to equip youngsters with the tools to naturally follow, extend, describe, and recount events on their own.

Monologues or Self-Talk

Language is learned in the framework of interactions—in the context of playing, learning, growing, and working. As young people engage in daily events, they often talk to themselves about what they are doing. Listening to youngsters at work and at play can delightfully fill our ears with their running commentary. It is natural for young people to talk (or sing) to themselves as they engage in childhood activities. Their interior monologue is an important part of their language and cognitive development (Vygotsky, 1987; Palmer and Bayley, 2005). Through their narrated passages, children play with words, sounds, meanings, and structures of language in ways that enrich and clarify their experiences. Youngsters will use self-talk naturally to convey thoughts, ideas and feelings when they engage in child-initiated activities or events that parallel their interests.

Parents and teachers need to allow children time to engage in self-selected activities they enjoy. Children may be better motivated if they have a variety of creative, playful and interactive indoor and outdoor activities to choose or develop on their own. These may include occasions and materials for discovery, craft making, hands-on learning, and imaginative play. Through self-activated experiences, children learn language naturally in the course of playful and purposeful interactions. In a world dominated by technology where schools are faced with the demands of accountability, opportunities for language learning are sometimes limited to television, computers, electronic toys, and structured activities such as tests and pencil and paper work. Spontaneous, self-initiated activities can make language learning more productive, meaningful, and personally engaging. Although these events help youngsters build vocabulary and explore language sounds and functions, at the same time children need interactive language opportunities to develop speech. The conversations that take place naturally during social engagements and ordinary activities at home and at school also set the stage for literacy learning.

Social Language Use and Conversations

Language learning is embedded in the conversations of everyday life. Learning to talk is a partnership between language users who offer their personal say and feedback to keep the dialogue, or social dance, going. Children need opportunities to explore the social uses of language in family circle conversations, class discussions, and peer interactions. These experiences provide young language

Language learning is embedded in the conversations of everyday life. Learning to talk is a partnership between language users who offer personal say and feedback to keep the dialogue, or social dance, going.

learners with recurring opportunities to talk and interact with others in different contexts (one-to-one adult-child or child-child interactions, small peer groups, large group gatherings). Through various discourses, young people discover the art of communication by learning to listen, pay attention, make eye contact, take turns, ask and answer questions, and develop other social language skills.

Children of different backgrounds may have other social and cultural language practices that shape the way they converse with others in the classroom or in the school community. Through consideration and respect for these traditions, the social behaviors and conversational skills of children of diverse ethnic backgrounds can be better understood. At times, it is important to allow young people to speak in the language that is most comfortable to them. Allowing youngsters to revert to the main language spoken at home can serve as a bridge in their development of vocabulary and grammar structures, and overall literacy growth. The key is to encourage children to talk with others about personal interests, life experiences, and the activities they are engaged in as they learn and grow.

Teachers and parents can provide the models and experiences for children to develop their listening and speaking skills by allowing them to engage in conversations with others in a variety of contexts, such as during circle time or in role-playing. As this chapter describes, there are many ways to encourage purposeful and productive talk in the classroom. At times, young language users need specific occasions to develop social language skills if they are to gain confidence as conversational speakers. The following techniques may help children to talk to others, one-on-one or in groups, throughout the course of the day:

Conversation Starters—Use prompts as a way to ease children into conversation during entry routines by displaying a series of objects or sentence starters on a table or news board in the classroom (wipe board, chart paper, chalk board, bulletin board). Invite students to select a featured item on display or chose a topic from a list to discuss with a partner or small group. Children can add their own topics or objects to the featured lists and displays.

Oral Presentations—Students can bring in objects from home to voluntarily share with others that may reflect their personal interests, life experiences or theme topics being explored in the classroom. Items can be portrayed during small or large group discussions where peers can ask questions or respond with related anecdotes of their own. Variations of these "show and tell" presentations may include objects that match a set of criteria or attributes (size, color, initial letter, or other concept being studied). These items can be revealed in a class game of 20 questions where children can use the criteria to guess the object that was brought in. Students can select the required criteria before collecting items from home.

News of the Day—Students can hold partner, small group, or whole class discussions at the start or end of the day sharing news stories or current events in the classroom, school, or global community. These conversations will allow children to share their own explanations and ask questions (5W and H questions) to clarify their accounts and descriptions of events. Recounting stories or activities of the day helps children develop narrative skills. These skills are also gained by sharing autobiographical experiences. Oral recounts are explored later in this chapter.

Allowing youngsters to revert to the main language spoken at home can serve as a bridge in their development of vocabulary and grammar structures, and overall literacy growth.

Language and Word Play

Language learning takes place naturally through pleasurable activities where children can have fun with language and get excited about words as they sing, act, and play. Apart from conversations, youngsters learn to talk through spontaneous, interactive, and lively childhood experiences in which they play with words, sounds, and structures they hear in rhymes, songs, and games. Word play activities help children develop a strong command of language by building vocabulary, growing familiarity with language structures, and encouraging repetition and innovation that are key to language learning and literacy development (Palmer and Bayley, 2005). Playful, engaging contexts for language learning include:

- Lap rides and bouncing games
- Clapping games
- Action songs and dances
- Finger plays
- Traditional and playground verses
- Nursery rhymes
- Chants
- Raps
- Children's poems and verses
- Music and song

The suggestions in Chapter 3 (Language Awareness and Word Play) provide further opportunities to develop oral language through dynamic literacy experiences.

Vocabulary Building Experiences

Experiences with poetry, song, rhyme, and verse are powerful vehicles for word learning. At the same time, children acquire new vocabulary and learn to master spoken language through strategic work or play activities that give them access to specific terms, phrases, and expressions. Hearing new words can lead to a "naming explosion" where youngsters are quick to identify objects and people in their environment from an early age (Hirsh-Pasek and Golinkoff, 2003). Learning familiar words and expressions through repetition and experience allows young children to use their new vocabulary in appropriate ways. Combining words to make sentences and expressions allows children to practice the grammatical part of language use. Young people play a major role in constructing their knowledge of vocabulary, grammar rules, and language structures. Children learn selected words and grammar forms through strategic activities and meaningful contexts, including:

- Stories and literature activities
- Drama games and role-play scenarios
- Theme studies or topic work in which target word lists and subject-specific terminology are used to narrate or explain activities (e.g., a science experiment)
- Name games in which explicit terms are used to identify and name objects and surroundings
- Word/concept games in which terms are used to denote concepts such as:
  - opposites (open, close; night, day; indoor, outdoor)
  - actions (eating, jumping)
  - positions (over, under, through)
  - sequence (first, then, after, later, next)
- Sensory descriptions that encourage children to use their senses to describe experiences using adjectives that relate to various attributes
- Expression banks, where children can keep records or lists and definitions of commonly-used phrases and expressions

Suggested activities and language games designed to build vocabulary and word usage are available in Sue Palmer's and Ros Bayley's book *Early Literacy Fundamentals* (Pembroke, 2005).

Through purposeful language activities that combine play and instruction, children can build storehouses of new words and expressions. Through balanced opportunities to learn language in different ways, young people have broad exposure to familiar words and expressions. Children need experience and practice with vocabulary to gain confidence using it themselves. Revisiting language in word games and vocabulary building experiences helps young people to become sophisticated language learners.

Read-aloud Events and Literature Activities

Reading aloud to children helps form the foundation for oral language learning that also leads to reading success and overall academic achievement (Wells, 1987; Hirsh-Pasek and Golinkoff, 2003; Peterson, 2007). Young children need to develop early reader strategies and oral language skills in order to learn to read.

Children who have better vocabularies generally become better readers (Hirsh-Pasek and Golinkoff, 2003; Peterson, 2007). To develop a broad vocabulary, youngsters need to be exposed to books from an early age. Through read-aloud events and literature experiences, children hear and learn new words in the context of a story or non-fiction book. Hearing words from books builds children's vocabulary and teaches grammar and language structures in a narrative way. The vocabulary, grammatical knowledge and narrative skills that children gain through reading activities form the oral language foundation that contributes to reading comprehension (Peterson, 2007).

Parents and teachers can use children's literature to help children build vocabulary, grammatical knowledge, and other oral language skills they need for reading success. Book experiences may include:

- reading aloud to children every day
- discussing the story and pictures
- inviting children to retell the story from their perspective or other viewpoints
- drawing attention to the author's style, word choices and descriptions
- asking children questions about the text that encourage the use of vocabulary (similar to dialogic reading of picture books as described in Chapter 5)
- challenging students to make predictions and explain their thinking
- having children participate in shared reading experiences and oral cloze activities (see Chapter 5)
- reading non-fiction books on topics that students like or are familiar with
- using children's literature to introduce and teach concepts in a range of subject areas so students experience the use of language and specific words in different contexts
- engaging students in book talks and literature circles that explore theme, word study, and other aspects of the text selection
- inviting children to respond to literature through writing and poetry, and other written formats to put new words to practice
- fostering interactive and imaginative engagements with literature through drama, role play, and visual arts

(Further literature activities are described in Chapter 5.)

Through read-aloud events, children can be inspired to use oral language as a way to interact with literature and respond to texts with a stronger command of language. These text encounters allow children to grow as language learners as they make use of new vocabulary, language structures, and narrative discourse to "talk like a book".

Choral Speaking Events

Children can enhance their oral communication skills by participating in choral speaking. Choral speaking turns poems, songs, rhymes, and children's literature into wonderful scripts for dramatic oral presentations. As youngsters work together to speak verses aloud, they practice saying words while attending to language sounds. Experiences in choral speaking often grow from shared reading events in which text selections are made and presented aloud with others through choral reading. As children move into choral speaking from shared reading events, like this, they encounter print and are introduced to various genres for the purpose of sharing these texts aloud. When children practice reading poems, rhymes, verses, and other texts with the support of others, they experiment with choral reading strategies such as voice, tone, and expression that are equally suited for choral speaking.

Before presenting a selection orally, children need time to practice saying words, dividing up parts, playing with sounds, and experimenting with voices. As students rehearse the selection and explore ways of presenting it aloud in choral reading and choral speaking, they learn to match spoken words with written language. Children can work individually, in pairs or groups to practice and share their oral interpretations in dramatic and entertaining ways using a range of strategies, such as, playing with phrasing, using sound effects, and incorporating gestures. Developing oral language strategies like fluency, clarity, and expression can provide children with effective vocal techniques they can use in reading and drama. Choral speaking events allow youngsters to become confident speakers and sophisticated language users who can draw in listeners and entertain audiences with ease.

Choral speaking events allow youngsters to become confident speakers and sophisticated language users who can draw in listeners and entertain audiences with ease.

Imaginative Play

Early childhood experiences in play provide youngsters with the settings, opportunities, and materials to learn oral language in authentic, engaging, and meaningful frameworks. As youngsters participate in pretend play, they discover words naturally in the context of "child's work" (Paley, 2005). Through the imaginative engagements and social interactions that are characteristic of play, children inherently demonstrate greater language confidence and linguistic ability (Palmer and Bayley, 2005).

Experiences in child's play take many forms. Through socio-dramatic play, youngsters often build on events from everyday life. As children explore familiar aspects of home and community living in pretend play, they imitate the social language functions and practices they observe in the real world. This form of reality-based play allows children to rehearse the oral language they hear in daily use. Sometimes, child's play moves into imaginary worlds of fantasy and make-believe. Engaging in *thematic-fantasy play* takes language learning to new heights above a child's ordinary use of vocabulary toward the development of narrative language and creative thought (Palmer and Bayley, 2005). As youngsters participate in dramatic play and make-believe, they adopt imaginative roles and improvise language using fantasy talk as they act together (Paley, 2005). Fantasy talk during play often mimics the language of books children are familiar with. When children absorb the book language they hear, they use similar words, grammar forms, and narrative structures to reconstruct stories and play sequences of their own. Through role play, youngsters use expressive language to communicate with others in both real-life and imaginative scenarios where words and phrases are learned and uncovered in the context of interactive, creative, and playful activities. Thus, play is a stage for building vocabulary and exploring complex grammar structures. Through both reality-based and theme-based play, children have engaging opportunities to practice and develop oral language as they talk through new concepts, relive familiar experiences, and explore innovative worlds and imaginative ideas in each episode.

Teachers and parents can create an environment that supports talk by providing time, space, and materials for children to enjoy spontaneous role play, drama, improvisation, and make-believe. With appropriate props and materials, indoor and outdoor learning settings can be transformed into recreational play centres where youngsters can actively participate in different forms of play. As recommended in Chapter 1, play settings might include:

- a home area (kitchen, work bench)
- theme centres for reality-based pretend play (retail or grocery stores, restaurants, post office, medical offices, hospital)
- drama corner for imaginative play

As you read in Chapter 1, demands for accountability and excellence standards in education have impaired early childhood literacy programs, limiting experiences in primary classrooms to traditional reading and writing tasks. Play needs to be restored to the curriculum and school life as an indispensible component of early literacy instruction. Adults have a significant role to shape play into purposeful and productive activities for children to learn oral language and develop literacy. Parents, teachers, and other language partners can:

- invite children to participate in a variety of hands-on play activities
- engage in different types of play with children
- model role play and language use in a variety of play experiences
- observe children's interaction during play and note the vocabulary and language structures being used in different contexts
- add new materials to play centres to extend children's vocabulary
- build on children's play sequences by making suggestions and extending the drama scenarios
- provide additional play experiences to give children more practice with language

Through play, children develop their language skills in an authentic and meaningful context that seems natural to them. Children's genuine attempts at communication through play reveal the depth of their literacy understanding and efforts to make meaning of their world. Play episodes support children's development of vocabulary and grammatical knowledge in practical ways. These engagements also move young people toward the use of narrative language as they imagine and pretend with others.

Building Narrative Skills—Learning the Language of Story

Children have a natural ability to describe things, recount events, and tell stories. Through emergent literacy activities, family literacy practices, read-aloud events, and play episodes, youngsters start to develop the literacy skills required for reading success, language development, and later literacy acquisition. Building a repertoire of words is important to literacy learning, but grammatical knowledge and vocabulary development alone are not enough to make meaning

To move from print to meaning, young people need to develop strong narrative skills that can give them greater control of written language. Understanding the structure of texts helps children make transitions in literacy from oral language to reading.

of print. To move from print to meaning, young people need to develop strong narrative skills that can give them greater control of written language. Understanding the structure of texts helps children make transitions in literacy from oral language to reading. Children learn the language of stories (known as narrative discourse) over time (Hirsh-Pasek and Golinkoff, 2003). This knowledge grows from experiences with narrative in the context of living, playing, reading, storytelling, and other oral language and literature events. Parents and teachers can foster the development of good narrative skills in children by planning oral language experiences.

Personal Recounts and Autobiographical Narratives

Children naturally develop their ability to tell stories when they share autobiographical experiences. Encouraging children to talk about events in their personal lives from an early age (as young as two years) helps youngsters receive the practice and guidance they need to develop the narrative skills required for later literacy acquisition (Engel, 1995; Peterson, 2007).

Personal stories may come from a wealth of sources based on everyday experiences and rich family histories. As life unfolds, children can draw on past events (cultural traditions, holidays, celebrations), daily episodes (school life, social programs, trips, family outings), and future plans or goals to share autobiographical stories with others. The following experiences may provide children with frameworks for constructing narratives:

Personal Timeline—Children can create timelines featuring important milestones or events in their personal or family history that mark each year. Holidays, celebrations, vacations, and childhood achievements (e.g., first steps, first lost tooth, or first hair cut) can be recorded. Students can chronicle their life stories using photographs or drawings too. Children can share their personal timelines or describe a featured event by presenting these accounts to others.

Scrapbook—Students can produce scrapbook pages highlighting important moments in their lives (favorite childhood memories, embarrassing moments, special occasions, sporting events they participated in). Children can present the pages they designed to others. Entries can be used to make a personal or class scrapbook featuring these autobiographical experiences.

Photo Albums and Baby Books—Ask children to bring in photos or baby books featuring important milestones in their young lives. Students also can assemble their own photo albums to feature significant people and special events in their childhood. Youngsters can present their albums or baby books to the class as they begin the school year.

Family Treasured Goods—Invite children to bring in a special object from home (item of jewelry, photograph, card, family heirloom, memorable gift) if they have permission from an adult family member. Children might also draw a picture or take a photograph of a treasured good that is important to them. Students can use the item or picture as a prompt to share its significance or meaning with others. With partners, in small groups, or as a class, participants can share personal stories based on family artifacts.

As children recount stories about their lives, they develop a sense of voice, narrative style and use of language that is uniquely their own. Telling personal event narratives gives children a stronger feeling of ownership and better command of language. These accounts provide context and structure for children's experiences that lead to a greater understanding of how stories are created and written texts are organized (Peterson, 2007). Narrative talk that grows from sharing autobiographical stories starts to mirror the decontextualized language, varied sentences, grammar structures, and sequence that are characteristic of literature (Peterson, 2007). As children gain confidence and proficiency in telling autobiographical stories, they develop the skills required to tell fictional stories on their own. Sharing personal event narratives moves children toward the kind of storytelling experiences that open up the imagination and further develop literacy.

Storytelling

Storytelling is an essential building block for early literacy development.Both research and practice have shown the importance of storytelling for language development, reading success, and later literacy acquisition (Hirsh-Pasek and Golinkoff, 2003; Palmer and Bayley, 2005; Peterson, 2007).

Storytelling is part of a strong oral tradition that delights audiences. Many oral stories are filled with mystery, joy. and excitement that draws listeners in and invites them to participate. Listening to stories helps children build their oral communication skills by developing attention span, auditory memory, and listening comprehension (Palmer and Bayley, 2005). Hearing stories retold allows young listeners to learn key phrases, patterned structures, and sentence constructions through repetition. During the retellings of a story, children often commit favorite texts to memory in an effort to take part in this oral tradition themselves. After all, many young people are natural storytellers who practice the skills of this art form to entertain others. Through the use of different vocal techniques, children develop fluency, expression, vocabulary, sentence structure, and linguistic ability as they craft oral stories with a style and voice that are distinctively their own. Storytelling helps children become confident, innovative, and sophisticated language users. Learning the art of storytelling gives young people dynamic skills in oral presentation and verbal communication needed in today's changing world.

Through storytelling children also develop the narrative skills required for literacy achievement. Recent studies have shown a strong relationship between storytelling and reading. As Hirsh-Pasek and Golinkoff (2003) explain: "storytelling is one of the bridges that move children from language to reading" (p. 103). The ability to tell stories is directly related to the ability to learn to read (Snow, 1983; Hirsh-Pasek and Golinkoff, 2003). Telling oral stories requires children to enter story mode, use book language, share literary details, and describe narrative elements in their storytelling presentations.

By listening to stories from a variety of sources and learning to tell stories themselves, children acquire an understanding of literary genres, story structures, fictional contexts, and narrative devices such as repetition and alliteration often encountered in literature. They discover characters, plots, settings, and other key features of story grammar that are used to shape narratives (Hirsh-Pasek and Golinkoff, 2003; Palmer and Bayley, 2005). When crafting oral stories, children play with storybook language (narrative discourse) and character dialogue as they interact in text worlds and make connections with literature.

As children recount stories about their lives, they develop a sense of voice, narrative style, and use of language that is uniquely their own. Telling personal event narratives gives children a stronger feeling of ownership and better command of language.

They use decontextualized language and discursive frameworks to construct a background for their own narratives. Learning the language and structure of stories helps young people better understand reading material. In storytelling, children are not limited by the challenges of print and decoding that can be obstacles in the reading process and sometimes inhibit the construction of meaning.

Listening to stories helps youngsters build sequencing, predicting, and inferencing strategies required to make meaning and understand print. Telling oral stories provides children with the narrative skills required for reading comprehension (Peterson, 2007). Through the playful practice of storytelling, young people can transfer their knowledge of oral language and literature to the reading of written texts. As children emerge as readers and writers, they will draw on the narrative skills and the language systems they developed through this oral tradition when they craft oral stories, read books, and write tales of their own.

Experiences in storytelling can provide children with skills, inspiration, and ideas to become writers and construct stories of their own. Listening to others tell stories can build an understanding of story sequence, text patterns, and genre formats encountered in print. As children craft oral stories, they incorporate the elements of story grammar and use narrative devices, decontextualized language, and literature frameworks that can influence their writing. Building a repertoire of characters, plots, settings, and book language helps children invent and write stories of their own. Through storytelling, young people can develop the vocabulary, sentence structures, grammatical forms, and language patterns of written language. Oral narratives, like printed texts, provide a model and structure for children's writing in different genres such as myths and legends. As children apply the language skills they gain through narrative experiences, they often experiment with different forms of writing until they find a genre preference and style that work for them.

The following will help parents and teachers to introduce children to narrative experiences in storytelling that can help them grow into proficient readers and writers.

Create the Environment—To establish a setting appropriate for storytelling, time, space, and materials are important. Set up a designated area in the classroom, school library, or other location where children can share stories. Decorate the area with a rug, rocking chair, treasure chest, and literature display (collection of multicultural stories). Enrich the environment with special objects that can be used as prompts for storytelling. Display these items in a Teller's Gallery or Storytelling Museum. Invite children to bring in and display items from home:
- toys (wooden toys, dolls/figurines, play sets, building blocks)
- old fashion games
- cultural goods and artifacts (ethnic crafts and hand-made goods such as pottery and wood carvings)
- trinkets, costume jewelry, and beaded ornaments
- folk music and instruments
- collection of objects related to a theme (e.g., animals, nature)

In addition, students can design ritual props, such as story hats, teller's vest, and talking sticks that can be used to tell a story.

Collect Storytelling Props—Children can build their narrative skills by playing with different props that incite the imagination and prompt story ideas (see the extensive list of materials in "The Play Environment" in Chapter 1). By gathering a variety of literature, play, and drama resources, teachers and students can build an inventory of tools to construct narratives.

The art of storytelling grows from imaginative and narrative experiences in early childhood in which youngsters can use props as aides to construct and present tales of their own. When children draw on creative resources that surround them as they interact with literature and engage in socio-dramatic and fantasy play, they begin to build narrative skills as storytellers. Young people develop these language abilities naturally through literacy events, shared oral traditions and play episodes. Through a variety of oral language activities that build on telling stories, children can develop the core skills needed to become crafted storytellers able to preserve this traditional art form for years.

Plan Storytelling Activities—Children need experiences in storytelling that invite them to listen and prepare them to tell stories on their own. Telling stories aloud enables children to learn about language, build vocabulary, explore genres, and rehearse forms to be able to communicate effectively. Teachers can assist young people by planning the following classroom events in storytelling:

Listening Activities—Provide an opportunity for students to listen to a variety of oral stories based on works of children's literature or tales from around the world. Introduce children to as many oral stories as possible by sharing different narratives every day. Establish a routine for telling stories regularly (following entry procedures). A daily storytelling ritual helps build a sense of community in the classroom. As well, invite professional storytellers, community and family members, librarians and other guests (older children, school administrator) to share oral narratives or allow children to listen to audio recordings of stories. Listening to others tell stories provides young people with examples to follow on their own.

Encourage children to be active listeners by sitting together as a group, maintaining eye contact with the storyteller, avoiding distractions, and refraining from conversations during the storytelling event. Involve students by engaging their imagination. Invite them to visualize the story as it unfolds. Have youngsters participate actively in telling parts of the story (e.g., call and response, chiming in), adding sound effects and vocal techniques (howling, whispering), and acting out scenes. They might also take on other roles that require audience involvement, such as introducing the storyteller or explaining the origin or significance of a story.

Responding to Oral Stories—After listening to experienced tellers share a story, invited the class to discuss the distinctive styles and performance skills used during the oral presentation. The storyteller may model the effective use of the following techniques:
- fluency
- clarity
- expression
- drama
- oral language/read-aloud strategies (chanting, word emphasis, repetition)

- listener participation (audience involvement)
- ritual prop or signal (bell chime, candle, story stick)
- sound effects (knocking, tapping, clapping)
- story symbol to represent narrative aspects
- other (music, instruments)

In *A Project Approach to Language Learning* (Pembroke, 2001), a variety of classroom activities that explore the art of storytelling with children are featured in detail.

After hearing a variety of stories told in different genres and styles, children learn to identify the features of a good story worth listening to. Engaging in the time-old tradition of listening to stories shapes children's understanding and appreciation of literature as they grow.

Encounters with oral stories allow young people to step inside the legendary tales and adventures they hear and interact with literature in creative ways. Apart from discussion, students can respond to story selections through the arts, writing, critical literacy and interdisciplinary activities.

Experiences in the arts, literacy, and related areas of study often challenge students to envision, extend, and use their imagination to respond to oral stories in ways that enhance the stories they hear. Through interactive engagements with literature, children find the inspiration, model, and voice to start telling stories themselves.

Building Collaborative Stories—To be comfortable with storytelling and be prepared to tell narratives on their own, children need practice with others. Start with experiences in which students can construct collaborative stories in pairs or small groups. Use story starters as prompts to develop narratives. Encourage children to listen attentively and build on what partners say as the story grows. After a read-aloud or storytelling event, encourage students to retell the narrative as a group. Ensure that all members have a voice and an equal chance to contribute to the story reconstruction. Telling cooperative stories allows children to develop narrative skills within a supportive framework.

Children Telling Collaborative Stories Using Puppets to Guide Them

Deanna: *Once upon a time, there was a princess with flowers in her garden. The princess went to see the flowers in the garden. Then she went back into the castle and fell into a deep sleep. Alas, when she woke up she turned into a flower. She cried and cried and cried (bows head and pretends to cry) Boo hoo. But she calmed down. Then she went to the witch's house. The witch scared her so she ran away into the forest.*

Adult: *Where did the princess go?*

Deanna: *The witch found the princess back at the castle sleeping on her pillow.*

Issabella: *The witch gathered gifts from the animals and insects in the flower garden to put into a magic potion. The frog gave up a croak. The ladybug gave up a spot. The butterfly gave up part of her wing. The caterpillar gave up her cocoon. The pig gave up mud. Next, the witch turned the potion and gave it to the princess. Suddenly, her face, skin, and hair turned back into a princess again. Finally, the princess was human again. The strange thing was when the princess returned to the palace that night, the king and queen heard her croak when she was asleep.*

Telling Guided Stories—Students can practice narrative skills in guided activities. Children often learn to construct oral stories by exercising props, play materials, literature resources, and art supplies that surround them. To begin, encourage young people to make use of pictorial information in texts to develop oral stories to share with others. Have students draw upon the illustrations in wordless picture books and other children's literature sources to create oral adaptations. As children explore the art of storytelling on their own, illustrated texts may serve them in their story reconstructions. Youngsters can also produce drawings and artwork to accompany their narratives.

Students may draw on literature itself for ideas to shape their oral stories. The characters and luxuriant settings that young people encounter in books often are the source of inspiration for tales they develop on their own. Although the stories children tell may depart from the original version, these text adaptations are filled with allusions to classical literature (characters, themes, conflicts). Through meaningful encounters with children's books, youngsters develop a framework for telling stories. Soon they are able to draw upon the traditional literature and contemporary tales they have heard and use these to guide the creation of narrative features and the development of their own storylines.

Students can also explore the language and techniques of storytelling through other guided activities. Often youngsters revisit the books and narrative experiences of childhood in dramatic play episodes in which a variety of early literacy materials and play resources become props in the narration of oral stories. Flannel storyboards, felt characters, puppets, dolls, and magnetic play sets may provide novice storytellers with both sources of ideas and tools to construct tales of their own. Stories that emerge through drama and child's play soon lead to experiences in which young people produce oral narratives using language alone.

Learning to Tell a Story—Learning the art of storytelling takes time, interest, and skill. Most storytellers begin by finding a story to share. Young people can draw on a variety of sources, from personal histories to traditional literature, when deciding on a story. Provide the class with a selection of quality picture books, short story anthologies (myths, legends, fables), and multicultural texts. Some works of literature, such as folklore and contemporary tales, are better suited for retelling. Encourage children to choose a story from their personal background. Many cultural tales are kept alive and passed down through this oral tradition (e.g., Anansi stories).

The art of storytelling is developed in many ways using a range of styles, tools, and techniques. After listening to or reading a story several times, students can use story mapping as an effective method to remember parts of the story they want to learn. Story webs, story grammars, storyboards, story cards, and other story outlines can be produced as aids for telling a story. In each graphic organizer, students record visual information, diagrams, illustrations, and key words and phrases in a format and sequence that helps them learn and remember the story. Story maps usually highlight the main events, characters, settings, problems, and other important narrative features that students want to learn.

Provide children with storytelling props or encourage them to make their own. For example, children might design story or picture cards that depict a range of characters, settings, scenes, symbols, and other important narrative elements from a collection of stories. Alternatively, they might create thematic story cards based on popular fairy tales, fables, legends, tall tales, or hero stories.

Encourage children to use these picture cards to share multicultural stories from around the world in different languages. Sharing multicultural stories in this way can help children embrace, accept, and learn to appreciate linguistic differences. It gives value to children's first languages and allows others to see and respect their peers as competent language learners. When sharing narratives using different languages, children can use visual story cards to guide them as they construct the story and help listeners follow along. Other students, adults, family members, and volunteers can serve as translators too.

Before sharing their selections with the class, students can work in pairs or small groups at listening and telling their stories to one another using their story maps as needed. As children practise their oral stories at home and at school, they can add gestures, change their voice, use props or other techniques (facial expressions, drama, symbols, and sound effects) to express themselves creatively. With time and encouragement, their fluency, confidence, enthusiasm, and skill at storytelling will grow. Through the shared practice, joy, and engagement of learning stories with language partners, young children can embrace the art of storytelling to become experienced storytellers who can fashion tales of their own. They will entertain wider audiences by telling oral stories with a distinctive style and format that all will appreciate and enjoy.

Storytelling sets the stage for literacy learning and language acquisition. As youngsters retell stories from literature, or construct tales of their own, they build up the language skills that shape them into readers and writers. When children produce oral stories, they use rich book language and story frameworks to deepen their understanding of narrative. They explore themes, genres and issues in literature that stimulate creative and critical thinking. According to Kim (1999), storytelling is a key cognitive skill in the process of intellectual development. It unlocks the powers of the imagination and capacity of the mind. As children generate their own stories, they build inner worlds and conceive places and adventures that go beyond their life experiences. The ability to imagine and create new worlds is "preparation for language, reading and problem solving" (Hirsh-Pasek and Golinkoff, 2003, p. 233). In storytelling, children face universal conflicts that challenge them to resolve human issues. Storylines and text adaptations expose children to other world views and experiences, broadening their perspectives and helping them find innovative solutions. Sharing stories from around the globe fosters a sense of community, encouraging children to work together and develop an appreciation and respect for other cultures. Becoming a storyteller builds confidence and self esteem in children's own language abilities too. Sharing oral stories provides authentic opportunities for children to become innovative and sophisticated language users. Storytelling supports the process of intellectual, social, and emotional development in young people of all ages.

Many experiences in early childhood contribute to the foundations of literacy achievement. Working with oral stories enriches children's love of language and enjoyment of literature while moving them closer to reading and writing. Oral language events that are rooted in talk, reader response, and imaginative play are cornerstones to literacy. Experiences in spoken language explored in this chapter promote word learning, vocabulary development, grammatical knowledge, and narrative skills in authentic contexts. Children learn about language and acquire literacy through delightful experiences in language play, word games, phonological and phonemic awareness, nursery rhymes, rhythm activities, and other playful engagements that bring words and language to life.

Storytelling sets the stage for literacy learning and language acquisition. When children produce oral stories, they use rich book language and story frameworks to deepen their understanding of narrative. They explore themes, genres, and issues in literature that stimulate creative and critical thinking.

3

Language and Word Play

Many steps along life's road are carved in strong traditions that give voice to the human experience. From the moment children enter the world, they encounter stories, songs, and verses through delightful shared practices that bring them joy and meaning. These early introductions to language often provide the richest learning experiences that guide the way to literacy.

Through play and oral language activities, young children take hold of words and build narrative skills of their own. Developing a strong language base in vocabulary and storytelling is central to emergent literacy (Hirsh-Pasek and Golinkoff, 2003). However, learning to talk is only the beginning. To become literate and be able to read, children need to gain a deeper understanding of language—a knowledge that grows with an awareness of sounds and other language features.

Children acquire linguistic knowledge and language competence in many ways. Opening a child's ear to language starts with experiences in play, music, read-aloud, and oral language. Before they begin formal schooling, many children are exposed to oral traditions of songs, games, chants, and rituals that are part of their homes and cultures. Through these delightful engagements, youngsters can develop an inherent love of language.

Children learn language through repetition, rhyming, chanting, and playing with words. When we listen to youngsters at work and at play, we often hear echoes of lyrics from songs and verses. As children experiment with patterns of rhythm and rhyme, they play with language—imitating sounds, manipulating words, and learning to control language. Through word and language play, young people grow to become sophisticated language users who can observe language, explore words, uncover structures, discover sounds, and learn other aspects that shape both written and spoken language.

Developing language awareness is an important cornerstone in building a strong literacy foundation. Experiences in word and language play form part of the groundwork for early literacy development. As children engage in playful language events with lively texts, they gain linguistic knowledge and language proficiency in ways that make literacy learning active, engaging, and fun.

Exploring Childhood Texts

Many early childhood experiences begin with lullabies, nursery rhymes, lap rides, universal songs, and traditional verses that tune a young child's ears to language. From birth, youngsters have been swayed to sleep by gentle lyrics of traditional lullabies such as *Twinkle Twinkle Little Star*. Lap rides, finger plays, action songs, and other traditional games that entertain children of all ages are part of a rich folk literature of childhood texts ideal for language play.

As they grow, young readers encounter various forms of literature in homes and classrooms. The language, verses, and stories of classic fairy tales and traditional nursery rhymes such as *Mother Goose* have delighted children for generations. Although traditional nursery rhymes may be unfamiliar to some children today, many well-known tales and verses have been reconstructed into modern rhymes and stories that echo the sounds, rhythms, and poetic verses of the classic works. Through parody, silly rhymes, and witty verse, these contemporary renditions offer an exaggeration or alternative to classic tales and nursery rhymes that appeal more to children of all ages and backgrounds. It is important to keep in mind that, in our increasingly diverse society, many children may not have been introduced to traditional nursery rhymes, stories such as *Mother Goose*, works by Dr. Seuss, or classic tales by Hans Christian Anderson or the Brothers Grimm. The literacy experiences of many children flow from a wealth of multilingual resources and multicultural texts.

In many cultures, rich oral traditions of folklore and song include children's lullabies, poems, nursery rhymes, old chants and verses passed down through generations. We can rely on these sources to provide an inclusive inventory of world folklore that children can use for language and word play. Apart from traditional nursery rhymes and classic fairy tales, children's literature collections should build on the oral traditions, songs, verses, and other childhood texts from a variety of cultures. Youngsters of diverse backgrounds come to school versed in other rhymes, chants, and songs they can share. Both teachers and students need to draw on the rich "linguistic, rhythmic and musical" resources that children of all backgrounds bring to the classroom (Compton-Lilly, 2004, p. 72).

When we turn our ears to the streets and playgrounds, we hear a rich source of language play in games, street songs, and urban verses (such as jingles) of popular culture. Incorporating these rhymes into classroom activities is an important part of linking a child's life with school texts (Barton and Booth, 2004). After all, the chants, rhythms, games, and cheers of the schoolyard are rooted in word play, silly rhymes, nonsense verse, and other fun language experiences. Even the street raps and road songs echoed on the sidewalk or shouted out in car rides move youngsters toward literacy through playful language learning.

To become literate, children need to interact with texts that are familiar to them. Teachers ought to find a place for the cultural resources, texts, and literacy experiences that young people encounter at home and in the community by using them as school texts and learning resources in the classroom. Connecting childhood texts (texts that are familiar to children's lives and are used and encountered daily) with the learning experiences and resources in schools (i.e., school texts) is important in building connections between home and school and bridging the learning gap that has taken place in traditional classrooms. By integrating traditional verses, multicultural rhymes, universal songs, and childhood games into the classroom, we give children language sources that are meaningful and relevant to them. Through rich collections of children's literature from around the globe, we introduce youngsters to texts that will be delightfully new to them. As children make these discoveries and connections, they begin to explore their curiosity about language through playful experimentation. Nursery rhymes, poems, songs, chants, and verses that are part of childhood culture are filled with spirited and animated language that is ideal for word play. These sources provide open access to language and fun-filled occasions for building literacy. By drawing on texts like these, teachers and students together can turn the folk literature of childhood into classroom learning resources.

To become literate, children need to interact with texts in the classroom that are familiar to them. Teachers ought to find a place for the cultural resources, texts, and literacy experiences that young people encounter at home and in the community by using them as school texts and learning resources in the classroom.

Gathering Sources of Language and Word Play

A child's ear is first tuned to the sounds of language in delightful engagements in songs, poetry, and verse, and through books that contain rhythm and rhyme. In children's literature, youngsters will encounter texts that invite them to play with words, language patterns, and sounds. By exploring the oral traditions of folklore found in early childhood experiences, cultural rhymes, historical verses, playground games, and street songs, we can discover other sources of language and word play to use in the classroom. To build these collections, teachers and students can work together to locate folk literature from different ethnic communities. Encourage children to involve family members in the search for multilingual and multicultural rhymes, songs, chants, and verses. Invite classroom guests to share examples with the children. Students can add to the growing collection by gathering samples and publishing them in anthologies for others to enjoy.

Children's Folk Literature

- Lullabies
- Finger plays
- Action rhymes and songs
- Lap rides
- Counting songs
- Alphabet chants
- Marching Songs
- Nursery rhymes
- Contemporary verse
- Nonsense verse (e.g., Dr. Seuss)
- Alphabet books
- Patterned books
- Poetry collections (e.g., Dennis Lee, Shel Silverstein, Sheree Fitch)
- Rhyming texts

- Sound books and poems (*Mr. Brown Can Moo*, *Peepo*, *Peek-a-Moo*)
- Old chants, prayers, and traditional verses
- Proverbs, psalms, and other religious texts
- Similes
- Metaphors
- Riddles
- Jokes
- Tongue twisters
- Puns
- Slogans and jingles
- Silly rhymes
- Parodies
- Playground verses

- Schoolyard chants
- Skipping rhymes
- Clapping games
- Counting-out rhymes
- Ball-bounce chants
- Join-in rhythms
- Jump-rope rhymes
- Sports/team cheers
- Road songs
- Street raps
- Neighborhood rhymes
- Lyrical verses
- Crosswords
- Word puzzles
- Songs
- Music
- Other childhood lyrics

Many early childhood texts are ideally suited for word play, language development, and literacy growth. This rich inventory of literature is filled with highly rhythmic, repetitive, and patterned language that can make word learning, language acquisition, and reading enjoyable and fun. Youngsters turn their ears to the sounds of language in poetry, books, and everyday life because the words and patterns they hear delight and entertain them. The rhythm and rhyme of playful verses and songs have an engaging quality that attracts children and invites them to spontaneously join in. Hearing the cadences of language in these works promotes play through oral language experiences, reading encounters, and writing events. The rhythms, rhymes, shapes, styles, and patterns of children's folk literature can magically inspire young people to grow in literacy.

The Importance of Word Play—Connections to Literacy

Children enjoy participating in word play. The babbling sounds of infancy soon turn into playful language adventures of early childhood that echo the sounds of nursery rhymes, playground games, action songs, and nonsense verses that youngsters discover or invent on their own. Through active engagements in word play, young people can develop the oral language, reading, and writing skills that are essential to early literacy.

The sounds of rhythmic and playful language in nursery rhymes, playground verses, riddles, tongue twisters, and catchy slogans can tune a child's ears to language. These childhood texts are rich in repetitions, patterns, and refrains that make them fun to listen to and easy to learn. As children attend to words and lyrics aurally, they develop attention span and auditory memory (Palmer and Bayley, 2005). Action rhymes, marching songs, clapping games, and other lively word play experiences also help youngsters recognize sound differentiations and develop auditory discrimination (Booth, 1998). Through repetition, play, song, and verse, children start to note sounds and patterns in language that enable them to tell words apart.

Remembering words, sounds, and phrases by heart allows listeners to contribute to rhymes, chants, and playful verses they know. As youngsters participate in singing, chanting, choral speaking, call and response, and other word play activities, they use spoken language in creative, expressive, and enjoyable ways. Reciting nursery rhymes, tongue twisters, riddles, and tunes helps children articulate words. The joys of language that accompany many early childhood experiences like these become natural lessons for developing listening and speaking skills.

Traditional verses, rhymes, playground games, and street songs are filled with vibrant language that is suited for word learning and language acquisition. As children engage with these texts, they discover new words that extend their growing vocabulary. When youngsters play with the sounds, shapes, and, rhythms of language and pull words apart, they stumble upon parts, roles, and meanings that contribute to word knowledge and language awareness. Experiencing the rhythms, patterns, and sounds of language allows children to uncover aspects that make it function, including parts that make up words, underlying sound structures, and technical features. As children play with silly rhymes, parodies, puns, and nonsense verses, they discover the absurdity of language too.

Soon, youngsters are able to recognize inconsistencies in language rules, patterns, sounds, and spellings (Booth, 1998). As children gain insights into the complexities of language, they acquire linguistic knowledge and competence that help them master and control the ways words work. Through repetition, chanting, rhyming, and singing, children become absorbed in language, rehearsing words that resound into whispers when they read. Often, youngsters hear the words in their minds and internalize the sounds so they can figure out what the print could be saying. Children draw on the jam-packed inventory of language they gather to find the meaning of, predict, or identify a word they first encounter on a page. Using rhymes, verses, and songs as texts for early reading helps children establish one-to-one correspondence between spoken and written language, acquire beginning sight words, and make visual discriminations (Compton Lilly, 2004). Through delightful engagements in word play, children gain knowledge of sound-letter relationships and form other reading strategies, like cueing systems (Booth, 1998; Wilson, 2002).

> The sounds of rhythmic and playful language in nursery rhymes, playground verses, riddles, tongue twisters, and catchy slogans can tune a child's ears to language. Like poetry, rhyming books, and songs, these childhood texts are rich in repetitions, patterns, and refrains that make them fun to listen to and easy to learn.

Musical engagements in word play and rhythm-based activities lay the early groundwork for children's ability to understand language patterns, rhythms and sound features. Hearing the cadences of a poem and beats of a song allows youngsters to become sensitive to the tunes and structures of written language, as essential part of both reading and writing (Palmer and Bayley, 2005). Experimenting with language in word play presents children with letters, spelling, rhyme, and other patterns they will find in literature. Learning language patterns by ear first helps youngsters better understanding them in print (Barton and Booth, 2004). Nursery rhymes, tongue twisters, chants, and playground verses are filled with rhyming patterns and alliterations that help children associate letters and sounds and blend words together, a strategy they may use as they read.

Interactive word play helps children to develop other strategies and skills to read and write. The rhythm and movement of action songs, schoolyard rhymes, and finger plays can help youngsters learn print concepts like directionality, form hand-eye coordination, and build fine motor skills required for handwriting (Palmer and Bayley, 2005). Poems, rhymes, verses, jingles, riddles, and songs introduce youngsters to the first genres they will meet in children's literature. The shapes, patterns, and models in these genres come together in children's variations of existing works and in their own compositions. Drawing on the literary styles, ideas, poetic devices, and frameworks of children's folklore, songs, verses, chants, and poems they know, young people become inspired to use word play as they innovate on rhymes and produce literature themselves.

Through active engagements in word play, children experience the joys of language at home, on the playground, in the gym, at the park, on the sports field, and in the classroom. Reciting chants, songs, rhymes, and verses makes language learning natural and fun in any environment. As children take part in these delightful adventures, they fine-tune their ears to the sounds that words make. Playing with words in puzzles, games, literature, poetry and everyday life builds language power and skills essential to early literacy development. When youngsters explore words, patterns, and rhythms through discovery and play, they form a deeper knowledge of how language works.

Understanding Language—Phonological and Phonemic Awareness

From the time that youngsters open their ears to the rhymes of *Mother Goose* and the nonsense verses of Dr. Seuss, they begin to focus attention on language. Through the oral traditions of songs, games, chants, and cheers, young people start to grow in language awareness as they play with words, sounds, patterns, and structures. At first, children need a strong understanding of spoken language before learning to read and understand print (Fitzpatrick, 1997). By the time they reach kindergarten, many young children have mastered the ability to understand and use increasingly complex oral language. Despite this, most youngsters do not know that spoken language is made up of discrete words, which are made up of distinct sounds (Sensenbaugh, 1996). Many children find this difficult because the sentences and phrases they hear sound intact.

Playing with words in puzzles, games, literature, poetry, and everyday life builds language power and skills essential to early literacy development. When youngsters explore words, patterns, and rhythms through discovery and play, they form a deeper knowledge of how language works.

Syllable: the largest unit of sound that can be broken down within a word

Onset: the part of the syllable that precedes the vowel; the consonant(s) at the start of a word (e.g., *c, t, ch,* or *ph*)

Rime: the letters that follow the first vowel; the vowel and any consonants that follow the onset (e.g., *–at, –ace, –eat,* or *–og*)

Phoneme: the smallest unit of sound that determines the difference between words and relates to letters of the alphabet

To become a fluent reader and writer, a child must develop a strong understanding of language, an awareness that grows from discovering that language is made up of sounds. To understand how language is constructed, children must be able to hear the sounds that make up words. As children develop the capacity to hear individual words and the distinct sound units used in spoken language, they start to grow in phonological awareness. Phonological awareness refers to an understanding of "the sound structures of language" (Yopp and Yopp, 2000, p. 130). It includes the ability to identify and manipulate units of sound that make up spoken words. To recognize that words are composed of more than one sound, children need to listen "inside" words to hear the specific sound units that make up spoken language (Fitzpatrick, 1997). As youngsters listen for sounds within a word, they discover larger "chunks" of sounds known as syllables and smaller units of sound within each syllable known as onsets and rimes. The path to phonological awareness begins with an understanding of words as units of sounds, the recognition of syllables, and an understanding of rhyme (Palmer and Bayley, 2005).

As children develop phonological awareness, they may notice phonemes, the smallest units of sounds that make up spoken language. Phonemic awareness refers to the ability to hear, distinguish, and manipulate individual units of sound within a word. Phonemes are what differentiate words and carry meaning. (It is a phoneme that accounts for the difference between the words *cat* and *hat*).

Phonological Awareness and Phonemic Awareness

Children who have a strong *phonological awareness* are able to:	Children with a strong *phonemic awareness* are able to:	
• identify rhymes	• hear rhymes and alliteration (repetitive initial sounds)	• find the different sound in a set of words (/cat/, /call/, /set/)
• produce rhyming words	• recognize that spoken language consists of a sequence of smaller sounds	• segment spoken words into distinct phonemes (ball into /b/ /a/ /ll/)
• break words into syllables	• identify the separate sounds, or phonemes, within a word (mat and fork have three distinct sounds (/m/ /a/ t/ , /f/ /o/ /rk/)	• blend individual sounds, or phonemes, together to say the word (/d/ /o/ /g/ into dog)
• count or clap out the number of syllables in a word	• recognize the individual sound in a word (initial sounds like /p/ in pot)	• substitute individual sounds, or phonemes, to make new words by replacing either initial (mop–top) middle (sat–sit) or ending sounds (dot–dog)
• identify the beginning and ending sounds in a syllable	• identify common sounds in different words (/t/ in toy, truck, tree)	
• separate the beginning of a word from its ending		
• recognize words with the same beginning and ending sounds		
• find smaller words within larger ones (i.e., "man" in "manager").		

Once youngsters are able to recognize individual sounds, they can break words apart into separate elements and manipulate them to make new words. Exploring the elements of language that can be pulled apart is an important aspect of phonemic awareness that can help children with reading. Acquiring an understanding of sound units can ease the transition into books and build in factors for reading success by providing youngsters with a schema for identifying words and analyzing texts.

Both phonological awareness and phonemic awareness lay the groundwork for developing early reading strategies like phonics and word recognition. The ability to tell sounds apart is an effective reading skill that young children use to decode words when they encounter print. Once children are able to hear,

The ability to tell sounds apart is an effective reading skill that young children use to decode words when they encounter print. Once children are able to hear, discriminate, and articulate a range of speech sounds, they are ready to connect spoken sounds to their letters.

discriminate, and articulate a range of speech sounds, they are ready to connect spoken sounds to their letters. Before children can identify a letter that stands for a sound they must be able to hear the individual sounds within a word. Drawing a letter-sound connection grows from having a strong phonemic base. Being aware of the phonological structure of language moves youngsters further along in their reading. Understanding the idea of syllables helps developing readers to handle more challenging texts and decipher larger words.

Phonological awareness and phonemic awareness have been the focus of considerable research in recent years (Sensenbaugh, 1997; Kropp, 2000; Yopp and Yopp, 2000; Hirsh-Pasek and Golinkoff, 2003; Peterson, 2007). Many educators believe that developing an awareness of sounds in spoken language is an important factor in learning to read. Studies indicate that both phonological awareness and phonemic awareness play a fundamental role in early reading acquisition. In fact, phonological awareness is one of the strongest predictors of children's success in reading in the early years of school (Yopp and Yopp, 2000; Peterson, 2007).

Phonological awareness and phonemic awareness are relatively new ideas and concepts that people often confuse. In most recent discussions on reading, the two terms are widely referenced and sometimes used interchangeably. Although the terms are mutually dependent, there are distinction between the two.

In addition to supporting early readers, strong phonological awareness and phonemic awareness contribute to greater success in later reading (Hirsch-Pasek and Golinkoff, 2003). Most children who have an understanding of phonological awareness have an easier time learning to read and, in fact, become better readers (Hirsch-Pasek and Golinkoff, 2003). The ability to segment and blend sounds together in spoken words also can help children increase oral reading fluency.

In past years, both the role of phonological awareness in early reading and the teaching of phonics explicitly in the language arts program have faced many debates. Lorraine Wilson examines this issue in her book *Reading To Live: How to Teach Reading for Today's World* (2002) by presenting new perspectives to inform our understanding and teaching of the reading process. As she points out, many phonics proponents believe that an awareness of speech sounds and the ability to manipulate them are essential prerequisites to learning to read. Building an understanding of the sounds that make up spoken words is a skill that relates more to oral language than to print itself. As children turn their attention to written language, they may draw on their understanding of speech sounds to analyze words and interpret symbols of print by linking phonemic awareness to letter knowledge. Developing sound-letter relationships through the old-style system of sounding out words is only one strategy that children may use to read. Yet, reading is more than a sounding out process. An increasing number of young readers are being taught and encouraged to develop a range of effective strategies to make meaning of texts and solve unknown words.

Many educators today are strong advocates for the teaching of phonemic awareness before children learn to read (Wilson, 2002). However, explicit instruction in phonemic awareness may push young readers into performing isolated tasks that are more skills-based. As a result, children may learn to identify and practice manipulating individual word sounds in decontextualized structured tests and activities that resemble traditional phonics lessons. When children are taught this way, their development of phonological and phonemic awareness is not sufficient to help them learn to read proficiently. Phonemic awareness instruction is only one part of a broader literacy program (Yopp and Yopp, 2000). Teachers need to balance the instructional methods they use to build language awareness.

A Balanced Approach To Literacy Learning

Building a balanced program in which students can develop word knowledge, language competence, reading strategies, and literacy skills requires careful planning. Effective literacy programs that enhance children's understanding and love of language require a holistic, balanced, and integrated approach. Teachers who adopt this approach effectively combine playful and fun learning activities with explicit instruction of literacy skills, concepts, and strategies in the framework of real reading, writing, oral language, and early childhood experiences.

Young children develop a growing understanding of how language works by participating in a variety of language activities that emphasize the sounds of language. Through literature, music, and language play, youngsters are drawn to the delightful sounds that words make. By combining stories, rhymes, chants, and songs with word games and explicit lessons, students can identify sound sequences, patterns, structures, and other important language features. The following guidelines may help teachers plan daily activities that build students' working knowledge of language. Children's experiences should be:

- engaging, playful, and fun
- practical and meaningful (avoid drills, rote learning, memorization or isolated tasks)
- purposeful and goal oriented
- social and interactive
- drawn from real language sources (childhood games, literature, ads)
- activity-based (focus on learning not evaluation)
- inclusive and respectful of cultural and individual differences
- mostly oral

Language and word play activities should also:
- invite full participation
- promote interest and inquiry (through curious investigation)
- encourage experimentation with language
- allow for explicit instruction and focused teaching of sound-letter relationship, word segmentation, sound blending, and other phonemic skills in the context of real reading and writing

By drawing on these principles, teachers can design balanced and effective programs and learning experiences in which children can develop a strong language base essential to literacy development.

Word Play Events

Children explore their curiosity about language through playful and interactive adventures that extend beyond the home or classroom. Their world is filled with rich sources of word play in the riddles, jokes, slogans, songs, ads, and jingles heard every day. Teachers can draw on these language encounters to provide students with learning experiences that build language awareness.

Word play activities allow children to put their growing knowledge of language to work. Language experiences ranging from traditional childhood rhyming and alliteration games to rhythm and music activities allow students to play with sounds, patterns, and words with others. Through sound explorations in shared reading and choral speaking, children learn to echo poems, verses, and rhymes with delight and ease. In literature encounters and word study, students grow more aware of print concepts and language features that move them closer to reading.

Word play challenges youngsters to pull language apart and make discoveries about how it works. Children's language adventures grow in complexity over time as youngsters uncover the intricacies of language. Word play experiences turn young language learners into sophisticated language users capable of twisting words, inventing riddles, and composing verses in clever, charming, and entertaining ways. Here are some of the many word play experiences that teachers can build on in school and beyond:

Early Childhood Games and Experiences

Many youngsters begin their childhood journey on the laps of loving family members, enjoying bouncing games and energetic rides filled with song. Early childhood events that start with gentle lullabies soon give way to traditional bouncing verses like *The Grand Old Duke of York*, clapping games like *Patty Cake*, finger plays like *Two Little Blackbirds Sitting on a Hill*, and action songs like *I'm a Little Teapot*. Through the strong oral traditions of songs, rhymes, games, and rituals from many cultures, young language learners can experience the delightful sounds of words as they grow. Playful adventures at home that introduced young children to language can be exercised in the classroom too.

Rhyming Activities

Children's songs, nursery rhymes, poems, and verses are filled with strong rhythms, patterned rhymes, and repetitive sounds that make them fun to listen to and easy to learn. Youngsters can share and delight in this literature collection by reading, singing, and saying them aloud every day. Playing with rhymes draws focus to the sounds of words and supports the development of phonological awareness. Rhyming activities allow youngsters to learn that individual sounds play a role in many words and make it possible for them to hear and identify the particular sounds of language that is fun to use. These experiences may include:

Rhyme Time

Provide opportunities throughout the day for children to listen to a variety of nursery rhymes, songs, verses, and other rhyming texts. Start with short verses that are quick to learn and call others to join in. Through repeated readings and sayings, youngsters soon memorize the words and are able to recite them on their own. Encourage students to repeat rhymes they have learned and share additional rhymes and songs they have grown to love. Allow children to say rhymes and sing songs from their own cultural backgrounds in the language or dialect they are most comfortable with.

Rhyme Search

Once children are familiar with rhymes, songs, poems, verses, and other rhyming texts, have them identify words that sound the same. As children point out similar sounds they hear, they begin to recognize rhyming patterns. After introducing youngsters to nursery rhymes, poems, and songs that they can enjoy repeatedly, challenge them to search for rhyming words in well-known verses and texts. Students can generate these rhyming words orally or make a list.

Cloze Activity

Nursery rhymes, songs, poems, and verses have an engaging quality that invites listeners to take part. When sharing familiar verses and text with children, leave off ending words and phrases and invite youngsters to fill them in.

Felt Board Rhymes

Nursery rhymes and traditional verses have a delightful way of telling a story. Youngsters can use felt board characters and story pieces to recite the words of popular rhymes and verses they know (e.g., *Hey Diddle Diddle)*. Children can also create their own felt board pieces to share favorite selections with others. These dramatic play props are helpful prompts for learning and telling nursery rhymes and verses.

Rhyming Games

Children can build an inventory of rhyming words by playing games that encourage them to look for rhyming patterns and the same sounds in a wider range of words. Producing a list of words that rhyme may require some practice at first. To start, select a word from literature, song, poetry, verse, theme, topic, or interest and share it with the class (e.g., *ball)*. Say the word aloud or record it for children to see. Provide students with time to think of other words that rhyme with the chosen word. Take turns saying, recording, or constructing a list of rhyming words (*wall, hall, mall, tall, call, fall)*. Offer clues of other rhyming words the child can add to the growing list.

A Phonetic Soup

Children can explore rhyming patterns and word endings in nursery rhymes, poems, songs, and verses by creating a phonetic soup. To help them do this, select a favorite nursery rhyme (e.g., *Humpty Dumpty)* or other rhyming text. Post the rhyme for the class to see. Display a cooking pot (real, cut-out, or drawing) that children can use to sort words and make lists. After reading the verse several times, encourage students to find rhyming words from the chosen collection. Produce a list of rhyming words they find (e.g., *wall, fall, men, again)*. Have students examine the rhyming words and look for patterns in words with the same sound (similar spelling, ending, or rime). Begin making a phonetic soup with words from the rhyme that share the same ending, rime, or spelling pattern (e.g., –*all)*. Have the class generate more words that belong to the same word family (e.g., *ball, tall, small, hall, mall)*. Words can be displayed on chart paper, word cards, or on the board when adding them to the phonetic soup. Next, explore rhyming words from the selection that share the same sound but have different endings, letter combinations, or spelling patterns (e.g., *men, again)*. Use a different cooking pot to make another phonetic soup featuring rhyming words from other sources that have different endings or spelling patterns (e.g., *ball, doll, crawl)*. Later, have children work in groups to explore other selections of rhyming poetry, song and verse and make their own phonetic soups.

Playing with Rhyming Sounds

When youngsters hear alliterative verses and repetitive sounds, they start to recognize the position of sounds in words and notice common parts they share. They pick out words that have the same initial sounds and recognize similar endings in rhyming words. This understanding of language grows from an exploration of onsets and rimes. Once youngsters can identify rhyming words, they are able to notice sounds that are the same in these words (usually the rime, or ending unit). As they make up rhyming words, encourage children to play with sound units by changing initial sounds (onsets such as *h, s, b, m, c, th*) and adding them to other sound units (rimes like *–at*). Allow children time to play word games in which they can make up rhyming words that share the same ending sound (*–ight, –ance*). This can lead to further word knowledge and language awareness.

Innovating on Rhymes

The rhythm of patterned verses, poems, songs, and rhymes inspires young children to join in with lyrics and silly verses of their own. When youngsters get hooked on a rhyme, they become familiar with the words, rhyming patterns, and structure. Soon they learn to echo the language and innovate on the rhymes they know. Children can have fun creating their own rhyming lyrics and adding verses to popular songs and poems. Building upon the structure of a familiar rhyme or song (e.g., *Down by the Bay*) allows youngsters to work with existing rhyming patterns and rhythms simply by adding to them.

As children innovate on rhymes, they may depart from the original text to produce their own variations. Encourage youngsters to play with structures and rhyming patterns to create original verses based on traditional favorites.

Having fun with nursery rhymes, songs, and traditional children's verses from a variety of cultures can inspire youngsters to make up rhymes too:

> *There were five little chickens sitting on a barn, one fell off and broke his arm.*
> *There were four little monkeys sitting in a tree, one fell off and broke his knee.*

Literature and Word Play

Tuning a child's ears to language often starts with books. Children's literature is filled with rich opportunities for word play and literacy learning. Reading nursery rhymes, poetry, patterned books, and stories that contain rhythm and rhyme allows youngsters to experience the joys of language through many literature activities. Through read-aloud events, shared reading experiences, and repeated readings of favorite storybooks that feature rhymes, poems, verses and patterned texts, children encounter words, patterns, sounds and structures that build language awareness in playful ways like these:

Reading Experiences

Share examples of traditional, contemporary, nonsense, and multicultural verses and rhyming books from around the world that youngsters find enchanting (e.g., Dr. Seuss, *Mary Had a Little Jam*). Allow children to revisit these texts through repeated readings. Encourage children to join in read-aloud activities by filling in missing words or reciting verses from memory. Use big books or record rhymes, poems, verses, or pages/stories on chart paper or overhead for everyone to see. Read the text aloud and have children follow along the print. Invite students to participate by reading along together. Through shared reading experiences,

The big fat spider
Went up a big oak tree
He slipped on some sticks
And landed next to me!
—Innovative rhyme Based on *The Itsy Bitsy Spider*

children can practice early reading strategies and develop print concepts such as directionality. Students can take turns pointing to words in the rhyme or text as the class reads it in unison. Children can divide up verses too. Through choral reading, youngsters can develop effective read-aloud techniques (e.g., changing voice, expression, fluency).

Sound Books

Many books are filled with repetitive sounds that youngsters can mimic orally. Storybooks like *Chicka, Chicka, Boom, Boom; Peepo;* and *Mr. Brown Can Moo* are filled with recurring sounds or spirited voices that call out to young listeners and invite them to participate. Starting with books that are filled with sounds is an effective way of moving youngsters into reading as many of these utterances become the first sight words that children can recognize in print.

Title Search

Many catchy phrases are found in the title of books and poems. Share examples of books and poems that use word play in the title (e.g., *Moose's Loose Tooth).* Have children search through literature anthologies, poetry collections, nursery rhyme treasuries, and other book sources for playful titles. Challenge students to generate their own creative and playful titles for possible poems and storybooks that are about different topics or characters. For example, a book about a ghost that likes to host parties might be called *The Ghost Hostess.*

Line-by-Line Rhyme Time

Provide students with a copy of a verse built on rhyming patterns and challenge them to pick out rhyming words and line patterns. By studying the words, lines, and verses closely, youngsters may notice:
- rhyming word pairs (e.g., *dish, wish*)
- words that sound the same and have similar spelling (e.g., *mean, clean*)
- words that sound the same but have different letter combinations and are spelled differently (e.g., *blue, shampoo; seen, bean*)
- lines that use the same rhyming scheme (e.g., *a, a, b, b* or *a, b, a, b*)

Children can mark the patterns they see using different colored crayons to show rhyming words that share the same sounds, have the same ending patterns (rime), or different spellings. Students can isolate word parts that are the same by underlining words that share the same spelling pattern. Later, discuss rhyming words that have the same sound but different spelling patterns or endings. As children focus on these patterns, they learn more about sound relationships and the structures of written texts in the context of reading literature.

Book Raps

Examples of Rhyming Word Pairs

mouse, house
cat, that
calf, laugh
fish, wish
sheep, sleep

Many works of children's literature are filled with rhymes and rhythms that are entertaining to listen to. Hearing the cadences of language can bring a text to life, making words leap from the page to become springboards for play.

Begin by reading books first for enjoyment and then for language play. Once children are familiar with a selection through repeated or shared reading, they are ready to take part in fun literature activities in which they can play with words from the book (e.g., *Charlie Cook's Favorite Book, Time For Bed*). First, have children tap, clap, or use a musical instrument to signal rhyming words found in the selection as it is read aloud. Produce a list of rhyming pairs they find. Later, students can examine the rhyming patterns and sounds of these words to produce a phonetic soup (see previous activity) or generate a list of other rhyming words by extending the word pairs into word families. Finally, encourage children to have fun with words by using musical instruments and voices to produce raps and chants of rhyming families inspired from the book.

Music, Rhythm, and Creative Movement Activities

Children communicate naturally through song. Singing rhymes, verses, street raps, chants, and action songs leads children to develop a joy and appreciation for music and rhythm that allow their language experiences to grow. Apart from singing songs and verses, youngsters can explore language through other word play activities that actively combine music or rhythm and movement.

Action Songs

Have children perform traditional action songs such as *Row, Row, Your Boat*; *I'm a Little Teapot*, and other childhood favorites. Youngsters can build up their repertoire of action songs by turning nursery rhymes, poems, verses, and other popular songs into action rhymes. Allow youngsters to work together to create their own action songs based on children's folk literature from around the world. These experiences help them to make meaning of texts and interpret language by creating actions to accompany the words and verses they have grown to love.

Puppet Shows, Shadow Plays, and Drama Activities

Children can explore the language of nursery rhymes, songs, poems, and contemporary verse by producing puppet shows, shadow plays, and dramatic presentations based on original texts (e.g., *Little Miss Muffet*). Encourage youngsters to make props and use costumes to act out characters, words, and verses. As children prepare for their performances, they will interact closely with language to draw meaning and share their interpretations of traditional or contemporary literature.

Rhythm and Music Activities

Youngsters can tap, clap, stomp or march to the beat in songs and poetry. Patting a drum or shaking a tambourine can add life and energy to children's renditions of favorite rhymes and verses like *Mary Had a Little Lamb* and *Sing a Song of Six Pence*. As children play with musical instruments and sounds, they become aware of the rhythms, patterns, and tunes of language that help them grow in literacy.

As children play with musical instruments and sounds, they become aware of the rhythms, patterns, and tunes of language that help them grow in literacy.

Playground Games and Jump-Rope Rhymes

Skipping rhymes, ball-bounce chants, clapping games, and counting-out songs heard on the playground are rich with opportunities for vigorous word play. Allow time for children to share action games, playground verses, jump-rope rhymes, and schoolyard cheers from around the globe. Use these rhymes as texts for early reading. Create books and posters featuring verses from the playground. Finding a place for this collection of folk songs can bridge the gap between the language of childhood and the texts of school and move children closer to reading.

Songs of the Neighborhood

Children can explore the rhythm of language through the musical sounds of street raps and songs heard in the neighborhood. Invite youngsters to share the beats and rhythms of the music of their cultural and ethnic community. Make up simple raps to accompany daily routines or devise more difficult ones that mirror the rap songs they hear. As children practice rapping to a beat, they use spoken language to produce vocal rhymes.

Sound Games

As children listen "inside" words, they hear specific sounds and begin to notice language components. As youngsters recognize initial sounds or ending word patterns in rhyming pairs or other words, their focus turns to sounds and language structures. Word play activities allow children to grow in language awareness while having fun breaking up words and bringing sounds together. Sound games give youngsters the opportunity to pull words apart and practice segmenting, blending, and sequencing sounds. Activities that focus on sounds within words (syllables, onsets, rimes, and phonemes) can help children develop phonological and phonemic awareness. Here are some word play events to help young children attend to the sound structure of spoken language:

Sound Discussions

As children experiment with language, talk with them about the sounds and structures of words. Show excitement when playing with sounds and having fun with language. Discuss the units that make up sounds in words. Encourage children to ask questions that will help them develop a better understanding of sounds and language structures.

Sound Museum

Encourage children to create a sound museum filled with a collection of artifacts they find at home, at school, or in the community that begin with same initial sound. As students grow more familiar with other specific positions of sounds within a word (middle, ending), they can create other displays to feature objects with the same middle or ending sounds.

Play "I Spy"

Have children look for objects around them with the same beginning, middle, or ending sound. As youngsters try to guess the item that shares the same sound, they are learning to discriminate the individual sounds within a word.

Sound Matching

As children learn about language, they discover patterns in words that share the same sounds. Youngsters can look for word patterns and sound relationships using objects around them (mug and rug) or practice matching sounds using picture cards that feature related items (apple, ant). Teachers can develop their own set of cards or use commercial memory games that feature word pairs. In addition, students can produce their own sound matching games by creating game cards for word pairs (e.g., sun, puppy) that share the same sound.

Name Chants

To introduce the concept of segmenting sounds, start with the syllables in names. As a class, tap or clap out the syllables beginning with the teacher's name. Encourage youngsters to work in pairs or small groups to tap or clap out the syllables in each student's name. Children can use musical instruments to tap out the syllables as well. Students can later chant the names of class members as they tap, clap or pat the syllables on a drum to a steady beat.

Clapping Words

Have children clap out words from songs, verses, rhymes, literature, or real life. These words can range from one syllable to many syllables (e.g., *coat, mountain, jacket, teacher, pencil, supermarket*). As youngsters clap the beats, they will learn to isolate sounds and segment words apart. Instruments such as tambourines can also to be used to break words into syllables by tapping out separate beats.

Exploring Compound Words

Since many compound words are made up of two or more identifiable words that children may know, youngsters may have more success pulling these types of words apart and blending them together. As children explore compound words in oral language activities, they have fun playing with the syllables, word chunks, and sound units they hear within them. At first, youngsters can practice putting words together to make a new word (e.g., *bed* and *room, side* and *walk, hot* and *dog, rain* and *bow, air* and *plane*). Later, children can say words with word chunks left out (e.g., remove "cow" from *cowboy*, "ham" from *hamburger*, "bath" from *bathtub*, "chalk" from *chalkboard*). By deleting or adding word chunks or syllables in this way, youngsters can better understand how words are made up of smaller parts or sound units. Starting with larger words that can be pulled apart or put together to form compound words gives children practice in segmenting and blending sounds. This can help them isolate and identify individual sounds within smaller words and later sequence them together.

Humpty Dumpty Words

Youngsters can practice saying words by leaving out different sounds (e.g., removing /l/ from *look)*. To begin segmenting sound units, play the following game inspired by a nursery rhyme children may know:

> *Humpty Dumpty sat on a wall*
> *What happens when you take away /b/ from "ball"?*

Next, have children pull apart other words from literature, songs, rhymes, and theme topics or interests.

Once children have had practice segmenting sounds by pulling apart onsets and rimes, they may be ready to bring parts back together by sequencing sounds. Begin by having youngsters put together the words they first broke apart. Have them use some of the words from the popular rhyme:

> *Though all the king's horses and all the king's men*
> *Couldn't put Humpty together again*
> *Words are quite different as you shall see*
> *The parts join forces quite easily*
> (provide example here: *What happens when you add /s/ to /ong/?*)
> *The sounds come together to make the word:* (say the word e.g., *song*)

Children can practice sequencing sounds by using words from the rhyme to blend onsets and rimes. For example, they can add an initial sound onto another sound unit (add /l/ to /ight/). Challenge youngsters with other words that can be brought together by sequencing and blending sounds (e.g., add /sh/ to /op/, /bl/ to /ack/). Through sound blending games like this, children have fun playing with language orally before seeing words in print. Playing sounds games helps youngsters begin to develop an effective strategy for reading.

Instrument Words or Keyboard Sounds

Many oral activities can work to emphasize the process of "sounding out" words by segmenting and blending individual sounds. Children can practice sequencing sounds together by focusing on simple words that can be easily pulled apart. Youngsters may grow to understand how words are made up of separate sounds when they play games that help them discriminate the beginning, middle and ending parts of a word. Teachers can start by choosing simple words such as *cat*, *dog*, or *big*. Have the children count out the number of separate sound units, or phonemes, they hear (e.g., /c/ /a/ /t/ = 3). Next, use a keyboard to demonstrate the segmentation and blending of sounds within the word. To show this clearly, separate notes can be played to represent the individual sound units (e.g., one note to represent /c/, another to represent /a/, and a different note to represent /t/). As each note is played, the individual sound is repeated. Finally, all the notes are played in unison as the word is said or sung aloud. (This process can also be demonstrated by playing musical chords). After giving several examples of segmenting and blending sounds using phonemes, invite students to repeat the individual sounds with other words as they are pulled apart and later, say the words as the parts are brought together. Finally, have children use the keyboard to practice breaking words apart and bringing them back together by sequencing sounds. (Note: Other instruments such as tambourines, drums, or maracas can also be used to practice segmenting and blending sounds).

Changing Sounds

Part of the fun of word play happens when texts get altered in silly ways. Substituting initial sounds in songs, poems, games, and children's books can turn popular rhymes and phrases into nonsense verse. Children are amused by the ridiculous sounds that nonsensical words can make. Encourage students to repeat songs, phrases, and verses several times by substituting the initial sounds of words in popular texts with other sounds:

> *Ring around the Rosie...*
> *Ping around the posie...*
> *Sing around the sosie...*
> *Ting around the tosie*

As children play with initial sounds in nonsense verse, they learn to manipulate language by changing sound structures beyond the limits of meaning and vocabulary to produce words and sounds just for fun.

Tongue Twisters

Tongue twisters are a fun way to involve children in sound discrimination and repetition games. Through the reiteration of alliterative phrases, youngsters can focus their attention on initial sounds while discovering an important literary device (e.g., alliteration) used in poetry and word play. Learning to repeat tongue twisters helps children to articulate and discriminate letter and word sounds. Seeing tongue twisters on a page moves youngsters towards making visual distinctions between letters and initial sounds and building letter-sound relationships. Begin by having students repeat simple tongue twisters until they can say them on their own. Encourage youngsters to find other twisters they can learn. Post alliterative phrases so students can see the repetitive sound and letter patterns. Invite children to underline the first letter of each word in the phrase and circle the sounds that are the same. Ask students to make up their own tongue twisters to share orally or to challenge others. Children can make up simple twisters based on their own names, people they know, or familiar experiences:

Mommy made milk on Monday morning.
Tony likes to eat turkey and tomatoes on Thanksgiving.

Nonsense Couples

Children's games, songs, literature, and films are filled with rich examples of language play in which words and sounds creatively come together to make nonsense phrases and verses that are easy to remember. As a class, make a list of rhyming pairs from these sources. For example:

Bippity boppity	*Cock-a-doodle-doo*
Itty bitty	*Mock–a- moodle-moo*
Teensy weensy	*Rock-a–roodle-roo*
Wibbly wobbly	*Sock-a-soodle-soo*

Have children make up their own rhyming pairs, or nonsense couples, using double words with similar sounds. As children play with sounds in nonsense verse, they discover patterns in language (rhyme, alliteration) that can lead to word study.

Word Study—Playing with Print

Through rhyming, chanting, playing games, reciting verses and singing songs, children experience the joys and sounds of language by sharing it aloud. These early childhood activities introduce youngsters to language by lifting words from the page and giving them a voice. As children engage in word play through oral language events, they grow familiar with childhood texts and soon encounter rhymes, verses, songs, poems, and literature in print. Many word play activities are based on print encounters. You will read about these activities in Chapter 4.

* * *

When children take part in word play, their understanding of language authentically grows. This creates a stronger foundation for literacy learning. Early experiences in word play invite youngsters into the world of children's literature by introducing them to playful genres and texts that ultimately motivate them towards print. As youngsters enjoy the fun of making up verses, rhymes, songs, and jingles of their own, they learn to play with words, patterns, sounds, and structures in ways that echo the literature they hear. Innovating on songs, rhymes, games, and verses helps children compose works of their own. In word play, youngsters skillfully draw on spoken language to formulate thoughts, arrange words, and construct texts orally as they step fluidly into the writing process.

The strong oral tradition of word play in early childhood provides youngsters with rich opportunities for literacy development. When children add verses to songs, expand on popular rhymes, and make up riddles and jokes of their own, they are learning to write naturally—using word play even before a pencil marks the page. As youngsters explore the sounds, patterns, words, and literacy devices of poetry, rhymes, games, and songs, they develop an understanding of the genre formats and techniques of children's literature. Knowing these language structures supports children in their reading and writing by providing strategies for comprehension and modeled frameworks for their own words and ideas. Word play experiences are a natural entryway into reading and writing by first introducing children to the authentic and rich print sources that surround them. Soon youngsters learn to make important literacy connections between oral and written language by recognizing symbols, visual messages, and graphic signs in the genuine print encounters in the environment that surrounds them.

Children's Book References

Ahlberg, Janet and Allan (1995) *Peepo.*

Barretta, Gene (2007) *Dear Deer: A Book of Homophones.*

Cimarusti, Maria (1998) *Peek A Moo.*

Clarke, Jackeline A. (2003) *Moose's Loose Tooth.*

Donaldson, Julia (2005) *Charlie Cook's Favourite Book.*

Dr. Seuss (1996) *Mr. Brown Can Moo! Can You?; Dr. Seuss's Book of Wonderful Noises.*

Fox, Mem (1993) *Time for Bed.*

Gilmour, Don (2005) *Sophie and the Sea Monster.*

Lansky, Bruce (2004) *Mary Had a Little Jam.*

Martin, Bill Jr. and John Archambault (1989) *Chicka Chicka Boom Boom.*

4

Print Encounters

The road to reading and writing is marked by print encounters in which young-sters discover the connections between oral and written language. In order to become literate, children must learn to crack the code by unlocking the mysteries of print (Wilson, 2002). They do so by discovering that print has meaning and carries a message. As part of literacy development, it is essential that children be exposed to print in its various forms—in written language, signs, symbols, and visual texts that appear all around us.

Developing print awareness is an important building block in the language learning process. Gaining knowledge of print, recognizing its forms, and under-standing its uses are key to developing in young people a motivation towards print. This motivation leads to an interest in reading, a desire to write, an eager-ness to communicate, and an enjoyment of literature. By being familiar with printed language and understanding its uses, children build positive relationships with books, gain confidence in reading, and see around them authentic models of writing in many visual and text forms. "The development of print awareness in situational contexts" is essential to literacy learning (Y.M. Goodman, 1980, p. 7). Through practical and meaningful encounters with print in environmental set-tings at home, in school, and in the community, young children acquire the print knowledge and motivation to grow into proficient readers, writers, and language users.

Code-breaking is an important reader practice that is part of Luke and Freebody's (1999) *Four Resource Model.* "Code-breaking is what a reader does to get inside a text or to unlock the mysteries of print to access the meaning" (Wilson, 2002, p. 45). In code-breaking, the reader learns to use a range of strategies to enter the text, crack the code, and make meaning.

Print Awareness—Discovering The Uses of Written Language

From a young age, children encounter print everywhere. Print awareness grows from family literacy practices, read-aloud engagements, shared book events, and other experiences that expose children to a variety of text forms and language uses. As young people explore the world around them, they discover and learn to recognize print on their own (Goodman and Goodman, 1979). Through natu-ral, purposeful, and everyday print encounters, children learn about written lan-guage and its uses in different contexts.

Written language functions as a sign and symbol system that carries meaning (Harste, Woodward and Burke, 1984). To uncover its meaning, children must discover how print works by learning to read its signs and symbols convention-ally and naturally. The system of signs and symbols takes many forms. Written language may appear in various text formats, alphabets, print layouts, commu-nication systems, and foreign languages. Through authentic examples in real-life daily use, children begin to recognize the nature and functions of print. Soon young language learners come to understand that written language and print carries meaning and is used for specific purposes (Hall, 1987). The meaning and purpose of print often depends on the situational context where it is found.

As children recognize words on a shopping list, recipe, instructional manual, or menu, they are interacting with texts, becoming aware of print, and experiencing language in different uses. When children use symbols, markings, or letters to record words or items on a grocery list, note, or page, they have challenged themselves to use written language to communicate in real-life ways. These genuine encounters with literacy often mark the beginning steps in young children's efforts to read and write. Children's first success at reading often begins with identifying environmental print.

Environmental Print

Look around and you will see print everywhere. Print is found on the products we use, the clothing we wear, the places we visit, and the routes we take to get there. Signs, symbols, words, and images surround us at home and in the community. Environmental print takes many forms.

Environmental print serves many functions. It is used to name, label, direct, signify, identify, and publicize many things (Martens, 1996). Environmental print uses signs, symbols, graphics, and other visual images to extend the meaning of texts.

Environmental Print

Type	Sources	Features/Variations

• Directional signs
• Road and traffic signs
• Street names/signs
• Safety signs/symbols
• Parking signs
• Advertisements
  – billboards
  – transit posters
  – bench ads
  – vehicle wraps (vinyl lettering and logos)
• Retail signage
• Graphic logos
• Trademarks/symbols
• Brand name labels
• Product packages
• Universal signs/symbols (e.g., restroom symbols)
• Digital lists (e.g., bus/flight schedule)
• Postings and local announcements
	• Clothing (e.g., hats, graphic T-shirts)
	• Cans, bottles, and similar packaging
	• Public buildings
	• Outdoor signs
	• Gas stations
	• Fast food chains and restaurant signs
	• Retail storefronts indoor signage (sales, notices)
	• Featured displays and product promotions
	• Food labels and consumer products packaging
	• Coupons and flyers
	• Brochures and pamphlets
	• Toys
	• Menus
	• License plates and bumper stickers
	• Electronics (telephone, computer)
	• Posters and billboards
	• Transit schedules
	• Mass transit vehicles
		• Font, style of lettering, handwriting
		• Pictures, graphics, symbols, visual images
		• Size of print (upper or lower case)
		• Color
		• Outline configuration of a logo
		• Geometric shapes of signs and logos
		• Limited or no text

Environmental print illustrates the use of written language and print in a social context in the community. Seeing print in a social context provides children with meaningful literacy engagements that allow them to learn about written language naturally. Observing print in different physical settings enables young people to understand the meaning of words, the use of language, and the purpose of print by learning them in context. Through environmental print encounters, children attach meaning to symbols and make sense of print based on where texts are located (e.g., on a stop sign). Although environmental print provides concrete, visual examples of written language in use, it may not look the same as conventional print or written texts. To draw children's attention to environmental print, it is important to be fully aware of the sources, features, variations, and locations where it can be found.

Early Reading Experiences—Identifying Environmental Print

As children grow in print awareness, they notice language all around them. From an early age, they recognize signs, symbols, and labels on items familiar to them. As young people participate in the social and cultural events around them, they discover what print is, learn it is to be read, and understand that it serves different purposes (Wilson, 2002). Through authentic language experiences in their environment, children become empowered with the tools to read print on their own. Print encounters build strong foundations for literacy development by moving children towards reading independently.

Through genuine print encounters, children come to realize that written language uses signs and symbols like the alphabet to construct messages and enable people to communicate. This understanding helps young readers to recognize signs and identify letters in their environment. Many youngsters gain alphabet knowledge and language awareness through recognition and practice with sounds on print sources and everyday items around them. For instance, they may start to notice initial letters on signs and labels on common items like salt and pepper shakers (S, P), hot and cold faucets (H, C), and parking signs (P) (Palmer and Bayley, 2005). As children learn to identify letters, they begin to establish letter-sound relationships, acquire phonological awareness, and develop language cueing systems (i.e., graphophonics).

The context provided by the situations where print is found gives readers powerful clues to make meaning (e.g., stop sign). As young people grow more aware of their environment, they learn to spot and read familiar signs and symbols based on the visual cues that these images give. Learning to interpret and identify environmental signs engages young children in the reading process and allows them to develop an important early reader strategy (e.g., using visual cues/picture clues). Through recurring print encounters, children learn to attach meaning and relevance to the words and symbols they see around them. From a young age, many children learn to recognize the words on signs, labels and packages even before they can read books conventionally. The familiar signs, labels, and graphic logos that children find in their print environment often become the first sight words they identify and can read on their own (Palmer and Bayley, 2005). As children learn the communicative role of written language, they soon realize that the print, not the picture, carries the message (Bloodgood, 1999). This understanding leads them to discover words and read print independently.

Through authentic language experiences in their environment, children become empowered with the tools to read print on their own. Print encounters build strong foundations for literacy development by moving children towards reading independently.

Through environmental print encounters, young people start to acquire alphabet knowledge, phonological awareness, and early literacy strategies that lead to reading success. When children have recurring experiences with written language in their homes and community, they learn to recognize words, understand what they mean, and identify them in real-life contexts. Learning words in the context of environmental print may help children develop other cueing strategies (e.g., semantics) that are fundamental to the reading process. As children explore written language in their environment, they learn to discover the nature, functions, and meaning of print and respond in different ways.

Responses to Environmental Print

When children learn to read environmental print, they may identify features of the products, signs and labels they recognize and use in their everyday life. As young people become familiar with common items in their environment, they respond in ways that help them make meaning and attach relevance to the words and symbols that appear on the labels, products and signs around them. In *Language Stories and Literacy Lessons* (1984), Harste, Woodwood, and Burke identify the following types of responses to environmental print:

- specific—the child may identify the product name, trademark, logo, product character, or manufacturer
- categorical—the child identifies the type of product by giving it a general classification (e.g., shampoo, toothpaste, cereal)
- functional—the child identifies the product's use or purpose (such as to brush teeth or wash clothes)

Although children's responses to environmental print may vary, their interpretations reveal the depth of their awareness, understanding, and experiences with language. In reading and responding to environmental print, young people learn to integrate language into their own experiences in ways that are relevant and practical. Through recurring print encounters in their everyday environment, young readers engage in literacy practices that challenge them to search for meaning and understand the various messages, symbols, and formats that appear in texts around them so they are "reading to live" (Wilson, 2002). When children practice reading for real purposes in their environment, the literacy skills they develop help them to become increasingly sophisticated language users.

As young people become familiar with common items in their environment, they respond in ways that help them make meaning and attach relevance to the words and symbols that appear on the labels, products, and signs around them.

Print Environment in a School Setting

When children enter school, they have many opportunities to grow in print awareness and use reading and writing naturally as part of daily activities. These purposeful classroom activities may include:

- reading music lyrics from a song sheet while preparing for a concert
- making a list of supplies and materials required for an art project or other classroom activity (baking, cooking)
- reading menu choices and taking orders for a school lunch or snack program
- checking the weather forecast for a class excursion or school event

To grow in print awareness and understand the many uses of written language, young people need an environment that is rich with print. Classrooms, playgrounds, hallways, libraries, offices, and other areas of a school provide authentic settings where real-life language models and print images are found. In addition to children's literature resources, young people encounter signs, symbols, visual texts, and written messages in their learning environment. Drawing children's attention to print helps youngsters to discover language on their own. In a learning environment filled with print, students are encouraged to experiment with language and practice reading and writing in natural, purposeful, and real-life ways. A print-rich school environment may include:

- Children's literature resources
- Magazines and local newspapers
- School newsletters, websites
- Brochures and pamphlets
- Posters and flyers (featuring upcoming school events)
- Bulletin boards and displays
- Labels
- Product packages at play centers or other displays
- Graphics (on clothing, footwear, school supplies)
- Maps and diagrams
- Directional signs
- Safety symbols
- Universal signs (restroom signage, EXIT signs)
- Food labels
- Parking and outdoor signs (crosswalk symbols)

A print-rich school environment may also feature signs, labels, diagrams, posters, and other displays that children can produce themselves. Hallways, learning centres, and other areas should be marked with print sources that young people can read and understand on their own. As children visit classrooms, the library, and other parts of the school rich with language, they become more aware of print and discover a variety of contexts in which it is used.

Environmental Print Awareness Activities

Environmental print awareness is an important stepping-stone in early childhood literacy development. To become effective language users, children need genuine opportunities to explore, discover, observe, and participate in literacy events that build environmental print awareness. Because children may have had different print encounters before they enter school, it is important to provide them with experiences in school and community settings that bridge any gaps in the growth of environmental print awareness. Here are some recommended activities.

Discovering Types of Environmental Print

Print Detectives

Work with children to create a list of environmental print examples they have noticed at home and around their neighborhood. Have students identify places where print can be found in their everyday life (e.g., on labels and packages, in lists, and on menus). Point out that print is everywhere to help children increase their awareness of language and its many signs and symbols. As young people become attentive to print in the world around them, they can train their detective eyes to discover signs of print on their own.

Signs Scavenger Hunt

Have students work in groups to find environmental print examples in different rooms and areas of the school. As students search for signs and symbols, ask them to note examples on a tracking sheet or discovery notebook. Children can record their findings in sketchbooks or detective note pads as well. Later, groups can share the print examples they found during their scavenger hunt.

Print Walks

Lead the class on a neighborhood walk to look for signs and environmental print examples in the community. Use a digital camera to take photographs of environmental graphics, advertisements, road and traffic signs, directional symbols, and other examples of print. Later, use the digital images to produce a book of environmental signs and local print sources.

Print Drives

Encourage children to look for signs and print sources as they ride in a car or a school bus. If your community has public transit, arrange a trip that requires the class to take a bus or subway. Ask students to note examples of print and advertisements on transit shelters, billboards, community post boards, and at places along the way such as retail locations and parks and recreation centres. Use a digital camera to record some of these examples.

Reproducing and Creating Environmental Print

School and Community Maps and Models

Students can produce maps of the school and local community and label them with signs, location names, and other examples of environmental print. Children can use art materials to create (and label) models of parts of the school (gymnasium, library, playground) or neighborhood (local shops, community areas) featured on their maps. Children can add new signs and symbols that may be relevant to them (e.g., a new stop sign or safety symbol needed in a local area, hallway names throughout the school). Finally, students can display their school and community maps and models in the building or other local venue such as a community centrer or public library.

Designing Storefronts

As children grow aware of environmental print, they learn to identify and recognize trademarks, brand names, graphic logos, and other print features on storefronts.. Children can combine this dimension of print awareness with media literacy and graphic art/design skills to develop environmental print of their own. First, have youngsters decide on a business, product, or service they want to create. Next, have them consider a company name or label for their product or business. Children can then experiment with print variations (e.g., fonts, logos or graphic configurations, color, shape and size of lettering) to design a new storefront or building. Students can use art materials and graphic design techniques (fonts and lettering) to produce retail signage to mark the shops and buildings they have created. Children can extend the activity by creating other sales-related signs (promotions, notices of in-store events, product giveaways) to display on their storefronts. Later, the class can assemble the display boards featuring the new retail shops that might appear in their community.

Community Poster

Have students design a poster that can be displayed in the neighborhood featuring event notices, local advertisements, and environmental awareness signs. Later, the class can visit places in their local community (public libraries, community centre, supermarket) and display their postings in different areas (on community notice boards, traffic light posts). Similar signs can be made and featured throughout the school.

Bench Ads About Me

Children can use bench advertising as a way to express themselves to others. Have students design and build model benches to feature their personal ads. Children can create symbols, signs, visual images, and text to represent aspects of their personality, interests, hobbies and background. Students can display their advertisements throughout the classroom or school for a parents' night or other community event.

Shopping Lists and Store Visits

Plan a class project such as a cooking, baking, art or drama activity that may involve a trip to a supermarket or arts and crafts store. Have students work in small or large groups to produce a shopping list of ingredients, supplies, or materials using words or pictures (brand name, trademarks, or their own symbols). Later, arrange for supervised store visits for students to find items on their list by reading and identifying labels, logos, brand names, or graphics on product packages. Encourage children to check off items as they practice using language and reading print in a natural, real-life way. Finally, students can work in groups to read and follow food recipes or instructions to create, costumes, props, settings, or crafts for their class project.

Designing Product Packages

A personal chocolate bar

Children can design packaging for a consumer product (cereal, chocolate bar, toothpaste) by creating unique logos, original trademarks, creative symbols, and product descriptions. Features might include personal labels and designs that represent themselves.

Designing an Ad Layout

Have students imagine themselves to be graphic designers or art directors as they design a magazine layout to advertise an existing product or something they create. Children can apply different print and layout features to have variety in slogans, logos, graphics, size of lettering, style of font, and color.

Signs in a Book

Students can create an environmental sign in response to an event in a story or after reading a non-fiction book. Children can respond to literature by producing signs, symbols, or graphic images to consolidate their understanding of reading material or express their reaction to a text. Readers can share their responses by displaying their environmental print signs in a book corner or during a literature circle discussion.

Environmental Print Art Museum

Students can display environmental print works they make (posters, ads, maps, storefront models, product packages) in a Print Art Museum. Children can act as tour guides for members of the school community as they visit the museum and study the items on exhibit.

The Importance of Children's Names in Literacy Learning

The most meaningful word a child will encounter in print is his or her name. Being able to recognize one's name is the first consistent sign of print awareness during the early years of language learning. As children grow in print awareness, an important step they take towards literacy is knowing and writing their own name (Clay, 1975; Ferreiro and Teberosky, 1982). As youngsters learn to recognize and produce their name, they discover ways of making sense of print and using written language. Children's name recognition provides insight into their emergent understanding of literacy.

Names play an important and powerful role in helping children develop their reading skills. Names often become the first words in young children's growing sight vocabulary. A name is a word that a child can successfully read and recognize in print. As young people begin to recognize their own name and those of family members and friends, they start to build a repertoire of words they can read independently. When youngsters read familiar names aloud, the letters and word forms they recognize allow them to make letter-sound connections (Martens, 1996). Children's early understanding of phonics begins to develop through name recognition. As youngsters see in print the representation of their own names and other related words (Mom and Dad, for example), they begin to grasp the relationship between oral and written language (Schultze, 2008). Matching sounds with symbols and spoken language with written codes helps children develop language systems that are essential to reading success. Names allow youngsters to practice early reading strategies (using graphophonic cues) and form other literacy concepts too.

Name knowledge plays a significant part in children's writing development (Bloodgood, 1999). Learning to write one's own name marks a child's first attempt at creating meaning through print and using written language. At first, youngsters may use symbols, drawings, signs, and other markings to represent their names on paper (Ferreiro and Teberosky, 1982; Harste, Woodward, and Burke, 1984). These early writing engagements allow children to exercise their emerging literacy skills as they learn to grasp and manipulate written language concepts (Bloodgood, 1999). As children grow in print awareness, knowledge of the alphabet, and understanding of word concepts, they may use initial letters or combination of letters to represent their name. Some youngsters gain greater control of the alphabet using known letters to produce their name. This knowledge may lead them toward making letter-sound associations, integrating the graphophonic system, and applying the alphabetic principle to writing their name (Martens, 1996; Bloodgood, 1999; Palmer and Bayley, 2005).

Name writing also can challenge children to work on letter formations and printing. As children begin to explore conventional forms in producing their name, they may discover other concepts about literacy and apply the syllabic hypothesis to writing (Ferreiro and Teberosky, 1982; Marten, 1996).Youngsters may start to match each syllable that is spoken with a separate character, symbol, or letter unit on the written page. Matching spoken words or syllables with written marks helps children form relationships between oral and written language, a skill that is essential to reading and writing. As youngsters work with known letter units or patterns to write their name, they may discover that these alphabet characters can be used to produce other words too. When used in varying orders and with added letter combinations, these language symbols can be manipulated to represent various messages in writing. This discovery helps children unlock the mysteries of print and learn the code to written language.

Name recognition and name production allow youngsters to explore and develop their understanding of literacy concepts in a personally relevant and meaningful way. To build print awareness and literacy skills, children can engage in the following language experiences at home or at school:

Name Recognition

Children first learn to recognize their own names in print when they see them on signs, labels, and materials. Encourage children to read their own name and those of other students or family members by creating personal labels and signs. Record and post names on name tags/cards, coat hooks, and personal items at home and in the classroom. Encourage children to look for their own names when locating supplies and materials that belong to them. This also helps create a welcoming place for children (Schultze, 2008).

Betty Schultze provides other lesson ideas for helping children learn to print their names in her book *Basic Tools for Beginning Writers* (Pembroke, 2008).

Name Production

Children learn to produce their own names in a variety of ways. They can practice printing the letters in the air as well as on paper. They can use crayons, paintbrushes, and other writing materials, as well as early literacy tools such as magnetic or felt letters, and modeling clay. Students can practice name writing by designing personal labels for school supplies, books, and clothing. They can also explore name writing in visual art lessons, using stencils, stamps, different fonts, or illuminated letters.

Children can learn to print the letters and spell their names in other activities too. Students can look for letters of their own name on environmental signs, product packages, and brochures. They can cut out individual letters from magazines and newspapers and assemble them to form their names. Youngsters can practice spelling their own names aloud through songs, call and response, clapping games, and similar oral language activities. They can also tap out the letters and syllables of their names using drums or other musical instruments.

As young children embark on the journey to learn language, their ability to recognize and produce names emerges collaboratively as they develop alphabet knowledge (Bloodgood, 1999). Names allow children to form important understandings about literacy by helping them make connections to letters, sounds, and words. Names provide young people with authentic language opportunities to develop print awareness, alphabet knowledge, word concepts, phonological awareness, and other literacy understandings essential to reading and writing.

To become readers, writers, and language users, children must gain control of the alphabet, make use of letters, and know their sounds. Letter recognition and alphabet knowledge are developed through emergent literacy activities that allow children to learn about language in genuine and playful ways.

Letter Knowledge and Alphabet Play

Youngsters learn about print through read-aloud events, environmental print awareness activities, name games, and similar rich, authentic literacy experiences. As children encounter print, they discover language forms that are used to make meaning and communicate with others. They learn to recognize signs, symbols, and characters in print sources. They learn that print carries the message more than pictures do, and that written language on a page maps onto meaning. The search for meaning challenges young people to unlock the mysteries of print by uncovering the secret code in written messages. Children are clever print detectives who soon realize that written language takes the shape of letters and words that carry meaning. Discovering these features of written language helps children gain knowledge of the print itself.

An important part of print awareness is knowing and being able to identify the letters of the alphabet. Letter recognition enables young people to decipher aspects of writing and learn the written code. Knowing the alphabet helps children make sense of squiggles and characters on a page. To grow in alphabet knowledge, children must:

- know what letters are
- be able to recognize letters around them
- be able to tell the difference between pictures and letters
- be able to identify letters from squiggles and designs
- know letter names and sounds
- understand that letters of the alphabet are different from one another
- be able to tell letters apart.

Early Literacy Fundamentals (Palmer and Bayley, Pembroke Publishers, 2005) and *Basic Tools for Beginning Writers* (Schultze, Pembroke Publishers, 2008) feature lessons and other engaging activities designed to help children learn the alphabet and play with letters.

Alphabet knowledge and letter recognition are essential steps in the reading process. "Studies show that knowledge of letter names and letter sounds is related to success in learning to read." (Hirsh-Pasek and Golinkoff, 2003, p.115)

In their early years, children need rich, engaging, and meaningful language experiences to play with letters and grow familiar with the alphabet before learning about reading and writing (Palmer and Bayley, 2005). Learning the alphabet and letter names should be an integral part of a child's early reading experiences at home and in the classroom. To ensure that children have the pre-requisite skills needed to read and write, teachers and adult family members can provide youngsters with creative hands-on activities based on alphabet and letter play. Drill and practice worksheets often focus on remote aspects of learning the alphabet (e.g., printing letters). Direct teaching of letter names should not be an end in itself. Children can learn the alphabet in the context of informal, playful, and rich emergent literacy experiences. Here are some examples:

- The Alphabet Song—Children can learn letters by reciting the alphabet song.
- Alphabet rhymes—Youngsters can practice the alphabet by repeating jump-rope rhymes, schoolyard chants, and alphabet raps.

> *Ice cream soda, ginger-ale pop,*
> *Tell me the initials of your sweetheart.*
> *A, B, C.....X, Y, Z.*

- Alphabet toys—Young children can learn to recognize letters by making alphabet puzzles, constructing with alphabet blocks, and playing with magnetic or felt board letters.

Cut-out picture alphabet letter

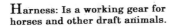

Page from picture dictionary

- The Alphabet Game—Play an attribute game that challenges youngsters to name objects that start with each letter (e.g., *A* is for *apple, B* is for *ball, C* is for *cat)*. Variations of this game can be played using, for example, names of foods, animals, or countries.
- Alphabet books—Read books that teach the alphabet such as *Chicka, Chicka, Boom, Boom* or *Dr. Seuss's ABC*. Encourage children to go on an "alphabet book search" for similar storybooks (e.g., *Alphabeasts)*. Point out and name letters when reading these concept books. Have students identify letters when reading children's literature too. Show children that the same letter can look different in print depending on the font or style of lettering.
- Baking letters—Children can use cookie dough to form different letters of the alphabet and then bake them for a delicious treat!
- Constructing the alphabet—Youngsters can use straws, stir sticks, toy building sets, and other materials to construct letters of the alphabet, including their own names.
- Alphabet raps, chants, and stories—Children can learn these to help them match letter names, sounds, and shapes (see Betty Schultze's book *Basic Tools for Beginning Writers* for sample stories).
- I Spy—Provide clues for mystery items that begin with letters of the alphabet and have children guess by locating objects around them that start with that letter.
- The Alphabet Museum—Have children gather and display objects that begin with each letter of the alphabet. Groups can work together to create a display of objects that begin with a given letter.
- Scavenger hunt—Challenge children to find and name objects in the environment that begin with each letter.
- Nature's alphabet—Have children look for shapes and objects in everyday life, nature, and architecture that resemble letters of the alphabet. Sample objects include playground equipment, tree branches, and arches/doorways.
- Cut-and-paste picture alphabet—Have children find (and cut out) pictures of objects in newspapers, magazines, and catalogues that begin with a letter of the alphabet. Using large construction paper stencils of each letter, children can glue the cutouts they find onto the letter. Make a classroom display of the cut-and-paste picture alphabet or use the letters to assemble a word wall.
- Word wall—Use a variety of materials (crayons, magnetic letters, chalk) to write words that begin with each letter of the alphabet. Feature the words on a classroom word wall. Focus on words related to topics of interest or other learning experiences in which children are engaged.
- Tracing letters—Children can practice making letters by tracing their shapes in sand, salt, grains of rice, or other granular substance that can be stored in a plastic bin. Later, children can trace their names and other words they know.
- Textured letters—Youngsters can use stencils to trace letters out of sand paper or other textured paper. Afterwards, children can use these forms to play with letter shapes and learn the outline of each letter.
- Letter prints—Using hand-made stencils, foam sheets, rollers, and paint, children can make prints to recreate the alphabet or decorate letters as illuminations.
- Model alphabet—Youngsters can construct letters of the alphabet using modeling clay, fabric, cardboard, or other craft materials.

- Picture alphabet book—Children can use a digital or disposable camera to take photographs of objects that begin with each letter of the alphabet. Later, students can glue each photograph on a separate sheet, label each item, and arrange the pages in alphabetical order to make an alphabet book.
- Picture dictionaries—Have children produce picture dictionaries of words that begin with each letter of the alphabet based on themes, topics, or content areas of study (e.g., pioneer words, community helpers, transportation).
- Alphabet poems—Read alphabet poems to the class. Encourage children to work together to create their own alphabet poems based on different themes. Students can use the alphabet to make a list poem about a topic too.
- ABC tongue twisters—Children can produce an alphabet book of alliterations and tongue twisters that begin with the first letter of their name or with each letter of the alphabet.

When children play with letters and learn the alphabet through fun and interactive activities, they gain confidence in themselves as language learners. The competence, knowledge, and skills that youngsters develop through alphabet and letter play prepare them for phonics, handwriting, and other language lessons. As children play with language forms, they discover how to link letters and sounds in order to translate print. Learning about letters in the context of rich emergent literacy activities and early reading experiences allows children to make word connections and get real meaning from texts. Knowing how to master language and understand print makes the task of learning to read and write seem within reach. Playing with letters may soon lead children to discover, make, and study words as they become increasingly aware of how print looks on a page.

Word Study—Playing with Print

Children's first encounter with words begin by reading environmental print, recognizing and producing names, playing with letters, and knowing the alphabet. Once youngsters have had these experiences with print, they may start to notice word sounds, language patterns, and writing features that lead to conventional reading and writing.

There are many ways to move youngsters from spoken to written language. Children can explore the sounds, patterns, and features of written language through playful word study. These activities provide emerging readers and writers with strategies they can use to predict or recognize words in print. Through word study, children play with letters and sounds, come across spelling patterns, and uncover meanings that can help them break the reading code. As children work with written language in interactive and fun activities, they build vocabulary, sight words and word knowledge in ways that lead them to become word sleuths and print masters.

Word Sounds—Onomatopoeia

Children are delighted by the playful sounds of language. As youngsters become aware of print, they start to focus attention on written language and notice words. Some words have the power to soar from the page and capture attention by their sheer appearance and sound. When read aloud, these words say their own sound in a resonating way (*crunch, pop, squish, splash, boom*). Children can explore language sounds and print features by studying words through onomatopoeia. Challenge students to make a list of words that say their own sounds. Have them find

Name: Deanna

My word is mountain

1.	cant	11.	nut
2.	out	12.	not
3.	mat	13.	tin
4.	main	14.	mount
5.	in	15.	unit
6.	it	16.	bun
7.	on	17.	at
8.	no	18.	nit
9.	man	19.	am
10.	tan	20.	mint

This is an example of a hidden word activity.

these words in print sources. Provide the class with art supplies and ask students to design and display posters that feature these words in ways that visually depict their sounds and meanings (e.g., drip).

Word Hunts

Once children are interested in written language, they can become word detectives searching for words in literature and environmental print that begin with the same initial, middle, or ending sounds. Students can produce word lists and show the relationship between sounds in words by underlining, circling, or highlighting the sound units, or word parts, that are the same or different.

Hidden Words

As children "look" inside words, they may uncover a treasury of other words hidden within the letters. Select a word and post it for the students to see (e.g., *kingdom*). Have students locate other words that appear in order within this word (e.g., *king, in, do*) or use the same letters to make smaller words (e.g., *no, on, dog, dig, kin, gin, ding, dong*). Challenge students to look for hidden words or make new words using the letters in their names (e.g., *Matthew: math, hat, that, mat*).

Word Building and Alphabet Play

Encourage youngsters to have fun with language by making words as they play. Begin by having children use toys as construction units for word building. Students can use a variety of play and craft materials (alphabet blocks, magnetic letters, alphabet beads, letter cubes, letter stickers) to work with letters, explore sounds, and construct simple words. Youngsters can build word towers, snap together linking cubes, or string together beads to form their names or spell beginning sight words, words from storybooks, and other new vocabulary using alphabet toys and craft supplies.

Word Games, Puzzles, and Brainteasers

As children grow in word recognition and vocabulary, they may enjoy playing commercial card and board games (e.g., *Scrabble, Boggle,* or *Upwords*) that challenge them to make words cooperatively with others. Classic word games (e.g., hangman) help children to make connections between letters and sounds as they spell out words, titles, and phrases. Children can search for words, uncover word meanings, and solve word dilemmas by completing word search and crossword puzzles, brainteasers, and unscramble word games.

Building Word Families—Word Twins, Rhyming Triplets

Children can discover word patterns and sound relationships by studying words that belong to the same word family. Often these words share the same ending sounds and spelling patterns (or rimes). Begin by introducing students to a word family (e.g., the *–ook* family). Next, have them identify two rhyming pairs, or twins, that belong to this word group (*look* and *book*). Ask them to extend the word pattern by naming three more words, or rhyming triplets, that belong to the same word family (e.g., *hook, cook, took*). Challenge students to add other initial sounds, or onsets (*br–, sh–, cr–*) to the word family to make more sets of rhyming words (twins like *nook, rook* or triplets like *brook, shook, crook*). Once students have had practice building word families, have them use other onsets (*d, l, fl*) and rimes (*–ance, – ight, –oat, –unk*) to make to more sets of rhyming words.

Letter Swap

Youngsters can use magnetic letters to make words in addition and substitution games. For example: Display the letters of a word family, or rime, on the board using magnetic letters ('it'). Next, ask: *What do I add to make it "sit"?* Invite children to find the magnetic letter ("s") and add it to the word part to make the word "sit". Then ask, *What do I change to make it "fit"?* Have children use the magnetic letters to change the initial letter, or onset, "f" to make the new word. Challenge the students to make new words by changing the middle and ending sounds and letters too. Adding and substituting letters in this way helps children build words and leads to more challenging word fun.

Word Ladders

Students can play challenging word games by changing letters in a sequence of steps or moves to create new words. To demonstrate this, draw a ladder with a given number of steps (e.g., four) on the board. Next, record a word (*hat*) on the bottom step and another word (*lid*) on the top step. Challenge the class to the game by having them practice changing a single letter on each step to make a new word until the old word (*hat*) becomes the new word (*lid*) in the specified number of moves that are indicated on the ladder (e.g., *hat, had, lad, lid*). Provide children with other sets of words they can change in a specified number of steps on a word ladder to make new words (e.g., *land* to *king* in five steps—*land, band, bind, kind, king*). Allow students to construct their own word ladder games to challenge others.

Heads or Tails

When youngsters look closely at words in print, they may find patterns in words that share the same root. As a class, produce a list of root words. Have students locate words in literature and print that have the same root by circling, underlying, or highlighting the root or base word (e.g., *build)*. Challenge the class to make a list of other words constructed from root words (e.g., *rebuild, building, builder)*. Have students identify the word parts that have been added (prefixes and suffixes) to the root word to change the context or meaning. As a class, produce a list of common prefixes and suffixes that readers may find tacked onto words. Challenge students to make new words by adding heads (prefixes) or tails (suffixes) to a series of root words. These activities can help children recognize root words in print and give them another effective reading strategy to use when they encounter unknown words. Building words from their roots is an interactive way for youngsters to explore word patterns, construct word knowledge, and process language.

Word Lists

Challenge students with activities in which they can look for patterns and inconsistencies in words by exploring sounds and written language. Charting words that share similar features can help children learn about the complexities of language, build vocabulary, and identify words in print. As children explore words and language sounds, they may uncover common attributes. Ask students to work with others to locate words in literature, environmental print, and other sources that share the same patterns. Have them produce word walls or other charts that feature the following word lists:

- word families
- root words
- words with the same prefix
- words with the same suffix
- words with silent letters
- theme words
- compound words
- words with the same vowel sound
- high-frequency or sight words
- words that rhyme that have a similar spelling (e.g., *dance*, *prance*)
- words that rhyme that have a different spelling (e.g., *ball*, *doll*)
- other attributes (plurals, contractions)

Word Duos and Double Meanings

Many words in the English language have both patterns and irregularities in spelling and sounds that are often confusing. Some words may be spelled and pronounced the same way but carry different meanings (homonyms). Other words may sound alike but differ in both spelling and meaning (homophones). Certain words may share the same spelling but have different meanings and pronunciations (homographs). Through language play, children can have fun exploring these discrepancies in sound, meaning, and spelling.

Literature (*Dear Deer: A Book of Homophones* by Gene Barretta) can be used to introduce children to the wonderful treasury of words that share the same sound but have different spellings and meanings (*hear, here; aunt, ant; hair, hare; ate, eight*). Challenge students to find and list homophones in books and recall other word pairs from memory (*red, read*). Have children produce game cards featuring these word duos (one word per card). Later, students can use the game cards to play a matching memory game.

Challenge students to find examples of homonyms and homographs in the print sources around them and make a list (e.g., *bat, rose, park, close, bill, project, pitcher*). Later, children can use language play to explore double meanings in words that are spelled the same way. Challenge students to make up crossword puzzles and trivia games that draw out the meaning of different homographs.

Jokes, Riddles, and Puns

Children delight in funny stories that play on words and make them laugh. Jokes, riddles, and puns are filled with simple language designed to entertain. These playful forms poke fun at language in a humorous way. Youngsters are drawn to dialogue, stories, one-liners, and puns that use wittiness and absurdity to play on the discrepancies of language. The comical aspect of jokes and riddles often hangs on the double meanings and common sound-alike words found in homographs and homophones.

Allow youngsters to collect and share a variety of jokes in the classroom (knock knock jokes, puns, riddles). Provide time for children to read joke books with others. Students can also produce their own collections of jokes, riddles, and puns.

> *What kind of paper do you build with? Construction Paper*
> *What type of book has wings and a tail? A Fairy Tale Book*

By telling, reading, and inventing jokes and riddles, students are able to explore language patterns, discriminate word meanings, develop communication skills, and use logical thinking with a growing sense of humor.

Ads, Slogans, and Jingles

Popular culture is filled with rich sources of word play in the jingles, slogans, catchy phrases, taglines and advertisements we hear or see in broadcast and print media. Children tune their ears to these language sounds from a young age. Often, we hear them cheerfully repeating words and verses they remember. The pattern, rhythms, sounds, and rhymes found in contemporary verses are fresh examples of how words and language can be manipulated into new shapes and forms. As a class, create a display featuring examples of word play found in media and advertising. Discuss the techniques used. Provide students with an opportunity to develop their own jingles, slogans, or taglines for popular consumer goods or new products they invent. Allow children to share their ads with others in mock television and radio commercials. As children work to create these advertisements, they may innovate on the rhymes, sounds, patterns, and verses they know from popular culture or creatively invent their own.

Text Reconstructions

Once youngsters have grown familiar with well-known children's verses, they may be drawn to written language as their eyes move toward words they start to recognize on the page. Through text encounters, children may come to note features (letters, words, sentences), structures (genres, shapes), and conventions (capital letters, punctuation) in writing that will help them gain reading strategies (visual discrimination, syntactic cues) and develop concepts of print (directionality, sentence breaks etc). Students can work on developing this knowledge of language by reconstructing texts they know.

Begin by selecting a memorable rhyme, poem, verse, or song that children have grown to love. Copy the words, phrases, or sentences onto strips of paper for youngsters to rearrange. Have students sequence the strips to reconstruct the text. Later, have children cut apart other poems, rhymes, songs, or verses and challenge their peers to reconstruct them. Familiarity with the text will enable children to identify words, phrases, and sentences more easily. In the process of sequencing the words in the rhyme, poem, song, or verse, youngsters draw upon their understanding of letters-sound relationships and schematic features to reshape the text. Through text reconstructions, children develop skills in code breaking and move closer to reading independently.

Print Concepts

As children grow in print awareness, they discover language and develop literacy through diverse learning experiences. Environmental print encounters, name awareness, letter recognition, alphabet knowledge, and playful word study provide youngsters with emergent literacy experiences that help them become language users. Print encounters form an essential cornerstone in building a strong literacy foundation in the early years. Discovering the meaning of print allows children to unlock the mysteries of reading. To crack the code, youngsters must find meaning in printed words, learn to master written language, and know how to handle books with ease. As these understandings emerge, children start to display essential reading skills that are linked to important concepts about print.

Book encounters move children beyond learning about print in situational and environmental contexts towards developing "print awareness in connected discourse" (Y.M. Goodman, 1980, p. 6). As children grow in print awareness, they begin to show an interest in books and an enjoyment of literature. This motivation towards print may inspire them to learn to read. Even before they can identify words, young children will often pick up a book and approximate reading themselves. As they pretend to read, many of them begin to imitate early reading behaviors that reflect their growing understanding of concepts about print (Clay, 2000).

Developing print concepts is key to literacy learning in the early years. Understanding conventions like linearity, directionality, spaces, and punctuation (Clay, 1975) provides readers with some of the essential guides to manage print and course their way through a text. By observing young people as they interact with literature and make meaning of print, teachers and parents can gain insights into the print concepts that growing readers are learning to use and comprehend. As children become literate, they may demonstrate the following reading behaviors and concepts of print:

- book/text handling skills (knowing how to handle a book/text)
  - pick up print sources (books, magazines, newspapers)
  - position the text for reading (place it conveniently in front of them on a table or their lap) (Jobe and Dayton-Sakari, 2002)
  - know how to handle a book or text (hold it upright not upside down)
  - know which way a book opens and how to turn the pages
  - hold the text a certain way (e.g., hold book or newspaper with two hands)
  - lean into reading material or move the text closer for ease of reading (Jobe and Dayton-Sakari, 2002)
  - replace the text when finished reading (Jobe and Dayton-Sakari, 2002)
- print tracking skills (knowing how to follow texts and words on a page)
  - read books from front to back
  - understand the directionality of print (text flows left to right, top to bottom)
  - follows the linear progression of print (follows lines of print in a sentence on the page)
  - pay attention to print (recognizes text, identifies letters and words)
  - distinguish between illustrations and print (pictures vs. text)
  - match print on the page to spoken words (matches written and spoken words)
  - finger points (word-to-word matching)
  - display an understanding of letter-sound relationships
  - have a sight vocabulary of some words
  - understand the use of spaces in written language
  - recognize word/sentence breaks on a line or page
  - pause and pace his/her reading (uses spacing and punctuation)
  - know when to turn the page (page-to-page matching)
  - stop reading while turning the page
- keep track of reading place
- finish story/text at exactly the last page

As children develop concepts of print, they learn to use a variety of early reading strategies to make meaning and comprehend texts (e.g., picture cues, monitoring, and self-correcting). Many strategies that children practice during their emergent reading development highlight their growing understanding of print concepts. Children's knowledge of print concepts plays an important role in the reading process. Knowing how to handle a book, track and follow text on a page, and match words to print draws youngsters into a story and prepares them to read on their own. While these print concepts help young children move into reading, knowledge of print itself is also necessary to break the code. Youngsters need to uncover the features of written language to be able to decipher texts. Understanding that letters make up words and that sounds are connected to letters is only one step in learning to read. Being able to recognize letters and match them to their sounds may not always ensure reading success especially if youngsters have no idea what the words and phrases they are decoding mean. The goal of real reading is being able to go from print to meaning (Hirsh-Pasek and Golinkoff, 2003, p. 120). To learn to make meaning, children need a range of literacy experiences that teach them about language in authentic and purposeful ways.

Along with play, talking, language/word games, rhyming, and music activities, print experiences are essential in forming the cornerstones for literacy development in the early years. Through a variety of genuine print encounters, children become familiar with how language works and start to take interest in reading and writing for different purposes. A growing awareness of print can lead young people towards literacy events in which they can enjoy books or use written language to communicate with others. As children develop a knowledge and motivation towards print, they step into reading and writing naturally and come to manage these "full-blown" language tasks with greater success and competency.

Children's Book References

Dr. Seuss (1963) *Dr. Seuss's ABC*.
Edwards, Wallace (2008) *Alphabeasts*.
Martin Jr., Bill; Archambault, John; and Ehlert, Lois (2000) *Chicka Chicka Boom Boom*.

5

Reading Events

Learning to read is one of the most important skills that children acquire as they become literate. Reading is more than naming letters, knowing sounds, and recognizing words in print. It is a complex language-learning process that involves constructing meaning and interacting with a text. To make meaning, children must learn to crack the code and unlock the mysteries of print (Wilson, 2002). Young children develop the ability to break the code and establish meaning through emergent literacy experiences. Reading events in early childhood play an important part in building strong foundations for literacy learning. As children participate in read-aloud engagements, shared reading experiences, and early literacy activities such as reader response, they develop essential reading strategies, literacy practices, and language knowledge that are the groundwork for learning to read independently.

Children's Literature—A Building Block of Literacy

From the moment that a child climbs onto an adult's lap to listen to a story, the journey into literacy begins. Young children's first encounters with stories start with the rich narratives they enjoy through read-aloud or oral traditions such as storytelling. Children's literature provides great pleasure to children and plays a significant role in their social, academic, and literacy success (Hoewisch, 2000). Reading aloud to young children contributes directly to their early literacy development (Teale, 1984). Through the emergent reading of favorite storybooks, many youngsters learn to read naturally even before they enter school (Sulzby, 1985). As children engage in book encounters, they build comprehension, vocabulary, phonological awareness, structural knowledge, and emergent reading strategies. When youngsters grab hold of a favored book, they often learn the pages by heart, correcting adults when they deviate from the original text and later pretend reading the book to themselves or others (Sulzby, 1985). Children even use texts as springboards for play, drama, and their own story compositions. Children's literature is an important tool in building early literacy. Memorable book experiences play a leading part in shaping youngsters into readers and writers.

Children's Literature and the World of Print

The road to becoming a reader is paved with books and children's literature resources. Selections of children's literature have grown over the years to include a wide range of genres, including novels, picture books, poetry collections, nonfiction resources, and traditional folklore. An expanding number of multimedia texts are being added to literature collections in homes, libraries, classrooms, and bookstores. These texts include graphic novels, CDs, DVDs, and mass-produced books (e.g., series books/novels, magazines, and comic strips). Many are based on popular culture in films and television episodes such as *Dora the Explorer, High School Musical,* and *Hannah Montana.*

With the rapid spread of technology, the appearance of print has been transformed. New literacy texts include websites, downloadable video segments, web logs/blogs, and other internet-based resources. Through digital messaging, gaming, on-line social networking, and similar popular pursuits, young people are participating in literacy events that reflect new forms and genres. Although the propagation of mass culture and digital technology are changing the face of print, a wide range of literacy encounters based on children's literature, new and old, continue to inspire and motivate even the most reluctant reader to interact with texts and print images. Together, novels, picture books, poetry collections, works of non-fiction, and multimedia resources offer countless opportunities for children of all ages to engage in and respond to various text forms that now fall within the realm of children's literature and the range of published materials available to them.

The Gift of Children's Literature

Children's literature enriches the lives of readers of all ages. Literary treasure chests around the world are brimming with tales and experiences that have the capacity to reach children and adults alike. Storybook collections and other children's literature resources have the power to engage us all through the compelling act of response. Books can entice our imaginations, entangle our emotions, provoke our thoughts, and inspire our ideas.

Children's literature can help people, young and old, make sense of their lives, and understand others and the world more deeply. Stories that speak of the human condition, that address the unknown or shared experiences of hardship, or that describe the joys that define daily life reveal the healing source of the human spirit. Through these stories, we can grow in character and connect more meaningfully with others. These heartfelt encounters with literature can invoke feelings of compassion and social and cultural awareness that help form the values, attitudes, and behaviors to inspire action and bring change to our world.

The transforming power of children's literature carries us into times and places beyond the realm of everyday life. Stories of fantasy or science fiction, books of past cultures or foreign events, and tales of mythic heroes or famous people are open tickets for our imagination to recreate the world we live in. These text encounters give children vicarious experiences to stretch the boundaries of their minds and carry them to faraway places. The works of children's literature are passports to learning.

Books promote thinking and learning in myriad ways. The wide inventory of children's literature in classrooms, libraries, and bookstores today holds storehouses of facts and information that students can draw on to learn something new. Once inspired, readers turn to books to acquire knowledge, gain understanding, and develop insights on subjects they are required to learn or topics that interest them. Through purposeful text encounters, young people are challenged to discover new concepts, interpret images/findings, evaluate information, think critically, question facts and opinions, and formulate judgments and perspectives of their own.

Shelley Stagg Peterson and Larry Swartz explore the sources, selection, rationale, and use of children's literature in classrooms as tools for literacy learning and reading/writing development in their book *Good Books Matter* (Pembroke, 2008).

Storybook collections and other children's literature resources have the power to engage us all through the compelling act of response. Books can entice our imaginations, entangle our emotions, provoke our thoughts, and inspire our ideas.

Children's literature provides rich models and authentic contexts for literacy learning and language development. Through playful and purposeful encounters with stories, poems, picture books, non-fiction texts, traditional folklore, and other quality children's publications, young people can grow as readers and writers. The crafted language of children's literature is filled with a rich texture of stories and information that offer creative ideas and literary structures that can shape students' own writing and sense of narrative.

Using children's literature in classroom reading events nurtures young people's language development. Children's literature helps emerging and developing readers and writers:

- learn narrative elements and story structures
- use patterns and text structures as models to develop a sense of story and create their own narratives complete with characters, setting, conflict, plot, and solution
- identify and apply literary devices (e.g., foreshadowing, flashbacks, and metaphors) and book language (traditional prompts like *Once Upon A Time*, and other phrases, expressions, and words learned from books)
- develop a wide range of vocabulary, spelling, and language structures (grammar, conventions, syntax rules) and learn them in context
- become familiar with a variety of literary styles, text forms, and genre features (patterns and structures of myths, legends, novels, short stories, poems, and works of non-fiction)
- understand various themes in literature (community, relationships, peace, environment)

Classroom events that use quality children's literature can inspire in students a growing interest in books, a pleasure in reading, and a love of literature to last a lifetime. Developing a lifetime of pleasure in reading and love of literature happens by giving children open admission into the world of books and quality children's publications.

Building Children's Literature Resources

Reading events and book encounters are essential elements of building strong literacy foundations. The resources that will be read to children or made available to beginning readers should be the finest literature available. Building a library of books worth reading and sharing with children carries the demand of making quality text selections. Often, the best choices are those with tattered bindings and worn pages earned through the delightful enjoyment of repeated readings. Hooking young people onto good books is an inspiring goal in the resource development and learning-to-read process.

Book Selection Criteria

To develop into lifelong readers, children need access to a wealth of literature. The selection, availability, quality, and range of children's literature resources have grown beyond the capacity that most bookshelves can hold. From this vast inventory, the task of selecting quality resources is rich with promise in the opportunity to shape young minds into readers and writers.

Parents, teachers, librarians, and other educators who work with emergent and developing readers often consider different features when making their text

The crafted language of children's literature is filled with a rich texture of stories and information that offer creative ideas and literary structures that can shape students' own writing and sense of narrative.

selections, depending on the reading event. Reading materials serve many purposes depending on the age, interest, and abilities of students.

Criteria for Classroom Book Selection

Read-aloud Events	Shared or Guided Reading	Independent Reading
• Age level and attention span of students • Expressive book language (including extended use of vocabulary for learning new word meanings in context) • Exemplary illustrations in picture books (that can be viewed as art) • Creative ideas that expand the mind and enrich the imagination • Diverse writing styles and different genre forms (e.g., poem, short story, novel, picture book, informational text) • Positive and authentic character and human portraits that reflect people from various cultures, backgrounds, and genders in different social roles • Powerful themes that address issues of equity and diversity, or convey universal messages • Texts beyond children's own reading level that may extend their reading interests, vocabulary, ideas, and book knowledge by exposing them to literature they might not read on their own	• Books that match readers' abilities and growing capacities (different leveled books that may be challenging for independent reading but still understandable) • Multiple copies of texts • Big books with large print and lines of text that can be pointed to or viewed and read from a distance • Material that engages readers and invites participation • Patterned texts or predictable stories with language, form, and structure suitable for repeated readings • Texts suited for explicit instruction of reading strategies and concepts in small or large group lessons • Books, poems, or other reading materials suitable for reading along with the teacher, choral reading/speaking, or reader's theatre (scripted stories where characters' dialogue is read aloud in parts by different readers) • Texts that provide authentic purposes for reading and may raise issues for discussion	• Texts that reflect children's interests and personal experiences • Books that match students' different reading and instructional levels • Books that are popular with the age group (genre, character, author series books) • Free choice of a variety of genres and texts forms including graphic novels, comic books, magazines, and non-fiction books • Materials that can be easily accessed, browsed through, sample read, and returned if not suitable

In *Reading with Meaning* (2002), Debbie Miller provides a range of texts features that students can be taught to consider when making selections for independent reading. These features can be considered in addition to the criteria described above:

- Type of font and size of print that is readable
- Number of words and lines on a page that readers find manageable and easy to process
- Pictures that carry meaning and support textual understanding
- Pattern and repetition in predictable texts suited for beginning readers
- Words and vocabulary that can most easily be read and understood independently or in context
- Content that reflects readers' knowledge about a topic, story, book series, or genre
- Schema or background knowledge used to understand texts and themselves as readers
- Motivation, willingness, and perseverance in learning to read books they are interested in
- Emphasis on a variety of books that reflect different genres, texts forms, and levels of difficulty

Selecting books for children should be driven by the effort to understand their lives, cultures, communities, interests, abilities, and experiences. When children have ready access to the quality selections available to them, books travel with them as invited guests on their life journey.

Building quality children's literature collections rests on different factors that may be shaped by the reading event, yet one criterion remains the same despite the kind of text encounter. Selecting books for children should be driven by the effort to understand their lives, cultures, communities, interests, abilities, and experiences. As teachers, librarians, parents and educators, we share an important role in children's early literacy and language development. By acting as tour guides as children discover the world of books, we can steer their reading choices to satisfy their growing thirst for knowledge, their fascination with narratives, and their appetite for literature. When children have ready access to the quality selections available to them, books travel with them as invited guests on their life journey.

Book Collections for Young Readers

Visit a children's bookstore, school, or public library and you will see shelves overflowing with books waiting to be held and pages longing to be turned. Over the years, the selection and variety of children's literature publications have grown to include a wider range of genres and styles suitable for young readers. Classroom collections available to primary students should include an assortment of books and literature resources to help children who are learning to read. After all, becoming a reader does not just happen. Young children require a variety of texts to handle, to come upon naturally through discovery and play, or to encounter in classroom reading events.

Many books for young children are published in a choice of easy-to-read formats that are accessible to early readers. These practical forms include board books, picture books (available in both hardcover and paperback), big books, wordless books, alphabet books and books with limited texts. Along with these resources, there are other forms of books geared to emergent and developing readers, including beginning-to-read books, high-frequency readers, and leveled book series, such as those featuring Maria Fleming's *What Grows Underground?* and *Lunch* by Gay Su Pinnell.

The language, pattern, and structure of predictable books provide children with natural entry into the reading process. Predictable, pattern books often contain recurring, rhyming words/phrases (Mem Fox's *Zoo-Looking*), repetitive or cumulative patterns (*Something from Nothing* by Phoebe Gilman and Audrey Wood's *The Napping House),* and interlocking or chronological sequences (e.g., Janet and Allan Ahlberg's *Each Peach Pear Plum* or Shel Silverstein's *The Giving Tree*) that call out to children to join in. The delightful, predictable, and engaging patterns of these books invite young listeners to participate aloud through choral reading and repetition, encouraging them to develop reading behaviors that are essential to literacy development.

Children's literature that entices young readers to discover, handle, and play with books should be part of classroom collections. Interactive texts like elaborate pop-ups, touch and feel, seek and find, or other concrete, tactile books (e.g., Eric Hills' *Where's Spot?* series) engage the senses and promote the curiosity of early readers drawn to them. Concept books that deal with a range of topics, concrete subjects, or abstract ideas also are important early learning resources for the primary classroom. Books such as Lois Ehlerts' *Color Zoo* examine different concepts including animals, shapes, and colors in an explicit, identifiable, and practical way that promotes learning through discussion. Other concept books deal with complex topics such as the growth and change of living elements (seasons, plants). Betsy Maestro's *How Does an Apple Grow?* is an example.

Children's book collections can be organized around works of much-loved and popular children's authors (e.g., Eric Carle and Mem Fox) or favorite stories and read-aloud resources that delight young listeners. Many of these collections are published as short story anthologies or in a treasury of shared literature that children can enjoy for years to come. Story collections such as *Much More Munsch!* by Robert Munsch and *The 20th Century Children's Book Treasury* selected by Janet Schulman are examples of children's literature anthologies that can be shared by everyone. Literature collections that feature poetry, nursery rhymes, fairy tales, and other genre studies are favored additions to classroom libraries too.

Multicultural books and traditional folklore that bring to light stories, tales, fables, myths, and legends from around the world enrich children's understanding of narrative and broaden their global perspective. Along with contemporary, fractured, or feminist tales (e.g., *Cinder Edna*), these diverse texts present stories from different points of view (e.g., *The True Story of the Three Little Pigs* by Jon Scieszka). Young children require literature engagements with culturally diverse books, traditional stories, and progressive literature. As Vivian Vasquez (2003) explains, these books "create space to talk about issues of racism, power and control" (p. 30). To reflect the diversity and experiences of all groups of children, teachers should make room for these books in their classrooms.

Multicultural children's literature serves to raise social, cultural, and political awareness of the realities faced by various marginalized groups in ways that even young readers can be made to understand. Books that address issues of power and inequality, challenge stereotypes and false assumptions, and confront oppression and injustice help young people acquire critical literacy skills at an early age. In addition to raising issues of injustice that arise from unequal power relations, multicultural children's literature celebrates differences in social class, race, culture, ethnicity, gender, age, ability, and sexual orientation (Peterson and Swartz, 2008).

Through powerful book encounters with multicultural literature (Rukshana Khan's *The Roses in My Carpets* is an example), young children see authentic portraits of people's lives in ways that help them embrace diversity, develop compassion and respect for others, and earn a sense of pride in the cultures, personalities, and identities that make each of us unique.

Classroom libraries can also be arranged around universal themes and special interest topics that are personally relevant to children. Stories that deal with family separation (e.g., *Two Homes* by Claire Masurel), human loss (e.g., Maria Shriver's *What's Heaven?*), and self-esteem (e.g., Diane Loomans' *The Lovables in the Kingdom of Self Esteem*; *Eggbert: The Slightly Cracked Egg* by Tom Ross and Rex Barron) can help young people deal with their emotions and make sense of their lives.

Literature collections can be organized around thematic books that focus on shared topics including relationships (e.g. *Oma's Quilt* by Paulette Bourgeois and other texts that centre on children's relationships with elders), seasonal texts and holiday stories (e.g., Allen Morgan's *Sadie and the Snowman* and Hans Christian Anderson's classic *The Little Match Girl*), or social action books that speak of the human condition (e.g., *The Quiltmaker's Gift* by Jeff Brumbeau). Many of these inspirational books convey universal messages that even young children only beginning to read can understand (e.g., Mem Fox's *Whoever You Are).*

Libraries of children's literature should also include celebrated works of fiction and books featuring renowned characters created in timeless masterpieces. A.A. Milne's *Winnie the Pooh* and Beatrix Potter's *Peter Rabbit* are legendary tales written generations ago. The animal heroes in these books have grown to become lasting symbols of childhood that will continue to delight young readers for years to come. Classic stories including *The Story of Ferdinand* by Munro Leaf and Frances Hodgson Burnett's *The Secret Garden* are accessible to young readers today in retold adaptations and abridged versions that still hold the magic and delight of the original works.

Books based on popular fictional characters continue to be published in whole volumes, series and collections of children's literature. Series picture books featuring familiar characters like *Madeline* (Ludwig Bemelman), *Franklin* (Paulette Bourgeois and Brenda Clark), *Curious George* (Margaret and H.A. Rey), and other favorites appeal to children in the primary years. Young readers first encounter these characters as friends in read-aloud events and shared book experiences. Through repeated readings and recurring text encounters, these characters soon become partners in the reading process, guiding beginning readers along the road to becoming independent readers (Peterson and Swartz, 2008).

Beginner chapter books, junior novels, non-fiction texts, and multimedia resources deserve a place on primary classroom bookshelves too.

Reading Events—A Cornerstone to Literacy

Storybook reading plays a significant role in early literacy development. As youngsters begin formal schooling, their book encounters continue through classroom read-aloud events and other shared reading experiences provide enjoyable and meaningful literature encounters in which youngsters can learn effective strategies that help them grow into independent readers.

Checklist of Early Reader Classroom Resources

Here is a checklist of the types of books that can be used to build classroom collections appropriate for young children. This list will be useful in developing book inventories and making purchases of children's literature resources that support early literacy development. The texts can be organized by genre, theme, or topic into book bins or reading baskets. Collections brimming with these sources can be arranged on bookshelves in a classroom library, resource centre, or other school display for easy student access. Books and other literacy resources should also be available in reading, writing and play centres.

- ❑ Board books
- ❑ Picture books (hardcover and paperback)
- ❑ Big books
- ❑ Short story collections
- ❑ Storybook treasuries
- ❑ Children's literature anthologies
- ❑ Beginning-to-read books
- ❑ High-frequency readers
- ❑ Leveled books
- ❑ Read-along books with CDs
- ❑ Concept books
- ❑ Alphabet books (e.g., *Chicka Chicka Boom Boom*)
- ❑ Counting books
- ❑ Wordless picture books
- ❑ Books with limited words/text
- ❑ Interactive books
  - – pop-up, three-dimensional, lift-the-flap books
  - – sensory books (i.e., touch and feel, scratch and smell)
  - – seek and find books (e.g., *Where's Waldo?*)
- ❑ Nursery rhymes and *Mother Goose* collections
- ❑ Rhyming books
- ❑ Poetry books
- ❑ Predictable books
- ❑ Pattern books
- ❑ Books based on popular songs/music for young children (e.g., *Five Little Ducks, Baby Beluga, Wheels on the Bus* by Raffi)
- ❑ Traditional folklore (fairy tales, myths, legends, fables, and folktales from around the world)
- ❑ Contemporary, fractured, and feminist tales

- ❑ Multicultural children's literature
- ❑ Multilingual books (books available in different languages)
- ❑ Dual track books (bilingual books that feature two translations—English and another language)
- ❑ Thematic books
- ❑ Special interest books
- ❑ Seasonal texts
- ❑ Holiday and traditional books
- ❑ Critical issue and social action books
- ❑ Universal stories
- ❑ Nonfiction books
- ❑ How-to books/procedural texts
- ❑ Arts and crafts books
- ❑ Recipe books
- ❑ Manuals
- ❑ Fiction and nonfiction books about art/artists/musicians
- ❑ Magazines
- ❑ Newspapers
- ❑ Beginner chapter books
- ❑ Junior novels
- ❑ Novels
- ❑ Graphic novels
- ❑ Comic scripts
- ❑ Plays and scripts for reader's theatre
- ❑ Mass-produced books based on popular culture
- ❑ Series picture books
- ❑ Multimedia texts (e.g., CD and DVD jackets)
- ❑ Classic works of literature

Pembroke Publishers. © 2010 *The Cornerstones to Early Literacy* by Katherine Luongo-Orlando. ISBN 978-1-55138-257-9

Read-aloud Experiences

Children delight in having stories read aloud to them. In many homes, read-aloud events including bedtime storybook reading are important daily rituals. Research shows that reading aloud to children is a fundamental part of early literacy development (Teale, 1984; Sulzby, 1985). For some young children, the experience of being read to can assist them in becoming early readers who learn to read before entering school (Durkin, 1966; Bissex, 1980; Doake, 1981; Taylor, 1983). Early studies have also found that reading aloud to children in the preschool years has lead to school readiness, academic achievement, and overall success in beginning to read. See Teale (1984) for a list of cited research.

Although reading aloud remains an important activity for ensuring success in reading and school achievement (Wells, 1986; Cameron, 1989; Booth, 1998; Hirsh-Pasek and Golinkoff, 2003), a diversity of equally significant literacy experiences and linguistic resources beyond emergent "storybook reading" can also be found in children's homes and communities (Auerbach, 2003; Cook, 2005). Family and home literacy practices (including culture-specific emergent literacy experiences) help form a strong foundation for literacy. These are explored later in this book.

In creating literacy programs, teachers can build on the read-aloud events, book encounters, and other family literacy practices that youngsters carry with them to school. Reading stories, books, and literature aloud everyday allows children to:

- build vocabulary
- discover how words are used in various contexts
- develop oral language
- improve listening skills
- learn about the reading process (through modeled demonstration)
- acquire literacy knowledge (e.g., by observing reading strategies)
- understand the features, functions and structures of language
- develop print concepts
- use and enrich their imagination
- make connections to and enjoy literature
- stretch their reading interests and abilities by giving them free access to books they may not be able to read independently
- attempt and be able to read the same text more successfully on their own
- discover a variety of text forms, genres, and literature choices they may not make on their own (e.g., poetry, mystery, narrative non-fiction, historical fiction)
- acquire knowledge and effective strategies on how to read different types of books
- uncover different purposes for reading
- focus their attention on different writing styles and ideas in a book
- develop a sense of narrative and how stories, informational books, and other texts are structured
- acquire information and ideas that may inspire further learning, reading, and writing
- use texts as models for their own writing
- learn about themselves, life, topics, cultures, others, and the world
- broaden their perspectives
- develop an interest in books and pleasure in reading

Reading aloud to children helps build a sense of community in the classroom. By coming together to share a read-aloud story, young children learn to talk about books in ways that deepen their appreciation of literature and the world.

Reading aloud to children helps build a sense of community in the classroom. By coming together to share a read-aloud story, young children learn to talk about books in ways that deepen their appreciation of literature and the world. Book talks that surround read-aloud events should move children beyond the task of simply identifying aspects of narrative or genre features. Conversations around literature should help children to address critical issues by raising questions and topics for discussion that may be more challenging to comprehend. Dealing with profound themes can strengthen students' understanding of texts, help them learn about human experiences, and invite them to respond to literature emotionally in ways that broaden their point of view and make personal connections.

Read-aloud Strategies—Bringing Literature to Life

Literature comes alive when it is read aloud. Suddenly, the characters step from the page and have voices that tell their story. Illustrations get woven together with mental images to create the most vivid pictures of the real and magical places we can visit in each storybook encounter. Books speak a language of their own, lending us words to shape our own narratives.

Reading aloud to children models the range of techniques and strategies that can be used to read a book. For children only learning to read, shared literature experiences such as read-aloud events and emergent storybook reading are crucial to developing print concepts and practicing early reading behaviors. Reading aloud to young children exemplifies the reading process by illustrating how books work and showing how others read. To model this competently, teachers and other language partners may need to practice reading a book, story, poem or other text aloud independently before sharing it with children. Familiarity with a text's content is important to reading aloud because it allows the reader to share the text with deep enthusiasm, interest, and expression. Through the reader's use of phrasing, tone, and fluency, listeners can hear the rhythm of a story, the cadence of a poem, or the style of a nonfiction text in ways that fully engages them. As we read aloud, young listeners hear the pauses, tones, wording, quality and ease of our voice in ways that bring literature to life and model proficient reading.

Reading aloud effectively demonstrates to children what reading is and helps them grow to become independent readers. Through modeled demonstrations in classroom and family read-aloud events, emergent and early readers can gain the reading tools and strategies that will enable them to enjoy books on their own.

Participation in Read-aloud Events—A Building Block in Learning to Read

Read-aloud events are opportunities for children to learn effective strategies they need to become readers and writers themselves. Storybook encounters that begin in homes where adult family members read aloud to children are invitations for young people to learn to read naturally. While listening to a family member read a story aloud, the child is able to engage with the book, look at the illustrations, touch the pages, handle the text, see the print features, and hear the language of stories in close proximity with significant others and the book. The interaction that grows from these shared literature experiences often mark a young child's early attempts at reading. Given the opportunity to listen to favorite storybooks, religious books, and other texts through repeated readings, young children soon take part in reading along by mumbling words, repeating phrases, or using the pictures to tell the story themselves (Doake, 1988).

Adults can engage young children in emergent storybook reading by posing questions about the story, the illustrations, the events, and other narrative elements. This style of reading picture books is called 'dialogic reading'. The technique challenges young listeners to construct the story, build their understanding of narrative concepts, and participate in the reading task in a more active way (Peterson, 2007). Asking open-ended questions and expanding on what children say allows adults and children to engage in conversations about literature as they read. By enticing young readers to join in, read-aloud experiences facilitate the development of reading-like behaviors, an important building block in learning how to read.

Read-aloud classroom programs build on the natural initiatives of family literacy experiences in emergent storybook reading, dialogic reading, and other home literacy practices in the preschool years. These shared literacy events provide children with the aspiring incentive to grow as readers by the sheer enjoyment and pleasure that they allow in welcoming their involvement. Through delightful literature engagements, teachers can share nursery rhymes, traditional verses, songs, favorite tales, predictable stories, familiar texts, and other charming book selections in ways that encourage young readers to join in. Here are some ways that teachers can structure read-aloud experiences to invite participation:

- Select children's literature that is filled with playful language, lively sounds, repetitive words/phrases, predictable patterns/sequences, delightful rhythms and rhymes, and recurring structures that young children can quickly learn and soon identify in print (e.g., *Brown Bear, Brown Bear*).
- Revisit texts through repeated readings of favorite storybooks, poems, and rhymes so that children become familiar with the content and book language. Through repeated readings, beginning readers learn to internalize the words, patterns, and structures that are embedded in the text.
- While reading stories aloud, ask the students questions about the text and illustrations. Build on children's phases and ideas into order to strengthen their understanding of vocabulary and content in the book.
- Have students introduce books for read-aloud by sharing the title and names of the author and illustrator with the class or small group.
- Discuss cover art and text illustrations. Examine ways that pictures help tell a story and support print.
- Invite children to tell a story using the illustrations in a wordless book or other picture book selection so they can develop the use of book language and practice making meaning themselves.
- Allow children to reenact a story as it is read aloud. Children can play different roles, act out narrative parts, or stage the story for other listeners.
- Encourage the children to repeat a line, phrase or sentence that has been read aloud to them. Through *echo reading,* children begin to share in the reading process and participate in reading-like ways (Doake, 1988).
- Pause at key words or a predictable part in the story and invite children to join in. Provide the first word, part of a sentence/phrase, or another cue. Then, wait for children to finish the sentence or complete part of story on their own. This oral-cloze activity, also known as *completion reading*, helps children develop early reading strategies too (Doake, 1988).
- Challenge children to read along with familiar texts by taking the lead at different parts of a story or reading aloud in unison with others. Using big books with large text and print features that can be easily seen by the group helps facilitate *co-operative reading* (Doake, 1988).

- Play with sounds in a book, rhyme, or verse by having the children practice different real aloud techniques such as changing the phrasing, tone, and expression in their voice so they can discover different ways of reading literature aloud effectively.
- Try reading poems, songs, and verses in unison as a class or group in choral reading events that use a variety of read-aloud techniques.
- Have children learn the dialogue in a familiar story and prepare scripts for reader's theatre. During a read-aloud story, ask students to read or act out speaking parts.

Following the read-aloud event, invite children to share their responses to the text by making predictions, comparisons, and connections to literature. Encourage children to revisit texts from read-aloud events, reviewing them either on their own or with others (peers, family members). Encourage children to use the read-aloud techniques and strategies they have learned in order to engage other readers and practice beginning reading skills.

By participating in read-aloud events, young people can experience delightful engagements with literature as part of a shared reading community. As members of this literate group, students make steps towards reading on their own with the support of their peers and teacher in an environment that supports and encourages their efforts as beginning readers. Read-aloud engagements that allow children to join in can provide some emergent or reluctant readers with their first successful reading experience. Through active involvement in classroom read-aloud events, young children often experience the success and enjoyment of sharing literature with others in ways that shape their confidence, interest, and motivation in learning how to read. Soon, they view themselves as readers who can enjoy books on their own.

Shared Book Experiences

While reading aloud remains an important activity in daily classroom programs, children can participate in other book experiences to enrich their love of literature and motivate them to read. Enjoying literature with others is a powerful driving force on the journey to becoming a reader. Classroom literacy programs that invite children to participate in shared reading events offer endless possibilities for students to work supportively with encouraging adults and peers become literate and learn to read. By providing opportunities for children to interact with others in shared book experiences, teachers and students can build a strong literate community where the classroom culture and rich language environment support literacy learning and early reading development.

The following teaching and learning strategies broaden the reading program to include a variety of shared book experiences that provide children in the early stages of literacy development with authentic and supportive contexts for learning to read. These same strategies can be used with older students to provide rich contexts for their literacy learning too. Children at all stages of literacy development benefit from shared book experiences. These practices carry the enjoyment and guided support of being part of a literate community that makes reading enjoyable and possible for everyone.

Classroom literacy programs that invite children to participate in shared reading events offer endless possibilities for students to work supportively with encouraging adults and peers to become literate and learning to read.

Parallel Reading

As children begin to show interest in books and take steps towards reading, they need time to enjoy literature in the comfort and space of a supportive environment they share with others. Visiting a bookstore, classroom/public library, or school literature display offers young readers an exciting way to discover the wealth of available children's resources. The quest to find the right book can sometimes be overwhelming. When making text selections, children often brush next to other students and peers as they search the shelves or book bins in a joint literature venture. This shared endeavor can mark the beginning of a parallel reading experience.

In parallel reading, children read books on their own in close proximity to others. They share a collective space, sometimes sitting side by side, reading and enjoying books on their own while in the company of others. As children read simultaneously, they may turn to students beside them to share ideas, make connections, or seek assistance. Since reading silently may be difficult for some emergent readers, they often read softly to themselves in a low voice while browsing through a book. As young children read next to others, they may demonstrate similar reading-like behaviors (print concepts, book handling, use of picture cues, and book language to tell a story).

Partner/Buddy Reading

Young children like to read with others at home and at school. Partner/buddy reading is a supportive learning strategy that helps beginning readers make steps towards reading books independently. This shared reading practice moves young readers beyond parallel reading to working directly with peers, family members, and other language partners on reading books aloud. Reading to a partner/buddy allows the child to actively engage in the reading process in ways that bring pleasure, provide entertainment, and give guidance. Sharing a book with different audiences provides extra reading practice for emergent and early readers. Through repeated readings of favorite storybooks, beginning readers develop word recognition, fluency, expression, and other reading strategies and read-aloud techniques.

As partners read to one another, they express meanings and strategies that help them make sense of the text. Suddenly, children are able to face reading challenges with the confidence, support and tools provided by a reading buddy. Through discussion, readers learn new and effective ways for making meaning and decoding (visual cue strategies, identifying text patterns) that increase their prior knowledge and help them build their own reading power. Experiences in partner/buddy reading equip children with a schema of tools and approaches they can use to read books successfully on their own. Children move toward reading independently through shared book experiences that make practice and enjoyment part of literacy learning. Home reading programs that encourage children to take home books to share with family members provide genuine opportunities for partner reading too. Independent reading also emerges from classroom reading events that provide frameworks for explicit reading instruction.

Shared Reading

Shared reading events extend the practice of reading aloud to children to a teaching strategy that provides a supportive and engaging framework for meaningful, explicit, and formal reading instruction in the classroom literacy program. Shared reading allows children to build confidence, develop skills, gain motivation and experience success at reading with others.

In a shared reading experience, students draw together at first to listen to, and observe a story/text being read aloud by a teacher or another adult language partner. Next, the teacher and students revisit the text by re-reading the same selection several times in order to grow familiar with its language, structure, and content. After several readings, students begin to internalize the words and embedded patterns and soon are able to read along themselves. Through formal instruction, the teacher might then focus on a particular reading strategy or specific concept that students need to develop as they practice reading the selection as a group. Explicit lessons might also focus on word usage, vocabulary, language conventions, story structure, or narrative elements. As children gain literacy knowledge, fluency, and reading skills, they are able to join in unison with the group until the entire class is able to read the same selection together.

For this reading strategy to be successful, all students must be able to see the text that is being read aloud. In primary classrooms, good text choices are big books with large font and print features that children can see clearly from a distance. Young readers are often amused by the large published format of these big books. Shared reading participation also grows from using predictable stories, patterned books, traditional tales with familiar plots, nursery rhymes, songs, poetry, and other children's verses popular with primary children who are just learning to read. Once readers have had plenty of experience and success with these texts, they can move on to more challenging selections such as narrative poems and informational text.

To help children during shared reading practice, teachers may guide students through the selection by pointing to each word or line of text. This can reinforce print concepts, such as directionality, or decoding skills, such as word matching and identifying letter-sound relationships. For this purpose, short literature selections written on a chalk/wipe board, chart paper, or overhead transparency for all to see can be used as texts in shared reading too. Experiences in shared reading may lead children to other literacy events that involve them in retelling stories, making predictions, sharing responses, innovating on text patterns, and inventing their own rhymes and verses. Drama and visual arts are other classroom activities that the literature selection may inspire.

Shared reading allows students at all developmental stages to experience the joint practice, reward, and sheer pleasure of reading that comes from being part of a supportive reading group. Children are free of the overwhelming pressures, expectations, and limitations of learning to read on their own. Through shared reading events, young people become members of a developing reading community that takes on together the challenging task of learning to read. For students who have lacked interest and motivation, or have had reading difficulties, group reading provides the gentle guidance, renewed inspiration, and common groundwork for learning to read proficiently. Since the goal of shared reading is for students to read a selection together, the emphasis moves away from a child's individual reading skills making problems seem less noticeable in group reading sessions. Hence, students come to enjoy reading with others because they are sucessful at the task of learning and practicing "good reader" strategies together.

Guided Reading

Guided Reading Framework

1. Observe and assess children's reading abilities.
2. Form guided reading groups.
3. Select and introduce the text to the group.
4. Allow children to read the selection independently.
5. Observe and note children reading.
6. Provide assistance when needed.
7. As a group, discuss the selection (story elements, reading strategies used).
8. Focus on specific reading strategies, processes and problem-solving skills through explicit teaching (e.g., modeled demonstration) and guided practice (mentoring and scaffolding individual children as they read).
9. Observe and assess children's use of strategies and reading development.
10. Note those children who are ready to move to another guided reading group.

Guided reading was introduced by Reading Recovery founder, Marie Clay (1991), and Reading Recovery trainers, Irene Fountas and Gay Su Pinnel (2001), whose foundational work in the area of early literacy and language development has fundamentally shaped literacy programs and reading instruction in the primary years and beyond.

In their early years, emergent and beginning readers typically encounter challenges in texts as they learn to read. Parents and teachers cannot expect children to face these difficulties on their own. Given the complexity of the reading process, students require continuous support of language partners to move forward in literacy development and expand their reading abilities. Even developing, competent, and fluent readers need to strengthen their literacy toolbox to handle increasingly difficult texts. Recognizing the diversity in children's abilities, prior reading experiences, and background knowledge is key to understanding students' needs. Through explicit instruction in guided reading, teachers can offer the wide levels of support that readers require.

Guided reading is a teaching strategy that provides supportive reading practice to students through teacher-directed, small group instruction. Guided reading meets the diverse instructional needs of all students in the class by providing the necessary levels of support to build their reading power. This involves grouping children who are at similar reading levels, or who have to learn particular reading strategies or concepts, for explicit teaching.

To form groups, teachers must observe and assess students' abilities by listening to individual children read and noting the processes and strategies they use to decode and make meaning (including fluency, miscues, self-correction, and comprehension). Next, the teacher brings together the students who share similar reading abilities or strategies in order to read a book especially selected to assist them in learning new techniques and concepts. These groups will change continuously throughout the year as children acquire new approaches and achieve different levels of reading success.

Once guided reading groups are established, teachers can begin by introducing children in each group to the book or literature selection. Multiple copies of books are needed as all members must read the same book. Texts should reflect children's interests, experiences, and reading abilities. Selections also should be accessible and manageable to all children who can then draw on their own reading toolbox, or background schema, as they read the selection independently. Texts for guided reading also should provide a level of challenge that is not too difficult but sophisticated enough that children can develop and apply problem-solving strategies they need to read successfully on their own. Essentially, students should be able to read and understand most of the selection without assistance. Since one of the goals of guided reading is to help children move forward in their reading development and learn new strategies to use independently, texts for guided reading should be suitable for practice and instruction as well. To help learners overcome challenges they may face trying to read the text, teachers can provide appropriate support by focusing on explicit strategies that readers can use to making meaning.

After reading the selection independently, invite children to talk about the book as a group. Through discussion, the teacher can help students explore the book's content, vocabulary, and context. Readers can share their insights and reactions, make text connections, revisit prior predictions, identify story elements, ask questions to clarify understanding, and examine their use of reading strategies with others. Since the purpose of guided reading is to help students grow as readers and develop new strategies for handling increasingly difficult texts on their own, teachers can use this time to provide explicit instruction. Begin by listing the strategies that group members used while reading the selection

David Booth offers practical teaching strategies for guided reading instruction in the primary grades in his book *Guiding the Reading Process* (1998).

independently. Identify other problem-solving approaches that helped students overcome challenges as they read. Revisit parts of the selection and model the use of specific reading strategies or processes that may lead to further understanding. Highlight new techniques on a list of reading strategies that students can access as reference when reading on their own. Have children reread the selection and provide supportive reading practice by guiding them in their application of new reading skills and knowledge.

Allowing students in a group to share in the task of reading the same selection enables them to grow in confidence, success, and ability as readers who delight in the act of reading alone and with others. This shared book experience carries authentic contexts for discussion and literature response that further engage children in the text and lead to greater reading enjoyment. Children can respond to selections used in guided reading through experiences in art, drama, writing, and research. Guided reading activities allow children to explore topics and aspects of the text through vicarious learning experiences that deepen their understanding and appreciation of literature. As children grow as readers, shared book experiences such as guided reading may evolve into reading discussion groups that allow students to further explore and enjoy literature as a literate community.

Literature Discussion Groups

Literature discussion groups provide conversational forums for readers to meet and talk about books. Even young children can participate in reading discussion groups as these meetings provide authentic frameworks for students to talk together. Participating in shared reading events like book talks allows children to develop as readers with the support of others. By working in heterogeneous groups, students can learn from more fluent readers while simultaneously having their own beginning efforts encouraged through shared, equal partnership in a reading discussion group.

The shared book experiences that grow from literature discussions help build a community of readers in the classroom. Within the community, all students share a voice and an equal role as members of a reading group that assumes responsibility for their literacy learning.

Shared literature engagements serve beginning readers in other ways. By providing opportunities for children to learn about literature and discuss books with others, teachers can help young people develop a lifelong love of books and interest in reading. Being part of a reading discussion group can motivate a child to read and take an interest in a book. For early and emergent readers, watching others engage in book talks, reading clubs, and literature circles can encourage them to read themselves. Hearing children talk about literature with interest and enthusiasm may spark an eagerness to read the same book or another favorite selection. The incentives that literature discussion groups provide in the primary years will serve students for years to come as they gain confidence and success as independent readers.

Children of all ages benefit from shared book experiences that allow them to enjoy, read, and talk about literature with others. Through discussion, children are able to:

- discuss their reading experiences (describe thoughts and images)
- express feelings and personal responses to literature
- provide insights
- explore ideas as a group
- question texts
- negotiate understandings together
- improve listening skills

(continued on page 108)

Forms of Literature Discussion Groups

Book Talks—A book talk is a way to introduce readers to a text and spark interest in a book. At first, book talks may be teacher-led and used to present literature to the entire class. Selections may be based on works by popular or well-known children's authors, new authors or titles, or books on topics and genres of most interest to the students. Discussions may centre on enticing narrative aspects (character profiles, descriptive settings, an intriguing storyline) or exciting facts and details from an informational text. To hook readers, a dramatic excerpt from the book may be read aloud. Following a brief introduction (one or two minutes), students make their literature selections. Once teachers have modeled how to talk about books in enticing ways, students can lead their own book talks and follow-up discussions.

Literature Circles—Literature circles are small reading discussion groups made up of a few students (three to five per group) who have selected the same book to read (Booth, 1998; Daniels, 2002). Group members take responsibility for making their book selection, reading, responding to literature, and holding a discussion. Together, students decide on the assigned reading for each discussion. After determining which pages will be read, students read independently and respond to the selection in a journal by recording notes, drawings, questions, and other response formats that can be shared in discussion. Later, group members meet to discuss their reading experiences (challenges, strategies, connections) and their interpretations of the literature (topic, narrative elements, literary devices, vocabulary, structure). At first, students may assume various roles that may lead them in the discussion and carry the dialogue to a deeper understanding of the text (by focusing on particular aspects of the selection). Eventually, students may be able to give up roles and engage directly in thoughtful, provoking, and meaningful discussions around literature. Teachers can guide students through literature circles as needed, helping them to form groups, stay on topic, keep focused, and prepare for discussion.

Reading Clubs—In a reading club, a group of children reads and talk about a small collection of books that are related to each other in some way (Collins, 2008). The clubs are organized around a group of texts, or text set, based on genres, topics, or literature selections that children want to read. Books for different reading clubs are arranged into baskets and may feature authors, characters, titles, or subject matter (Dinosaur Club, Whales Club, Human Body Club) that students can use during a nonfiction, author, character, or literature study (Collins, 2008). The books should reflect the students' independent reading levels to ensure that group members can read texts with fluency, accuracy, and understanding. As a result, more than one reading club basket may be available to students on the same topic, genre, or literature study focus.

To form a reading club, two to four students meet together with a basket of books during the course of a one week to two week cycle to work with the texts they are interested in and can read independently (Collins, 2008). In *Reading for Real: Teaching Students to Read with Power, Intention and Joy in K–3 Classrooms* (2008), Kathy Collins recommends that students begin by working with a partner who shares their reading interests, and who is at a similar reading level, to choose a reading club. Once partners have decided which texts to work with, they can establish their own purposes and plans for reading. During a cycle of reading clubs, students read and talk about books by expressing ideas, raising questions, pondering issues, conducting inquiries, sharing findings, developing reading strategies, clarifying meanings, and strengthening their understanding of the literature by becoming experts about the books and topics in their reading club baskets (Collins, 2008). Teachers can meet with students in their reading clubs to support and extend their learning by providing lessons on focused reading strategies and offering ideas on how students can grow as readers.

Reading Conferences—Reading conferences are literature discussions between an individual student and a teacher on a book the child is reading. Initially, teachers may meet with a student to assess the child's instructional reading level (Szymusiak & Sibberson, 2001). While listening to a student read aloud, the teacher can determine the reading strategies used, the level of accuracy and fluency, and the skills the student needs to work on. Through discussion, the teacher can learn the extent of the child's comprehension of the text and the ways the child responds to literature (makes predictions, inferences, and connections). Teachers can use individual reading conferences to guide students on their road to reading independently by matching readers with appropriate books (Szymusiak & Sibberson, 2001).

Students can meet together to hold their own reading conferences as well. These literature discussions can move readers to a more in-depth analysis of the text, such as examining a character's motives and relationships, to understanding the theme or universal lesson in a story. Time in reading conferences can be spent on sharing related experiences and opinions of a text that can form new contexts and purposes for reading. Students can also model and discuss effective reading strategies that can help other children develop the habits of proficient readers.

- develop social skills
- build communication skills
- clarify meanings and concepts they may have found confusing
- strengthen their understanding of the text
- develop and apply higher-order thinking skills (analyze, critique, compare)
- take responsibility for their learning
- make text, life, and world connections
- share their opinions or point of views
- develop new perspectives

Participating in book talks deepens the literature experience. Children work together to construct meaning and understanding in ways that enrich their reading of texts. The shared book experiences that grow from literature discussions help build a community of readers in the classroom. Within the community, all students share a voice and an equal role as members of a reading group that assumes responsibility for their literacy learning. Allowing children to take ownership and lead the literature discussions in various formats moves them towards independence in reading.

Other Classroom Reading Events

Many classroom reading experiences invite children to be part of a growing community of young readers. Children become familiar with the processes and strategies of reading through shared book experiences including read-aloud, parallel, and partner reading; discussion groups; and classroom reading events that involve formal instruction (shared and guided reading). As they do so, students acquire the interest, confidence, literacy knowledge, and practices needed to read literature on their own. In addition, young people discover the pleasure, purposes, and functions of reading by watching teachers and other adults model how it is used every day. These language partners demonstrate reading strategies that all readers can practice on their own. As mentors, teachers can give students guidance, support, and instruction to sharpen their own reading tools and be able to read independently and successfully throughout their lives.

Students' Independent Reading

Classroom literacy programs that include independent reading among a variety of book experiences help build the foundations for literacy learning in the early years and beyond. Teachers should provide time for students to practice reading on their own by establishing independent reading periods in their classroom literacy programs. To ensure the success of these events, review with students the criteria for independent book selections described earlier on pages 94 and 95. This helps early, emergent, developing, and even fluent readers make good book choices. When students are given time to select and read books independently, they assume ownership of their reading choices and responsibility for their growth as readers. Teaching children to make thoughtful book selections empowers them to be in control of their own reading development. The literature choices they make should be "just right" in ways that enable, challenge, and interest them to read and construct meaning independently (Fountas and Pinnell, 2001; Miller, 2002).

In the early years, teachers can facilitate students' independent book choices and reading practice in several ways. Literature selections can be presented through classroom book talks that introduce students to new texts, another book by a favorite author, books on special interest topics, or publications by a new author, illustrator, or genre the children may love. Discussing the title and author, showing the cover art and illustrations, reading aloud a book excerpt, posing a question, providing a brief summary of the text, describing part of the plot, setting, or a character, making literature connections, and sharing personal responses to a book are ways that teachers can lead students to a book that may interest them and entice them to read on their own (Fountas and Pinnell, 2001).

Teachers can support beginning readers in their growing independence by equipping them with tools to read books on their own. During independent reading periods, children can be taught effective reading strategies through explicit instruction in large class, small group, or individual mini-lessons on a specific skill (e.g., unknown word strategies, inferencing). This instruction will help students to develop reading competence, stay focused, and work more productively. By conferring with individual students during independent reading time, teachers can listen to, observe, monitor, and support children as they learn to read texts on their own. Listening to children read aloud enables them to build confidence, gain practice, and improve their reading skills. Showing interest, offering praise, and encouraging children as they read independently is a positive experience for growing readers.

When listening to children read aloud, adult family members and teachers can help them develop important skills (e.g., word solving, correcting miscues) by being patient and allowing readers time to figure out unknown words on their own, monitor their own reading, re-read, and self-correct. After listening to children read aloud, or providing time for learners to read silently, teachers and other language partners can engage them in book talks and literature discussions. Discussing independent text selections allows children to make connections to literature and share their personal responses with others. By focusing on a book of their choice, students can use the independent reading period to hone in on reading strategies they need to improve and work supportively with others to overcome challenges in the text.

Children gain fluency, understanding, and independence in reading through mentorship and example. When students observe adults and children reading literature independently, they see the reading process at work as others model the effective use of the strategies, literacy knowledge, and reading tools. The supportive practice and exemplary models that come from independent reading experiences allow children to gain confidence and expertise as readers who can fully enjoy book selections on their own.

Modeled Reading

Teachers, family members, and other adult language partners are guides on the road to reading by providing children with authentic demonstrations of modeled reading in everyday life. When young people see adults reading manuals, textbooks, non-fiction (newspapers, magazines), novels, and other special interests books, they are exposed to a variety of genres and texts being read for different purposes. Modeled reading at home and in the classroom exemplifies to children the further purposes, enjoyment, and enrichment that reading provides at different stages of life. In building a classroom literacy program that serves readers at any age, teachers ought to naturally model reading for various purposes and in different contexts throughout the day. Through modeled reading, children see authentic demonstrations of functional, meaningful, and purposeful reading in everyday life that they soon learn to imitate.

Becoming a Reader—Early Literacy Strategies and Activities

A child's journey to becoming a reader is marked with emergent literacy experiences in the home and local community that build the concept of story and the meaning of print. As young children enter school, the literacy experiences they encounter in the classroom lend further enjoyment and support that enables them to grow as readers. The reading events explored in this chapter make up essential tools for early literacy learning and reading development. Children learn to read by having others read aloud to them, by watching others read, by being part of shared book experiences, by talking about literature, by reading independently, and by having others listen to them read aloud (Booth, 1998). The following early literacy strategies will help young children acquire further knowledge and skills about reading in rich and meaningful contexts.

Revisiting Texts

Children often revisit favorite books during classroom read-aloud events and bedtime reading episodes when they ask again and again for the same story to be read. Revisiting a text is important to early readers as it helps them grow familiar with the content and language of a book (Wilson, 2002). By listening repeatedly to favorite storybooks, children learn parts of the story, and soon the entire text, by heart. Knowing the words of a story can help a child discover the signs of print, recognize text, and make connections between spoken and written language (Wilson, 2002). Revisiting a favorite book allows young children to develop meaning in the story too. When books are available for children to revisit on their own, young readers become more familiar with what the text is about and learn to grasp the essence of a story.

Teachers can use this reading strategy to strengthen a student's understanding of a text by providing different purposes for each book encounter. During each reading of the text, the student may have a particular focus, such as exploring a character's feelings or motives in a story, examining the themes or story lessons, observing the relationship between illustrations and print, or making personal, text, or world connections (Wilson, 2002). By revisiting a text in this way, the students can extend meanings and perspectives while making important print connections.

Recognizing the language of a story and understanding the meaning of a book are important building blocks for children as they become literate and begin to unlock of mysteries of reading. Revisiting favorite texts helps children grow into readers. Many of them use this strategy to learn to read favorite stories by joining in the act of reading themselves.

Repeated Readings

Early reading efforts often flow from listening to favorite storybooks that have been read aloud several times. Repeated readings build on the experiences of revisiting a text. Through repeated readings, children are able to deepen their understanding of the content and language of a story and use this knowledge to make print connections on their own. In order to match book language with print features, children need recurring encounters with storybooks, rhymes, poetry, and other early reading materials through repeated readings. This literacy strategy assists emerging readers in moving towards reading independently by engaging them in the task of reading books with others.

Listening to stories repeatedly invites children to participate in reading the story in a variety of ways. Through repeated readings of favorite books, children come to learn these stories so well that they often correct adult readers when they deviate from the text or omit parts of the narratives they have grown to love. Knowing the language of a story can help young children *mumble read* (Doake, 1988) along with the reader, or complete a word or line of a well-known book. By occasionally stopping the reading and leaving out words, teachers can use an oral-cloze strategy to encourage the children to predict and insert missing words/parts into the story reading. As children draw on their knowledge of words, grammar, and story context, they are able to predict the missing words and make meaning of the text. Apart from completion reading (Doake, 1988), children can participate in repeated readings by echoing a patterned verse or phrase in a book or saying it in unison with others. Through echo and cooperative reading (Doake, 1988), young readers can practice the language of stories orally before encountering the words in print.

Reading from Memory—A Stepping Stone in Learning to Read

Reading from memory helps children unlock the mysteries of print. Young children's early attempts at reading start with favorite storybooks they know by heart. Being familiar with a book enables the child to read it independently. Hearing a story repeatedly attunes the listener's ear to the language and content of the book, making it easier for the child to predict the text and learn the words on his or her own (Wilson, 2002). Knowing a book by memory helps emerging readers make links with print. As described in Chapter 4, making print connections marks a significant point in young children's early reading development.

Reading from memory facilitates the learning-to-read process. At first, children use pictures to tell the story. Learning a story by heart allows them to know from the pictures which print is on the page, recall the story, and use repetitive language, patterned phrases, known words and other familiar features (e.g., dialogue) as they share the book. As they page through the illustrations, young children may form their own stories using language that sounds like the written text (i.e., book language) but may depart from the actual wording of the book (Sulzby, 1985). When children recite language that sounds like reading, they move closer to matching their stories to the actual text. Soon, the young reader's eyes move from the illustrations to the writing on the page, allowing them to begin making word-print connections (Wilson, 2002). This leads children to discover that print on the page carries meaning and plays a role in the reading process (Doake, 1988).

Reading from memory helps children manage a text independently and learn to read conventionally from print. The ability to retain the language and meaning of a story they have encountered several times in a book allows young children to use spoken language to reconstruct the same story on their own. Children's growing awareness of print and recognition of words on a page allows them to make the significant transition from spoken to written language, a precursor to reading (Sulzby, 1985; Wilson, 2002). Reading from memory helps bridge this gap as children move from memorization of a story to making print connections by matching the spoken and written text. The more encounters children have with a familiar book, the more they can attend to written language, recognize print features, identify words on the page, and start to read texts conventionally on their own. As children learn to unlock the mysteries of print, they begin to act like readers and develop the early reading processes and strategies needed to read successfully and independently.

Reading-like Behavior

Children are crafted language learners with a novice talent to weave stories together using pictures and language that sounds like a book. As they draw on memory, book language, and other effective techniques, these gifted language users are able to reconstruct stories in reading-like ways (Doake, 1988). Reproducing stories using "reading-like behavior" (Holdaway, 1979) marks an important step in the learning to read process. In the early stages of their reading development, young children use reading-like behaviors in their literature encounters to gain independent access to books and self-control over their own reading process (Doake, 1988). Acting in reading-like ways provides beginning readers with the confidence and motivation to read successfully on their own. As David Doake tells us in *Reading Begins At Birth* (1988), "… behaving like a reader serves an extremely important purpose to becoming a reader" (p. 41). The moment a child picks up a book and starts telling a story, the child's lifelong journey into reading begins. Even before they can recognize print, children engage actively with books in literate ways and view themselves as readers. The enjoyment that comes from this activity can inspire them to take control of their own reading development. The image they have of themselves as readers serves as a stronger driving force in their desire to learn to read. Behaving in reading-like ways equips children with the intrinsic tools, positive attitude, and self-efficacy to achieve their literacy goals of becoming competent and independent readers.

As children become literate, they may act in reading-like ways and demonstrate early literacy behaviors that move them closer to reading actual texts and reading print conventionally. Reading-like behaviors extend beyond retrieving stories from memory to a growing awareness of print. Beginning readers may demonstrate the following reading-like behaviors:
- combine their own language with the author's words when sharing a story
- use book language (narrative discourse) to convey the meaning of the story
- embellish the story with the use of dialogue
- use details of illustrations to tell the story and predict ahead
- maintain fluency or flow through skillful transformations between using book language and their own words to share the story (Doake, 1988)
- turn the pages at appropriate points in the story (page by page matching)
- stop reading while turning the page

- slow down the reading process to focus on print
- make approximations while reading
- use words and language conventions that are more consistent with the written text
- start to match words to print on the page
- connect spoken language with written text
- point to a word on the page as it is spoken
- recognize words in context
- attend to sound in words
- finish the story exactly on the last page

Children demonstrate a variety of reading-like behaviors as they become literate. These reading-like techniques are closely linked to early literacy strategies and print concepts (see Chapter 4). Together, they provide beginning readers with a literacy toolbox to make meaning from texts. By observing and monitoring the development of early readers, teachers and adult family members can gain insight into children's skills as language learners. The knowledge and practice that grows from using reading-like strategies in the early years will serve children on the road to becoming literacy users themselves.

Reading and Literature Games

Before children can read conventionally from print or even recognize words on a page, they adopt attitudes and behaviors that support their reading development. The experiences, models and engagements that children have with literature, reading, writing, print, oral language, play, and other authentic encounters with literacy provide the essential frameworks for learning to read. Teachers and adult language parents can provide children with meaningful, purposeful, and enjoyable language activities to support literacy development. In addition to read-aloud events and shared book experiences, literature games and other playful reading activities allow children to develop and practice early literacy strategies, print concepts, and reading-like behaviors.

Picture Walk through a Book

Storybook pictures and text illustrations give readers cues to reading books. To help children understand the role of illustrations, have children examine a wordless picture book and use details from the illustrations to retell the story as a class, small group, or individually. Later, have children revisit favorite storybooks and check that the illustrations support the known text. Next, have the children recount a story using only the pictures and visual information in an illustrated text. As children grow familiar with this strategy, challenge them to use the pictures to predict and identify some of the words ahead. When reading illustrated texts, ask the children to stop at words that are clearly pictured on the page, match the item in the illustration to the word in the text, name the object, and read the word in print. This strategy may assist young children in learning to read an unknown word. Taking a picture walk through a book helps young readers develop visual cue strategies (i.e., picture analysis) they can use to read and understand texts on their own. Using pictorial information to read texts also helps children make meaning of print (Wilson, 2002).

Storybook Trivia

A child's first encounters with literature often begin with picture books, board books, and other stories that are published in easy-to-read formats. Through delightful book engagements with fairy tales, myths, legends, realistic fiction, multicultural texts, and other stories experienced through read-aloud, young children are introduced primarily to narratives when they begin to read and show an interest in books. To read and understand storybooks, children must grasp the concept of narrative as a genre of literature. By exploring folktales, fables, and other books that fall under the narrative genre (such as adventure and mystery stories or historical fiction), teachers can help students build the concept of story. To understand story structures and aspects of narrative, adults and children can engage in literature games such as storybook trivia.

After sharing a picture book, traditional story, or other work of literature with the class, discuss story features such as plot, character, and setting so that students become familiar with these narrative aspects. Challenge children to a trivia game in which they must identify a specific story element from the literature collections they are familiar with (e.g., Guess the Character, Guess the Setting). Begin with prompts like, "*I am thinking of a character who…*" and then offer clues and insights into this story element (such as physical characteristics, traits, personal descriptions, actions, events, surrounding features, and comparisons). Variations of these games may challenge children to explore other complexities in stories they love to read (Guess the Evil Character, What's the Problem?, Find the Solution, Guess the Enchanted Object). In challenging children to identify story conflicts and offer solutions that may depart from the actual narrative, young people are also encouraged to develop problem-solving skills.

Cloze Reading Activities

In order to learn to read, children must understand how language works. Understanding the order of, and relationship between, words, phrases, sentences and other grammatical structures is key to uncovering the mysteries of print. This knowledge of English grammar emerges from oral language experiences and read-aloud events that provide children with practical models of how language works. The ability to read also requires children to predict ahead and understand the meaning of words in the context of the story and life experiences. To become an efficient reader, children must be able to draw upon their knowledge of language structure, or syntax, and life experiences/meanings, or semantics, when they read (Goodman, 1967; Wilson, 2002). Teachers and parents can help children develop these non-visual cue strategies through the following cloze reading activities.

When reading aloud a favorite storybook, poem, nursery rhyme or other predictable text,, occasionally stop and leave out words and phrases. Then, invite children to fill them in. Drawing upon their memory of the text, their understanding of the language patterns and structures, and the meaning or context of the literature selection, children are able to predict ahead and complete the text during this oral cloze activity.

To help children understand that reading is a process in making meaning of texts and not naming each word correctly, teachers can engage children in a cloze reading task that encourages young readers to make meaningful word substitutions while predicting ahead. To do this, select a big book to read aloud and cover some of the content words prior to reading. As you read the book aloud, have individual children predict what each covered word might be and produce a list of possible words that would make sense in the text. Later, reveal the covered word and practice reading the sentence with both the actual word and other suggestions. Although these predictions may depart from the actual text, they may not interfere with the meaning. As children draw upon the context of the story to predict unknown words, they learn to construct meaning and make suitable word substitutions as they read.

Cloze activities challenge readers to use semantic and syntactic cueing strategies to make predictions while reading. As children learn to read conventionally from print, they draw upon these and other cueing systems to construct meaning of texts. In order to identify the early reader strategies that young children develop and practice as they grow to become efficient readers, we must first understand the reading process at work and be able to recognize the cueing systems used to unlock the mysteries of print (see Appendix page 156).

Supporting Young Readers—Developing Early Reading Strategies

Think-Aloud Technique: a comprehension strategy that children use as they read independently to themselves or read aloud to others. Throughout the reading process, the child stops reading to express ongoing thoughts, feelings, understandings, strategies, and questions while working through a text to make meaning (Pintrich, Wolters, and Baxter, 2000).

Metacognition: Children's self-awareness of the knowledge, information, and strategies they use to learn or read. Students develop metacognitive strategies throughout the reading process by reflecting, monitoring, and controlling the learning techniques and understandings they use to decipher a text and make meaning for themselves. (Pintrich, Wolters and Baxter, 2000).

From the moment a young child picks up a book, the child discovers ways to interact with texts and personally engage with literature. As children grow into fluent readers, they learn to use an array of strategies and processes to make sense of print. When readers demonstrate literate behaviors that give them access to print and methods for understanding texts they are well on the road to reading independently.

Along the path, early readers need direction and support. Both family literacy practices and school literacy programs should provide beginning readers with successful reading opportunities to increase their interest and motivation. Teachers, adult family members, and other language partners can nurture a secure environment where emergent readers feel safe to experiment with the reading process, explore text choices, make errors/miscues, and develop effective strategies in ways that scaffold and reward beginning efforts and novice achievements. To help children unlock the mysteries of print and break the reading code, adults and other readers can model aloud the strategies they use when reading texts. To make this concrete, teachers and other language partners can demonstrate how they read, verbalize the ways they read, and describe the specific strategies they use to read unknown words and new texts. Soon children may learn to use a think-aloud technique to communicate this metacognitive strategy themselves.

There are countless ways to support growing readers as they learn about the reading process. Discussing familiar concepts and words before reading a literature selection may prepare beginning readers for the task of reading the text themselves. Allowing children to make errors, self-correct miscues, and self-monitor their reading can lead to further development too. Acknowledging children's efforts with praise and guidance makes learning to read a positive and less challenging experience. Building supportive frameworks at home and in the classroom will assist young readers as they develop strategies and processes of their own. When early reading encounters are filled with positive models, encouragement, success, and pleasure, children's lifelong affair with literature grows.

Observing Young Readers—Assessing Early Reader Strategies

As we observe children in libraries and bookstores while they search bookshelves and reading baskets, explore titles, and select books to read, we learn about their personal interests and their developing reading tastes. When young readers engage with literature, the nature of their interactions with texts reveals aspects of their reading growth and literacy development. Teaching children to read and watching them become readers themselves requires on-going observation and assessment so we can guide their steps along the way.

On-going assessment and observation of children is an essential part of building a strong literacy program that supports all learners throughout the reading process. Planning effective reading experiences that ensure success for all students means understanding each child's progress, strengths, and challenges in reading. As each child reads and interacts with texts, teachers, adults and other peers can note various aspects of the reading encounter, including:

- the book(s) selected
- the types of books the child can read successfully on his/her own
- the amount of time the child can read independently
- the amount of material read in one sitting (number of pages or books)
- the strategies used (e.g., use of specific strategies)
- the child's understanding of the reading process
- aspects of the text the child finds challenging
- methods used when encountering unknown words or challenging texts
- the child's attitude toward reading (pleasure, enjoyment)

Observing children closely and listening to them read aloud give strong indictors of their reading growth. To assess each reader's progress, we need to watch for and note specific strategies the child uses when reading texts and the degree of success the child experiences. There are many effective methods for assessing readers' strategy application and overall reading strengths and challenges. Assessment tools, such as anecdotal observation notes, reading conferences, running records, personal reading inventories, checklists, observation guides, portfolios and students' self and peer assessments help provide a complete analysis of each child's reading abilities. To build on readers' strengths and develop other areas of growth, teachers can use these assessment procedures to inform their teaching and plan effective literacy programs for children at all levels of reading development. By planning on-going assessments using various methods on a regular basis repeatedly over a period of time (i.e., throughout the term), teachers can gain valuable information on a child's reading progress during the year.

All readers use a range of strategies to help them understand texts and monitor their reading. Some readers use visual tracking (e.g., finger pointing) and sequencing to guide them through a page. Others learn to interrogate the text by asking questions and raising issues. With practice, many children grow into clever word detectives who find ways to gain meaning from new words they encounter. Proficient readers even go so far as to use critical reading strategies (e.g., text analysis) to gain a deeper and more complex understanding of the literature they are reading. The strategies and processes that children use as they grow into fluent, independent, and competent readers are multifaceted and elusive.

Because of this, we need to look closely and specifically at the various ways that readers interact with and make sense of literature. The checklist and observation guide on pages 118 and 119 was developed to determine the early reading strategies that children successfully use as a way of understanding their development as growing readers. This tool can be used to make close observation of children as you watch or listen to them read. These findings can later be shared with readers themselves as they monitor their learning, reflect on their reading growth, acknowledge their strengths, and identify skills they would like to improve.

Responding to Literature

Literature has the power to engage readers through the compelling act of response. Exploring children's responses to literature can broaden our understanding of the ways that readers construct meaning in their experience with a text. How readers identify with characters, interpret visual images, relate autobiographical experiences, or reinvent the text world vary. Children learn to construct meaning and consolidate their understanding of a text by responding to literature before, during, and after a reading event using different formats. Readers should be encouraged to:

- make predictions
- create alternative endings
- suggest new titles for a text
- raise questions
- hold book talks and discuss content or issues
- make connections
- draw comparisons
- contrast texts with other reading material (e.g., books on related topics, story adaptations)
- examine text features and genre forms
- explore different perspectives and points of view

Types of Reader Response

As readers interact with texts, they respond to literature in different ways based on their reading experience. The reader's attention, purpose, or stance can significantly shape the literature encounter and the response method. Some responses are text-centred and focus primarily on the reader's knowledge of the genre, text features, language conventions, story elements, or content of the literature selection. This type of *efferent* response allows readers to gain information, share understandings, or carry out an action following a reading event (e.g., recount events, follow a recipe, or conduct a science experiment).

For many readers, the process of responding to a text is experiential. That is, readers respond to a text first by reflecting on their feelings, attitudes, beliefs, interests, and personal experiences. Then, they relate these to the literary work. Such responses are reader-centred and focus primarily on a reader's experience with a text. This type of *aesthetic* reading allows readers to attend to the images, emotions, ideas, personal knowledge, and opinions they form throughout the reading experience. "In aesthetic reading, the reader's attention is centeed directly on what he is living through during his relationship with that particular text" (Rosenblatt, 1978, p. 25). A reader's "lived through" experiences with a text can lead to powerful book engagements, as shown in the examples found on this page.

A Look at Children's "Lived Through" Experiences with a Book

After listening to the story *The Butterflies' Promise,* one child shared an autobiographical experience of shelling peas with her grandfather just as the main character does in the book.

Following a read-aloud event, a young child made a text-to-text connection between the books *Olivia* and *Katie Meets the Impressionists* by relating the main characters' experiences of visiting a museum and identifying similar works of art they both saw.

Through stories like *The Little Match Girl, The Quiltmaker's Gift, Uncle Willie and the Soup Kitchen,* my own children have learned about social problems such as hunger, poverty, and homelessness that moved them towards social action and inspired works of charity (e.g., clothing and food drives) as a form of response.

Observing Young Readers: Early Reading Strategy Checklist

Name: _____   Date: _____

Title of Book/Selection: _____

Amount Read: _____

Length of Observation: _____

The reader:

❑ distinguishes between pictures in a book and real objects

❑ differentiates between pictures and text

❑ uses visual cues (e.g., picture clues, text organization)

❑ analyzes visuals and pictures in illustrated texts (examines character/group representation)

❑ tracks reading by finger pointing

❑ uses other tools to help guide him/her along a sentence or follow a line of text (e.g., bookmark, ruler)

❑ matches spoken to written words (e.g., word-to-word matching)

❑ stops reading, retells events or recounts information

❑ uses a think-aloud strategy (shares interpretations/ideas while reading)

❑ rereads to establish or consolidate understanding

❑ revisits parts of the text to confirm meaning (rereads earlier parts of a story)

❑ draws on personal experience and prior knowledge to make sense of texts

❑ make predictions and anticipates what comes next

❑ visualizes the text to form context and gain meaning

❑ draws inferences

❑ seeks assistance when needed

❑ uses word focus strategies

   ❑ is familiar with sight words

   ❑ identifies other high frequency words

   ❑ recognizes letter clusters

❑ uses word solving strategies such as:

   ❑ analyzes the word for letter sounds

   ❑ matches print to sound

   ❑ uses knowledge of letters and sounds (graphophonic cues) to decode words (sound out strategy)

   ❑ uses phonemic strategy (segmenting and blending sound units within a word)

Pembroke Publishers. © 2010 *The Cornerstones to Early Literacy* by Katherine Luongo-Orlando. ISBN 978-1-55138-257-9

❑ passes over unknown or difficult words

❑ revisits unknown words after reading ahead

❑ guesses unknown words

❑ predicts a word's meaning based on context cues and background knowledge

❑ rereads the sentence to ensure understanding

❑ breaks word into smaller, manageable parts (sounds, letter clusters, or syllables)

❑ makes use of features of unknown words (initial letter, ending sounds)

❑ recognizes smaller parts of an unknown word (e.g., root, prefix, suffix)

❑ looks for familiar or known words in new or challenging words

❑ uses known words to solve new words

❑ makes word analogies and associations when encountering difficult words

❑ makes connections to literature to build understanding

❑ raises questions and issues

❑ draws analogies from the text

❑ monitors his/her reading and comprehension

❑ self monitors by matching words and noting miscues

❑ makes meaningful word substitutions or miscues that do not effect meaning

❑ self corrects errors and miscues that do not make sense while reading

❑ paces his/her reading

❑ uses phrasing to communicate meaning

❑ shows fluency as he/she reads

❑ demonstrates speed, accuracy, and comprehension

❑ determines pronunciation as he/she reads

❑ changes tone of voice or expression while reading

❑ examines text features (narrative structure, genre format)

❑ understands text organization

❑ uses sequencing to comprehend

❑ identifies text patterns and genre forms

❑ uses genre characteristics (contents page, table of contents) to navigate texts and monitor reading materials (e.g., novels, information books)

❑ uses syntactic cues (e.g., sub-headings, captions, graphic charts)

❑ uses dictionaries, glossaries, index, and other support resources

COMMENTS:

Strengths: _____

Areas of growth needed: _____

Goal(s)/Next Step(s): _____

Pembroke Publishers. © 2010 *The Cornerstones to Early Literacy* by Katherine Luongo-Orlando. ISBN 978-1-55138-257-9

The transactions that take place between a reader and a text may shift back and forth between efferent and aesthetic reading modes (Rosenblatt, 1978). Even young children can experience these different reader-text transactions and learn to respond to literature in different ways.

Making Text Connections

Making connections to literature deepens a reader's experience with a text by allowing the reader to form personal, intertextual, and universal relationships. Making connections with literature is a reading strategy and a framework for response. Readers can extend their experiences with a text by making the following literature connections:

- text-to-self connections (connections the reader makes between the text and his/her past experience and background knowledge)
- text-to-text connections (connections the reader makes between the text and other texts, such as books, poems, scripts, songs, films, and printed texts)
- text-to-world connections (connections the reader makes between the text and the world including universal issues, events, and social problems/concerns)

Response Activities

The language of stories can move us all. Apart from narrative, texts can reach us in many forms. The many faces of print can capture readers' attention with lasting appeal. Exploring text forms and responding to literature provide us with many adventures in reading. Reading gives us occasions to make meaning of print in ways that bring literature to life.

In the process of constructing meaning, readers mark their entry into texts with an assemblage of tools that they use to interpret and respond to the works they are reading. Together, their experiences, knowledge, and natural abilities allow them to make meaning in differing ways. Allowing children to share their different understandings and responses to a text can enrich the literature experience.

Literature engagements that encourage readers to participate with texts in meaningful and active ways contributes to children's lifelong love of reading. Children's understanding of language structure, narrative elements, and literary points of view are developed through playful response activities. Readers may respond through discussion, writing, drama, role play, visual arts, and other artistic forms. Aesthetic experiences can also enrich a child's relationship with literature. Classroom reading activities should carry the enjoyment, entertainment, and amusement that will inspire and encourage all children to participate fully. The response strategies that readers use to make meaning, interact with literature, and participate with texts vary depending on the purpose. Many response formats are described here.

Guided/Illustrated Retellings—Children can use picture clues to retell a story or read a book from memory. Through detailed picture analysis, readers learn to identify, label, and name objects in a book and examine specific elements such as animal characteristics, physical features, and landscapes. They can also examine complex literary devices such as personification in illustrated texts. Students often make sketches to use in their guided retellings. These illustrations may feature book covers, character portraits, or story scenes.

Oral Recounts—Children can share storybooks they have read with the class or small group through oral language activities like retelling. Use prompts such as *Remember when...?* to encourage students to recount important story events from a book or literature collection as they retell and/or compare plots and other story aspects in different narratives.

Literature Scrapbook or Photo Album—Children can explore narrative aspects in a storybook by creating a scrapbook or photo album illustrating the characters, setting, and other elements in the story. Students can collect photographs, write captions, create drawings, write journal entries, and produce their own snapshots to represent different aspects of the story (characters, setting, symbols, important events). Encourage children to use a variety of art materials and scrapbook tools to decorate the pages of their literature scrapbook or photo album before sharing it with others.

Literature Passport and Suitcase—The world of children's literature is filled with adventures that invite readers to journey to different times and places. Students can mark their travels in a literature passport, or reading log, to highlight the texts they have read. Children can share their book encounters with others by developing a literature suitcase filled with facts, symbols, images, and artifacts that represent the genres, texts, and resources they have explored. Travelers' notebooks complete with personal journal entries and reflections can be part of children's literature passports and suitcases.

Story Games—Students can consolidate their understanding of narratives through rich and complex story games inspired by literature. Locate commercial story games based on popular children's books (e.g., *Goodnight Moon, The Very Hungry Caterpillar)* and challenge students to play. Later, children can produce their own storybook trivia or board games based on literature they have read. Story games can be used to help readers make text-to-text and text-to-world connections by challenging players to find the relationship between characters, events, and narrative elements in books they have read, and story features in classical literature, traditional folklore, or actual life events and history.

Literary Talk Shows and Panel Discussions—Readers can explore issues in literature and seek alternate points of view through discussion forums that challenge them to raise questions, examine problems, prod for solutions, and study themes. Prior to discussion, students can gain insight into forum topics through further inquiry. Later, children can adopt roles (host, expert panel guests) and use their expertise to share understandings with other talk show/panel members.

Literature Word Power—Readers can discover the language of storybooks and the writer's craft by focusing on the author's choice of words and the rich vocabulary of stories. As you read aloud, give examples from the text of unusual words (e.g., compound words), descriptive vocabulary (e.g., adjectives), and colorful phrases. Help students find words and phrases from books they are reading that create powerful imagery and demonstrate the evocative language that authors use to write effectively. Readers can record words, expressions, and phrases from literature in an author's/writer's workbook.

Writing—Students can respond to literature through countless writing experiences that move beyond worksheets and comprehension questions. Thoughts and personal reactions can be recorded in a response journal during or following a reading event. These written responses can be shared with others during book

Text comparison chart for Cinderella and Cinder Edna

talks in literature circles or in a dialogue journal format that allows students to comment on each other's entries and reflections. Students can learn about language, forms, and structures by writing their own pattern books, constructing their own verses, or extending on rhymes and stories based on literature they know. Innovating on rhymes, pattern books, and predictable stories encourages beginning readers and writers to produce narratives and other texts (story sequels, short stories, poems, reports) of their own.

Book-Related Dramatic Play—Literature provides authentic contexts for children's play episodes. Following a reading event, encourage children to use props like puppets, felt boards, dolls, construction sets, and other toys and materials to retell traditional stories, recreate storybook settings, share familiar tales with new characters, produce narratives with alternative endings, carry out story sequels, or develop story adaptations based on literature they have read (see Chapter 1 for other ideas).

Drama and Role Play—Through imaginative engagements in drama activities, children can explore the world of literature in creative and empathetic ways. Readers can produce text reconstructions and literature adaptations through drama sequences such as listening, speaking, and writing in role (Close, 1993). These role play enactments invite students to participate with the text more intensely and sensitively as they learn to empathize with the characters they are portraying. Students can retell narratives from different characters' points of view, using diary entries, letters, poems, and other personal recounts written from their perspectives. Readers can respond to texts through experiences in choral speaking, storytelling, and improvisation, as well as in tableaux and other drama games (e.g., monologues) inspired by literature. Children can interpret narratives and entertain others through reader's theatre as well. After selecting a text to share with others, students practice reading it aloud by assuming the parts of different characters (including the narrator). Parts of the story may be scripted for reader's theatre before performing it for the class.

Visual Arts, Music, and Dance—Children can respond to literature through powerful art experiences that inspire them to transform symbols, meanings, and images from texts into paintings, sculptures, and other visual art forms. Using a variety of media, students can reproduce settings, character portraits, and story features in sketches, watercolor paintings, pastel drawings, collages, and other works of art. These aesthetic experiences enrich children's understanding of the descriptive aspects of narratives, poems and literary texts and allow others to see the powerful images their mind has allowed them to create. Students can also present their interpretations through music, song, and dance sequences. Composing lyrics, producing song medleys, and choreographing a dance enable children to explore themes and express feelings in response to literature.

Multimedia Projects—Producing multimedia projects is an interactive way to engage children in response. Students can use a variety of audio-visual tools, technology resources, and multimedia equipment to create films, documentaries, photo essays, websites, newspapers/magazines, interactive games, digital presentations, CDs, blogs, advertisements, bulletin boards, and other multimedia texts based on literature they have read.

Visual and Graphic Responses—Students can use a variety of graphic forms to respond to literature. They can consolidate and present their understanding of reading material in illustrative and symbolic ways by producing charts, maps, webs, tables, labeled drawings, lists, graphs, and schedules. As readers organize content in these various formats, they learn to analyze texts, synthesize information, and closely re-read the text.

Instructions and Procedural Tasks—Through reading, children learn to carry out instructions and complete a range of procedural tasks from following a recipe, to playing a new game or conducting a science experiment. As children explore different genres in classroom programs, they learn to respond to literature in practical ways. Students can extend their experiences with texts by performing procedural tasks that require them to carry out instructional methods and achieve different text purposes. Many of these practical engagements challenge readers to use texts and learn to read for real-life purposes.

Research/Inquiry—Reading literature inspires children to learn and discover more about topics that interest them. Students can respond to texts through inquiry projects that allow them to gain insights and knowledge on intriguing concepts and subjects. Conducting research and sharing findings through report writing, oral presentations, and visual displays help children learn to summarize, take notes, and develop inquiry skills. Interdisciplinary projects can grow from children's meaningful and purposeful text encounters. Inquiry-based learning allows readers to extend the literature experience into different content areas across the curriculum.

Community Participation and Social Action Projects—Literature has the power to inspire readers to social action by raising awareness of the social, cultural, and political issues that affect the human condition. As children develop critical literacy skills, they gain an understanding of the injustices and inequalities faced by people around the world and in their own community. Readers can respond to texts that raise and challenge these issues through social action projects. Children can organize food and clothing drives, support charity events, and participate in community outreach programs (e.g., environmental projects) in their response to literature.

* * *

Literature provides rich opportunities for children to respond to texts in myriad ways. Through countless engagements, readers can represent what literature means to them using a range of art forms, media, and genres. Students can use their imaginations to design literature responses that reflect their individual interpretations, creative talents, and interests. Suddenly, the act of reading is transformed into an innovative and purposeful literature event that inspires children to work with different media to share how texts affect them. As students expand their repertoires, they explore various response forms and make imaginative use of the resources and frameworks available to them.

The cornerstones to literacy rest on many early childhood literacy experiences that we have seen. Together these early literacy events enrich children's lifelong affair with reading and enhance the quality of their lives by opening doors to greater learning opportunities. Learning to read can inspire an interest in writing. In becoming readers, youngsters may draw connections to favorite children's writers, make powerful connections to stories, and discover worldly interests that motivate them to pick up the pen and release the author within.

Children's Book References

Ahlberg, Janet and Allan (1978) *Each Peach Pear Plum.*

Anderson, Hans Christian (1987) *The Little Match Girl.*

Anholt, Laurence (2003) *The Magical Garden of Claude Monet.*

Bemelman, Ludwig (1958) *Madeline.*

Bourgeois, Paulette (2003) *Oma's Quilt.*

Bourgeois, Paulette and Clark, Brenda (2001) *Franklin's School Treasury.*

Brumbeau, Jeff (2001) *The Quiltmaker's Gift.*

Dickins, Rosie (2006) *Usborne The Children's Book of Art.*

DiSalvo, DyAnne (1997) *Uncle Willie's Soup Kitchen.*

Ehlert, Lois (1997) *Color Zoo.*

Falconer, Ian (2000) *Olivia.*

Fleming, Maria (2003) *What Grows Underground?*

Fox, Mem (2001) *Whoever You Are.*

Fox, Mem (1996) *Zoo-Looking.*

Gilman, Phoebe (1992) *Something from Nothing.*

Handford, Martin (2008) *Where's Waldo? The Complete Collection.*

Hill, Eric (1980) *Where's Spot?*

Hoffman, Mary (1991) *Amazing Grace.*

Hodgson Burnett, Frances (1987) *The Secret Garden.*

Hopkinson, Deborah (1995) *Sweet Clara and the Freedom Quilt.*

Jackson, Ellen (1998) *Cinder Edna.*

Khan, Rukhsana, (1998) *The Roses in My Carpets.*

Leaf, Munro (1936) *The Story of Ferdinand.*

Le Tord, Bijou (1995) *A Blue Butterfly: A Story of Claude Monet.*

Loomans, Diane (1991) *The Lovables in the Kingdom of Self Esteem.*

Martin Jr., Bill; Archambault, John; and Ehlert, Lois (2000) *Chicka Chicka Boom Boom.*

Martin Jr., Bill and Carle, Eric (1992) *Brown Bear, Brown Bear.*

Masurel, Claire (2003). *Two Homes.*

Maestro, Betsy (1993) *How Does an Apple Grow?*

Mayhew, James (2007) *Katie Meets the Impressionists.*

Milne, A.A. (2003) *Winnie the Pooh.*

Morgan Allen (1985) *Sadie and the Snowman.*

Munsch, Robert (2007) *Much More Munsch!*

Ovenell-Carter, Julie (1999) *The Butterflies' Promise.*

Potter, Beatrix (2002) *The Tale of Peter Rabbit.*

Raffi (1997) *Baby Beluga.*

Raffi (1999) Five *Little Ducks.*

Raffi (1998) *Wheels on the Bus.*

Rey, H.A. (1973) *Curious George.*

Ross, Tom and Barron, Rex (1997) *Eggbert: The Slightly Cracked Egg.*

Scieszka, Jon (1989) *The True Story of the Three Little Pigs.*

Shriver, Maria (1999) *What's Heaven?*

Silverstein, Shel (1964) *The Giving Tree.*

Shulman, Janet (ed.) (1998) *The 20th Century Children's Book Treasury.*

Su Pinnell, Gay (2000) *Lunch.*

Various Artists (2003) *Dora's Storytime Collection.*

Wood, Audrey (1984) *The Napping House.*

6

Writing Experiences

From the moment that youngsters run their fingers through paint, trace images in the sand, or copy messages onto a steamy mirror, they are practicing writing. When children use crayons and pencils to produce marks on paper, they have started the journey to become writers. From an early age, youngsters discover that writing is used to communicate meaning through messages. The shapes and symbols that appear on a page translate into signs and print that others can read. Many children learn naturally to make meaning by inventing ways to write. The early markings, squiggles, and drawings that first appear on a page carry messages that move children into conventional writing. The transition from scribbles to print takes time, encouragement, practice, support, and meaningful experiences that turn children into young authors.

Writing develops in many ways. Early childhood experiences provide natural opportunities for youngsters to learn about written language—through reading, writing, talking, playing, and working with others. Engaging in different forms of play, building vocabulary, telling stories, identifying print, reading books, and playing with letters, sounds, and words are activities that lay the groundwork for children's writing development and literacy growth. Early writing experiences form an essential cornerstone to building a strong foundation for literacy learning. Learning to write is key to language acquisition, reading development, communication, and later literacy achievement.

Learning to Write

Children learn to write even before a pencil and paper are in front of them. Oral language experiences and word play events help children build communication skills, organize ideas, and compose texts verbally. Talking, storytelling, chanting, rhyming, singing, and making up verses allow youngsters to construct language by first experiencing it aloud. When children play with texts as young storytellers and poets, they take natural steps to becoming writers.

Early writing experiences form an essential cornerstone to building a strong foundation for literacy learning. Learning to write is key to language acquisition, reading development, communication, and later literacy achievement.

Writing grows by means of discovery with oral language and with books. Through encounters with stories, novels, and other children's literature, young people develop literacy skills in both reading and writing. Reading and writing together form cornerstones to a strong literacy foundation. They are parallel processes that are mutually dependent on each other. Children build reading and writing skills simultaneously when the skills are taught together. Students learn to write by writing and by reading daily. Every act of reading and writing provides practice with literacy skills. When reading and writing experiences are connected, learning in both areas is enhanced (Reid, Schultze, and Petersen, 2005). Therefore, children need many opportunities to both read and write.

Writing plays a central role in early reading development (Pearson, 2002). Children who are encouraged to write from an early age perform better on reading. Learning to write helps unlock the mysteries of print by empowering readers with the code. The task of writing helps children develop word recognition, language awareness, and letter-sound knowledge (phonics) in an incidental way (Pearson, 2002). Writing daily shapes children's vocabulary, builds fluency, and improves comprehension. When students are encouraged to respond to literature in writing, they become more engaged in the text, enter a dialogue with the author, and comprehend the content more fully. Writing also gives children a structural knowledge of texts that can facilitate reading comprehension (Tierney et al., 1988).

Reading and writing serve each other in many ways. Reading literature gives youngsters a growing motivation to write. Books offer a rich source of ideas and models for children to hang words and frame their own sentences. As youngsters encounter texts with aspiring interest, they learn to read as writers, looking for styles, forms, and content to make their own. With a new sense of authorship, a student will take hold of a pen and begin composing with a voice and technique that may echo the works that inspired him or her. Using books as models enables young people to see samples of writing in polished form. To read and write, students need to understand and communicate information using language conventions (punctuation, spelling, grammar, decoding, and encoding). Reading books and composing texts help children develop these skills naturally.

Learning to read and write together helps students grow as authors by bringing them into the process naturally. As children compose their own texts, they learn to read back their own writing, edit, conference, and revise their work. When students engage in the writing process in this way, their writing abilities and cognitive skills improve as they gather and organize ideas, clarify thoughts, and add details to their work. This moves children closer to producing logical and coherent pieces of writing. Perhaps the greatest incentive for children to improve their writing is in the hands of those who read their work. Reading literature and revisiting their own writing helps children develop a sense of audience and purpose as they grow more aware that the books they read and the stories they write become texts for other readers (Pearson, 2002). Awareness of audience enhances the power of children's writing by inspiring children to produce quality literature for others to learn from and enjoy.

Supporting Early Writers

Many children find writing to be difficult. Some are hesitant to write. Others avoid the task or feel anxious even before the process begins. There are many ways adults can help youngsters feel comfortable with writing from the start. Children grow into writers with the support of caring family members and teachers who serve as knowledgeable guides to lead the way. To facilitate beginning writers, we need to revisit assumptions about writing instruction and form new understandings of how children learn to write. This requires a departure from the practices of traditional, conventional teaching. We need to change our view of young writer's work, create a safe environment, and provide rich opportunities and resources for children to write naturally.

A View of Young Writers

From the time that young children use a paintbrush or pencil to make their first drawings or marks on paper, they need to see themselves as writers. They need to know that the early scribbles and pictures they make communicate ideas and express messages in formats that others can understand. Youngsters must feel that their early attempts at writing will be accepted and that each product will be greeted with praise, excitement, and celebration. We celebrate the efforts of beginning writers by acknowledging that every symbol, drawing, squiggle, or letter on a page is an act of writing. The early graphic representations that children produce are rich reflections of what children experience and imagine. As children use tools to draw and write, many are committed from the start to making works of literature and fine art. By viewing their products as masterpieces, we inspire youngsters to grow in their writing and reinforce the belief they have in themselves as writers (Reid, Schultze, and Peterson, 2005).

The Writing Environment

A supportive environment invites young children to grow into aspiring writers. Settings that are rich with literature and print surround youngsters with models and formats they can use as springboards for their own writing ideas.

A fundamental feature of a print-rich environment that inspires young writing is a safe and secure atmosphere where risk taking is encouraged. Beginning writers need freedom to experiment with ideas without the fear of making a mistake. Many children allow their anxieties of being wrong to inhibit them from taking risks—from using new words, trying other forms, or playing with ideas. Providing a nurturing environment where children feel free to take chances in their writing is critical. A classroom setting that allows students to explore ideas, use formats, and try out spellings despite their own uncertainty shapes writing into an adventure. The focus at first should not be on spelling, punctuation, and similar conventions. Expectations related to these may limit a child's creativity or expression of ideas. By accepting student's approximations and invented spellings, we convey respect and support to beginning writers as they work their way through the writing process. Although conditions of a productive writing environment should not be too demanding, students still need to be challenged if their skills are to grow. Supportive prompts, encouragement, and direct instruction are needed to nudge children along. However, the greatest success and achievement comes from celebrating the changes and progress we see in students' writing. Acknowledging these breakthroughs builds a stronger environment for children's success.

Invitations to Write

Children need occasions to write—at home, at school, and outdoors on the playground and in the community. Everyday life experiences provide open invitations for youngsters to write, from producing family grocery lists to taking restaurant orders during play. Through models and daily events, children discover the practical ways that others use writing.

Early childhood is filled with genuine opportunities for youngsters to be drawn into the writing process. Children can practice the skills and forms of writing in many ways. Teachers and adult family members can encourage children to:

- use chalk, paint, markers, and other art supplies and writing tools to produce marks, drawings, scribbles or "pretend" writing on paper, chalk/whiteboard, murals, or art displays
- make chalk drawings on playground walkways and in driveways, if permitted
- look at home, at school, and in the community for examples of writing in action (people writing lists, cards, or notes; making sketches, labeling diagrams, composing stories or poems, publishing reports)
- engage in word play and language awareness activities including games, songs, rhymes, and chants
- practice making words using materials such as alphabet blocks/cards/cereal, magnetic/felt/tile letters, or stickers
- produce their own names and those of friends and family members
- sign cards, letters, notes, and messages
- make signs, posters, and invitations
- work on the computer
- respond to literature and learning experiences in writing (in journals, writing-in-role)
- use writing in other program areas (to explain concepts in math, share observations and understandings in science, express facts and learning in social studies)
- mark calendars with important school, personal, or family events
- write as they play (see Chapter 1)
- explore writing for other authentic purposes (e.g., recipes, instruction booklets)

Through rich literacy experiences and practical daily episodes, young children can discover writing in its many forms and uses. Early practices like these support children's writing development and naturally move them into process.

Providing Resources—The Writing Centre

Children need to experiment with letters, words and print by practicing writing skills and playing with tools. They require time, space, supplies, and materials to ease the task of writing and make it enticing. Begin by creating a teaching area where models and lessons are provided. Designate a space for instructional materials such as a chalkboard, chart stand, wipe board, and a range of writing supplies. Having access to a variety of writing supplies and related art materials allows youngsters to uncover resources that may motivate them to write. Establishing a writing centre in the classroom plays a vital part in opening up spaces and opportunities for children to write.

Having an area for children to write or conference with others turns the classroom into a space where children may step into the role of authors and practice writing. Rich samples and a wealth of materials give students the incentive to write. As children play with the tools at their fingertips, they may become inspired to produce works of their own.

Materials for a Writing Centre

- pencils
- crayons
- markers (felt, dry erase)
- pens
- water cans
- paper strips
- glue
- tape
- scissors
- erasers
- white tape or blank sticker labels (to cover up errors)
- chart paper
- chart stand
- easel
- white board, magnetic board, chalk board (large and small for student use e.g., magic slate)
- chalk (white, colored)
- paper in various colors, size, and type (e.g., draft, construction, computer)
- cardstock, poster board
- stationary
- blank greeting cards
- notepads
- list pads
- index cards
- paint
- a variety of paint brushes of different sizes
- cover pages
- envelopes
- ready-made booklets
- stapler, staples, and staple remover
- date stamp
- paper clips
- folders
- letters (magnetic, felt, sticker, tile, block)
- alphabet books
- children's literature
- a variety of texts (e.g., manuals, non-fiction)
- dictionary
- thesaurus
- word wall and lists of high-frequency words
- theme word lists
- environmental print
- visual aids (lists, diagrams, charts, webs, drawings)
- writing samples, models, and displays

Stepping into Writing—Early Writing Characteristics

The journey to becoming a writer begins in homes and classrooms where children experience the joy of having a caring adult read aloud and tell stories to them. When youngsters find a place for books in their lap and turn the pages, they begin to uncover text features independently. As children engage with literature, they see models of written language in books and other reading materials that are filled with print. Youngsters often take interest in storybook illustrations, photos, graphics, and other visuals too. For many children, especially reluctant readers, these images are their entranceway to a book. In time, emerging readers and writers are able to distinguish between text and pictures. Being able to differentiate between drawings and print marks an important step into writing. Early reading experiences lay the groundwork for emergent writing development by allowing youngsters to examine texts, study illustrations, and make the "drawing/ writing distinction" (Martens, 1990, p. 12).

Children take natural steps towards writing when books, print materials, and writing resources are available for them to explore. Apart from picture book encounters, young children's next steps into writing happen when they use crayons or pencils to make marks on paper. Soon, the squiggles and scribbles that youngsters produce grow into lines, circles, and other figures that represent their early drawings and simple pictures. Initially, children use drawing as a form of writing (Ferreiro and Teberosky, 1982). Youngsters believe that the symbols and shapes in their pictures carry meaning and communicate messages (Martens, 1990).

The path from scribbles to picture-making moves children further into writing. In time, children's drawings grow in detail to include letters, labels, words, and stories they produce on their own. Oral language plays an important role in children's early writing development. As youngsters construct pictures and texts, they use talk to map out their early compositions (Harste, Woodward, and Burke, 1984). Vocalizing helps them express ideas and make sound-letter matches that eventually lead to conventional writing (Reid, Schultze, and Petersen, 2005).

The growth of early writing is an important part of young children's emergent literacy development. Emergent writing is marked by a progression of skills that develop at various stages of childhood. While the path from scribbles to script may show some natural progression, it is important to remember that children do not develop consistently and may acquire skills at different ages. Youngsters learn to write by discovering and inventing techniques, strategies, and unique forms of their own in diverse ways. By observing the changes that occur in children's writing as they grow, parents and teachers may note a general sequence of skills that young writers develop over time, changes that are well-known in research (Ferreiro and Teberosky, 1982; Harste, Woodward, and Burke, 1984; Burke, 2010).

The transition to conventional writing takes time. As children's writing matures, it begins to resemble conventional forms. Writing first takes shape from the scribbles and drawings that youngsters start out producing and grows from adventures with letters, words, and print that children discover in their language journey. Along the road, children leave trails of papers that show the inventions and breakthroughs made in their writing. These jewels reveal strengths in children's writing and offer directions for our guidance and teaching. By encouraging young children to write from an early age, parents and teachers can facilitate their emergent writing development and move youngsters along the path from picture-making to script.

By encouraging young children to write from an early age, parents and teachers can facilitate their emergent writing development and move youngsters along the path from picture-making to script.

Moving Children Along in Their Writing

From the moment that youngsters begin making marks on paper, they need encouragement to write in order to become authors. Finding ways to help emerging writers develop starts by knowing where each child is. Recognizing the strengths, skills, and ability of each student as a writer enables teachers to assist the child better through the development process. When we begin teaching from this point, we can nudge youngsters along the path from scribbles and drawing toward writing personal narratives and other genre forms on their own.

By scaffolding students, teachers can develop the supportive building blocks to move children along in their writing. To help children progress, adults can encourage young writers to:
- draw pictures with details
- tell oral stories from personal events, photos, pictures, or wordless books
- label pictures/drawings
- apply concepts of print (e.g., directionality)

(continued on page 132)

Early Writing Characteristics

Student's Name: _____ Date: _____

The writer practices or uses:

- ❑ random scribbles and marks (sticks, wavy lines, squiggles) on paper that represent writing
- ❑ early concepts of print (e.g., beginning awareness of directionality, starting point on a page)
- ❑ scribbling that looks like writing
- ❑ graphics and symbols to convey messages in print
- ❑ shapes (lines, circles) in writing that start to resemble letters of the alphabet (letter-like symbols)
- ❑ some random letters, known letters, strings of letters, or approximations of letters that are familiar (letters in child's name or in names of those around the child)
- ❑ directionality (write from left to right and top to bottom on a page)
- ❑ sequences of letters in random order
- ❑ mostly capital letters
- ❑ no spacing between letter clusters or words
- ❑ combination of upper and lower case letters
- ❑ letter forms that are reversed (e.g., *b*, *d*)
- ❑ initial sounds (e.g., beginning letters) are used to represent words
- ❑ words recorded with more than one letter or sound (usually start with consonant sounds)
  - ❑ growing knowledge of letter-sound relationships (matches letters to the sounds they hear in words)
  - ❑ words recorded with both the beginning and ending sounds
  - ❑ vowels are eliminated or used incorrectly at first
- ❑ spacing and punctuation begin to appear
- ❑ the ability to spell and use a small bank of known words or high-frequency/sight words
- ❑ book language in writing (e.g., *Once upon a time*)
- ❑ invented spelling and approximations to record words
- ❑ letter combinations that are reversed (e.g., *uo* for *ou*, *ght* for *hgt*)
- ❑ letters that are omitted from words
  - ❑ conventions (punctuation)
  - ❑ spacing, fonts, punctuation, and genres
  - ❑ recognizable words and sentences in their printing/writing

Comments (strengths, focus areas to develop, next steps): _____

_____

_____

Pembroke Publishers. © 2010 *The Cornerstones to Early Literacy* by Katherine Luongo-Orlando. ISBN 978-1-55138-257-9

- print letters they know on a page to represent their writing/story
- copy words (from books, word walls) before they spell them on their own
- use known sight words in their writing
- experiment with form (use spacing)
- begin to use conventions (capitals, periods, other forms of punctuation)
- use sentence starters/frames as leads into writing or the beginning use of sentences (should be used sparingly)
- write sentences on their own
- experiment with invented spellings
- make letter-sound matches using alphabetic knowledge and phonemic awareness
- visualize events in a story they want to write
- extend writing by adding more details
- use the writing process (editing, revising)
- improve on grammar, word usage and conventions
- start to explore other genres (move from narrative to poetry, non-fiction, and other genres)
- study the works, formats, and style of published authors for models and ideas

In *What's Next for this Beginning Writer?* (Pembroke, 2005) Janine Reid, Betty Schultze and Ulla Petersen provide a series of lessons and instructional strategies designed to assist teachers in working alongside students to move their writing to higher levels of competency.

To learn the writer's craft, children need models, practice, support, time, and experience. With prompting and guidance, students' efforts will be marked by change. The transitions children make will shape the view they have of themselves as writers and lead them through an exciting process. When we celebrate their attempts at every stage, children are motivated to improve. When opportunities for learning are built on success and praise, young people's writing will develop fully. To show progress, students' samples can be collected, dated, and kept in an individual writing portfolio that illustrates the improvement that each child has made on the road from scribbles to conventional writing. However, the journey to becoming a writer depends on more than just time, independent practice, growing confidence, and experience. On occasion, young writers need direct instruction to further their writing craft.

Building on What Children Know through Writing Instruction

As children learn to write, they experiment with language in inventive ways. They produce their own codes and invented spellings. They innovatively play with symbols, letters, forms, and conventions to express themselves. With each discovery, youngsters fill the page with new words, punctuation marks, and other approximations. All of us have seen eager young writers overuse a new language rule. With growing sophistication, they mark the text with apostrophes, quotations, or other print features they have noticed. Children's early attempts at printing, spelling, word usage, and conventional writing often reveal fundamental learning breakthroughs that show their current understandings about writing. Teachers can build on what students know by using this evidence to plan for explicit instruction. The key to effective teaching is starting with children's abilities, needs, and interests and allowing their writing to show us what to teach next. Through observing and recording changes in children's writing, we will encounter teachable moments to guide our instruction. When we link our teaching to what children are ready to learn, the likelihood of success is very high.

As we note the developments in children's writing over time, we may recognize essential skills and strategies that students need to learn. To ensure that students are taught at an instructional level that is appropriate to them, some lessons may need to be given to small groups or individually. Apart from mini-lessons, explicit whole group lessons may need to be taught to the entire class, especially when students seem ready and excited to learn a new skill, strategy, or form together. When planning our teaching, it is important to keep in mind that students may need direct instruction in a range of writing skills, from basic tools to editing strategies. The following topics may provide teachers with ideas for mini-lessons and whole class instruction.

- the fine motor skills needed to hold a pencil and form letters
- grasping and using a pencil
- making shapes
- drawing and labeling pictures
- alphabet knowledge
- letter recognition
- printing and letter formation
- printing their name
- printing legibly on lines
- word concepts
- sentence building and sentence structure
- punctuation (use of capitals, periods)
- grammar
- word usage
- letter-sound relationships (hearing and representing sounds with letters)
- phonological and phonemic awareness
- sound-symbol correspondence (linking oral and written language in sound-letter matching)
- phonics
- spelling strategies
- steps in the writing process (editing, revising)

Teaching children to write requires balance and innovation. Through modeling, examples, practice, repetition, and creative teaching approaches, learners can acquire the essential writing skills needed to express their ideas effectively. Instruction plays an important part in children's writing development. When focusing on formal lessons, the goal should be on making learning fun so children do not feel inhibited in their writing efforts. Beginning writers need to see that using basic tools such as printing, spelling, and language conventions will enrich their craft. The emphasis on form and skills (e.g., proper letter formation, printing legibly, using grammar) should never stifle young people's ideas. Creative expression must always come first. In the course of teaching, workbooks and commercial programs are best avoided. Providing authentic opportunities for students to develop fundamental tasks allows their abilities and ideas to take shape through meaningful rehearsals. Experiences in art, music, dance, literature, and creative writing can provide children with the motor skills, phonological knowledge, and effective writing strategies that authors use. Students gain understanding and practice through genuine print encounters where they can search for conventions, spelling, formats, and styles to enhance their writing. Through lessons, daily routines, and other early literacy experiences, young people can build the essential foundation to further develop their writing.

Early Writing Strategies—Routines, Practices, and Activities

Although everyday life experiences provide youngsters with early invitations to put writing to use, many teaching strategies, classroom procedures, and learning events give critical support to writing development in the formative years. Young people can discover the practical uses of writing during pragmatic experiences and real demonstrations that immerse them in authentic writing tasks. Through the following classroom practices, daily routines, and early literacy activities, emergent literacy learners can begin writing on their own.

Morning Message

A common daily routine in early primary classrooms (Kindergarten and beginning Grade 1) is the Morning Message. The Morning Message may greet students as they start their day with a few short sentences written on the chalkboard, wipe board or chart paper for them to read (or complete together). The message often contains information about what will happen throughout their day (e.g., field trip, library visit, guest visitor, art lesson). Pattern sentences and known phrases are used repeatedly each day to record the message. This way, children grow familiar with commonly used words and are able to read the message successfully on their own or as a class:

> Good morning… (class, boys and girls, students, everyone).
> Today we will… (visit the library, read a new book).

As children become familiar with this morning routine, additional information can be added to the morning message. Information may be related to calendar work (date, weather) or other classroom rituals (welcome songs, a student's special day). Students can be involved in writing the Morning Message by filling in pattern sentences with known words.

> Today the weather is … _____ and _____.
> The special helper today is … _____.

The teacher may also use the morning message to teach print concepts and aspects of writing. This daily routine provides an explicit demonstration of how print works to convey a message and communicate with others. Composing the morning message as a class enables teachers and students to practice writing sentences, using punctuation, spacing, and other conventions properly to write a common text. Discussing information for the morning message and recording ideas together also enables children to see how oral language maps onto writing. As they read or write the message together, teachers and students can talk about letter-sound matches and other phonemic concepts by stretching out the sounds that words make. This routine should take only 15 minutes or less.

Cloze Activities

Young children can build their writing skills by completing written cloze activities. To do this, present students with a passage that features deleted parts of words, whole words, or phrases that can be completed as a class. Display a large reproduction for the whole group to see. Teach a lesson that demonstrates the process of filling in missing letters, words, and parts of the written text by brainstorming, predicting, and using context cues and prior knowledge. As a class, discuss, debate, compare, and select appropriate letters, words, and phrases for each deletion. Challenge students with written cloze activities they can complete in pairs or small groups. Passages can be recorded on chalkboards, wipe boards, chart paper, or worksheets for students to work through.

When designing cloze procedures for young children, start with texts they can read independently based on shared experiences, familiar stories, or topics of interest. Then, move on to other genres that students may know and have success with (friendly letters, recipes, instructions, songs). Selecting familiar passages allows children to use experiential knowledge and contextual cues to anticipate, predict, and figure out missing words and phrases. To help young children solve the puzzle, provide visual aids (rebus symbols, initial letters, word meaning/definition) or use dashes to indicate the number of letters deleted from the passage.

As students scan the text, notice gaps, and fill in missing letters, words, and phrases, they build essential language skills, including comprehension, reading strategies, and writing abilities. Cloze procedures enable children to strengthen sight vocabulary, letter and word recognition, and spelling (Booth, 1998). The focus on language structures also reinforces students' understanding of grammar and genre forms.

Word Games

Games provide children with word play experiences that build their writing skills. As children compose words and phrases while playing games such as *Scrabble* or Hangman, they use cloze procedures and word-solving strategies. Word games like these provide incidental practice at stringing letters together to spell words and threading words to make phrases and sentences that can progress naturally into writing. As children uncover the vowels, consonants, and first, middle, and final letters that make up these words and phrases, they learn to solve language puzzles using word recognition and phonological knowledge as well.

Building Sentences

Sentences starters can make it easier for children to take the first step into writing independently. For many emerging writers, sentence starters act as prompts to spark ideas. In addition, students can use sentence strips and pocket charts to construct ideas before their thoughts meet the page. Using classroom resources, teachers can show students how to use sentence starters and sentence strips to structure words into sentences. However, these leads and resources should be used sparingly. The goal is to motivate youngsters to write expressively and freely on their own.

Sentence Scramblers

Through scrambled word activities, children can practice sequencing words and ideas into clear sentences. To begin, teachers can record sentences on strips of paper that are later cut apart for students to rearrange. Learners can use pocket charts or magnetic boards to reconstruct the words into coherent sentences. As children play with word order, they incidentally learn language structure, grammar rules, and syntactic forms. Once students are able to reorganize sentences logically, they can write their own sentences, cut them apart, and challenge others to put them back together. Concrete language activities like these turn writing into an active, constructive process that is fun and engaging.

Language Experience Stories

Children can write about events in their personal lives by creating language experience stories as described previously in Chapter 1. These stories can be written in many ways. Youngsters begin by sharing their personal experiences with others. Children can then draw or write about the event in a journal or personal narrative. Later, students can read back their writing or describe their drawing(s) to others. Children from diverse backgrounds can write their personal stories in their first language. Encouraging students to use their first language to write about their experiences makes it easier for them to read back the text. Afterwards, these texts can be translated for others to read. Sometimes, young children may record their personal experience stories using "pretend" writing (scribbles, wavy lines, strings of letters). When the student's writing is not legible, the teacher can seek permission to transcribe the work and write the text in conventional writing. At times, children can share their personal narratives by having others scribe for them. Although this can help move reluctant students into writing, scribing for children should be used in moderation. Emerging writers ultimately need to control the pen, write, and do the work themselves. When scribing children's narratives, the teacher or adult records the experience as the student talks about it, using words, structures and forms that are naturally spoken by the child to describe the experience ("I felled down in the grass."). Using the child's natural language in this way enables youngsters to read back their own language experience stories. As students read back their own writing or ideas, they are able to predict the text using both their experiential and linguistic knowledge (Wilson, 2002). By creating language experience stories, children are able to use meaningful reading materials they have produced themselves as a source of language acquisition and literacy development (Wilson, 2002).

Book Making

The experiences that children share at school (e.g., field trips, class visits, assembly, school celebration, bake sale, science fair experiments) provide rich topics for writing together. School events and classroom experiences can be made into experience books using a variety of formats (big books, individual booklets, chart stories, illustrated retellings) for all the children to read. These books may feature rhymes, songs, news events, letters, narratives, or instructions that teachers and students can write, illustrate, and publish together.

Making class books is an inviting way for beginning writers to enter a literate community where they can learn to write with the support of their teacher and peers. As children compose class-made stories and experience books, they learn to gather and organize ideas; use language structures; and produce genres like procedures, recounts, explanations, and reports as a way to write for different purposes such as to explain, instruct, or entertain others. Teachers can use this writing strategy to teach print concepts (directionality), word features (phonemes), letter-sound matches, sentence building, and aspects of the writing process (drafting, editing, punctuation and spelling strategies) in an authentic way. Making books together may inspire young writers to produce texts on their own.

Pattern Books

As children discover the joy of writing, they may take steps towards composing stories, books, and other texts independently. Emerging writers can begin by creating pattern books. These texts have repetitive, predictable structures on which young authors can hang their ideas. Teachers can make printed booklets featuring patterned sentences that relate to a theme or topic based on children's interest (e.g., recess, wintertime). These simple texts may include sentence starters on each page that include high-frequency words that students can use as springboards into writing (e.g., In winter, I like to _____). Children use the repetitive language and patterned text on each page to frame their thoughts and complete the book. Building on familiar structures in this way can helps students develop writing strategies to innovate on other texts.

Text Innovations

Once children are familiar with the structure of pattern books, they may be ready to produce text innovations based on popular stories, rhymes, verses, songs, and other texts they know. To innovate on a text, students must first recognize the particular pattern of the text. Once learners are aware of the text format (words, organization, rhythm, rhyming pattern), they can add lines or verses or write a new text by drawing upon on the familiar one.

Innovating on texts develops children's writing by turning children into young authors. Children use the framework of popular stories, poems, songs, and rhymes as models for their writing. Using this strategy enables emerging writers to compose texts on their own:

> *One little bear cub*
> *Jumping on the clothes*
> *She fell off*
> *And bumped her noise*
> Issabella, Age 5
> (based on *Ten Little Monkeys*)

Text Reconstructions

As young writers become aware of text structures, they begin to notice words, sentences and formats that encircle print. When children are familiar with a story, poem, or other known text, they may be able to reconstruct it in sequence. Students draw upon their knowledge of form and content to recompose the familiar text. After children have been introduced to a work of literature (news article, poem, non-fiction, short story) through repeated readings, the teacher can write the text, or parts of the selection, on separate sentence strips. Next, have the children work in groups to reconstruct, or arrange the text back in order. Young children can start by reconstructing simple sentences and texts before moving to other selections. Students can challenge their peers with further text reconstructions by selecting their own passages from literature, copying them onto charts, cutting the sentences apart, and having peers rearrange them in sequence.

To reconstruct texts, children draw on their familiarity with the text to identify the next sentence. To recompose the text in sequence, they must rely on their understanding of sentence structure, form, and content. Reconstructing texts gives children practice in using alphabet knowledge and phonological and phonemic awareness to identify letters, sounds, and words in each sentence. As learners recompose texts, they also learn to recognize print features, build on sentences, and shape texts into different forms. This strategy prepares children for writing independently by strengthening their understanding of how literature is constructed using different sentence structures, genre formats, and other schematic features.

Response Journals

Keeping a response journal allows students to break through the task of finding something to write about. Thrilling stories and exciting characters provide a rich source of ideas for children's own writing. Students can respond to reading material by producing drawings, letters, questions, and recounts in their journals. As young people develop their written responses, they may explore various formats, such as diary entries and friendly letters. The process of writing down thoughts and reactions to a text helps children to compose opinions, organize ideas, and clarify meaning. In addition to building comprehension strategies, students try their hand at writing within the supportive context of reading literature and responding to books through print activities. Later, both teachers and peers can respond to entries that learners make in their journals.

Many of the routines, early instructional practices, and emergent literacy activities that take place daily in primary classrooms are genuine occasions for young language learners to step into writing naturally. Real demonstrations and pragmatic experiences invite children to write in the context of authentic, engaging, and fun learning events.

Teaching Strategies for Young Writers—Types of Writing Experiences

When children find their writing voice, they want to share with others what they have to say, both in oral language and in print. In their efforts to communicate, youngsters may pick up a pen and start to write. Making symbols on a page marks the beginning of their writing experiences. To grow as writers, emergent literacy learners need the support of teachers and peers in order to control the pen on their own. The following teaching strategies and writing experiences can move children towards independent writing.

Modeled Writing

In modeled writing, the teacher or another adult language partner demonstrates how writing works by composing a text in front of students. While constructing a story, literature response, personal narrative, or other genre form, the teacher illustrates how to generate and record ideas, form sentences, produce a draft, and revise and edit a text. Students get to see the steps of the writing process at work in modeled writing lessons. Youngsters learn how oral language transcribes into print as the teacher "thinks aloud" and records ideas. Through modeled writing, the teacher maintains control of the pen while showing how letters, words, print concepts, and language conventions are used to produce a text. The explicit examples can guide students towards composing a common text with others.

Shared Writing

During shared writing, the teacher and students work together to discuss, and then write, a common text based on an experience, topic, or book they collectively know about. Using an easel, the chalkboard, or an overhead projector, the teacher acts as a scribe, writing down what the children have to say. Students can compose texts together in small groups, as a class, or one-on-one with the teacher. In shared writing, the teacher maintains control of the pen while students construct the ideas. Together, they can build lists, label objects, record concepts, retell events, keep schedules, or write a group story. As children work with others to compose texts, they develop and share ideas without the restraints of pen and paper they must use themselves. As teachers scribe students' writing, they can illustrate language conventions including print concepts, word building, letter-sound relationships, and sentence construction.

Interactive Writing

In interactive writing, the teacher and students share the pen as they work collectively to write a common text. Through discussion, the children and teacher collaborate on topics and ideas before assuming the task of writing together. Drawing on their conversations, the students work with the teacher's support to create a common text that has a real purpose (e.g., procedure, explanation, recipe). In interactive writing, the pen is shared and passed among the children as students take turns composing the text. Constructing texts in this way allows youngsters to put into practice explicit lessons and models from their early writing experiences. Students can try out language conventions, make letter-sound connections, and experiment with spacing with the support of others.

Parallel Writing

A child's journey to becoming a writer happens alongside others as youngsters work in parallel to compose texts independently. In parallel writing, students produce their own stories or genres, with other writers working next to them. As children begin to construct texts independently, they may turn to their peers to share ideas, ask for assistance, or talk about the stories and works they are creating. Through parallel writing, students find a supportive environment in which to work through the writing process and construct individual texts with the help of others if needed. As teachers observe young writers working alongside one another, they may notice students who have similar needs for instruction.

Guided Writing

Guided writing is an instructional context used to group children for the explicit teaching of writing skills and strategies. After reading and assessing students' writing, the teacher may note learners with similar needs and form small temporary groups for specific writing instruction. These groupings will change, depending on how students' writing develops. While working with these groups, the teacher meets with students to discuss aspects of their writing and guide them in explicit strategies and skills to help them improve. Guided writing sessions can focus on writer's craft lessons (writing an effective lead, using descriptive words), grammar structure (the use of conventions), spelling strategies, genre forms (reports, legends), text organization (the use of paragraphs), and other style features.

Independent Writing

In independent writing, students are inspired to write and are able to work on their own to compose their texts. Most often, learners select their own topics to write about, though occasionally some topics are assigned. Children draw upon a wealth of resources to produce works in various genres and for different purposes. As students explore the forms and functions of writing independently, the teacher offers additional support and strategies through individual writing conferences and daily mini-lessons. Gathering ideas, drafting, revising, editing, publishing, and sharing their work with others allow children to become authentically engaged in the writing process.

Becoming a Writer

Through powerful teaching and learning experiences, children gain initiative, competence, and autonomy to write with growing expertise. Through modeled, interactive, guided, and other shared writing activities, young language learners can practice putting pen to paper with growing confidence, skill, and ease. Having daily opportunities to write, children can learn both the joy and work of being a writer. Once children discover their voice and begin using a writer's tools, they are on their way to becoming writers themselves. Along the way, students can join paths and take steps together in a writing workshop.

The Writing Workshop

Through the work of Donald Graves, Nancie Atwell, Lucy Calkins, Frank Smith, and other prominent educators, teachers have inherited best practices in the teaching of writing and the development of literacy. One routine that has become well-established in language classrooms is the writing workshop. A writing workshop offers a program model that allows time for independent writing, explicit instruction, and sharing of students' work. It gives children opportunities to write throughout the school day and offers specific, targeted lessons that learners need to improve their writing. Since the writing workshop is designed to provide the instructional support that students need to become proficient writers, it is suitable for early literacy programs and primary classrooms too.

A typical writing workshop (Atwell, 1999) allows students time to write on their own on topics that are generally chosen by them. As children work independently, the teacher meets with an individual student, or group of writers, in a writing conference. After reading and assessing young writers' needs, the teacher plans and presents a daily mini-lesson (10–15 minutes) that focuses on a specific writing skill, strategy, procedure, or craft that children are ready to learn (Fountas and Pinnell, 2001). These short lessons are designed to help students learn aspects of the writing process from important workshop routines, to the use of language conventions, to the study of quality literature in the discovery of authors' crafts and techniques. Interactive mini-lessons can be introduced to the class at the start of the workshop or be taught during guided writing sessions with smaller groups of students. As the daily writing workshop draws to an end, students are provided time to share their work with others in a large group. Work is later collected for teacher evaluation.

Young writers may find success in a writing workshop when procedures are predictable and easy to follow; when conferences are respectful, supportive, and encouraging; and when lessons are practical, purposeful, and relevant. The following suggestions can make a writing workshop run smoothly in primary classrooms and beyond:

- Schedule the writing workshop for about 30–45 minutes daily at approximately the same time each day.
- Begin the session by:
  - reading samples of children's writing from a previous session
  - using students' works as models of good writing (point out strengths, improvements, areas of growth)
  - sharing a story, picture, personal event, artifact, or other prompt that may inspire students with topics to write about
  - reviewing procedures or routines that will help the session run smoothly

Genre Forms for Young Writers

- Personal writing (journals, diary entries, calendars)
- Personal experience stories
- Scrapbooks
- Photo essays
- Recounts
- Pattern books
- Dual track/bilingual books
- Poetry
- Procedures (recipes, game instructions)
- Lists (e.g., top ten)
- Captions and labels
- Signs, posters, and advertisements
- Letters
- Narratives (fantasy, adventure, humor, fairy tale)
- Short story
- Invitations, announcements
- Greeting cards and thank-you notes
- Post cards
- Menu
- Joke books, riddles, tongue twister books
- Non-fiction (reports, explanations)
- Chapter book
- Songs and verses

- offering positive feedback from students' work that has been evaluated
- teaching a mini-lesson to the class
- examining the work, style, and craft or a professional writer
- providing time for independent writing while working with students in guided writing groups or writing conferences
- Set reasonable, clear goals and expectations for the session that students can reach that day (e.g., starting a first draft, copy edit for spelling)
- Meet with individual students in writing conferences while other students are working independently
- Schedule time (10–15 minutes) to work with small groups of students on guided writing lessons as needed
- Provide a rich source of literature and resources that students can refer to as they write
- Establish the use of a writer's notebook, or individual folder, for each child to record and organize writing tools, resources, samples, and finished work
- Allow students to work with partners, at times, on parallel writing and peer conferencing
- Collect, review and evaluate students' work daily to determine writers' needs and plan daily lessons

Source: *What's Next for this Beginning Writer* (Pembroke, 2005) by Janine Reid, Betty Schultze, and Ulla Peterson

Providing time for daily writing is an important part of building a comprehensive and balanced language program in the early years.

Independent writing is as essential to young children's emergent literacy development as daily reading. By making writing part of the school day, teachers create space for children to step into the shoes of real author's and write themselves. In writing workshops, students learn aspects of a professional author's life or their craft. A fundamental part of the writing workshop is guiding students in using the writing process. Like professional authors, students must think of topics to write about, plan and compose their ideas, and later, edit and revise their work before sharing it with others.

The Writing Process

As children learn to read and write, they encounter the work of professional writers who have published quality literature for readers to enjoy. Before an author, playwright, or poet sits down with pen or paper or a computer keyboard, they begin composing by first exploring ideas to write about. The writing process continues from the moment an author starts exploring ideas to the time the work is published and ready to share with others. Using the writing process is a key to learning how to be a writer. Here are some ways to guide young children through the stages:

Pre-Writing Activities—Before putting pen to paper, young writers need time to explore ideas and discover what they want to write about. To develop topics for story writing, children can begin with personal narratives that portray events in their daily lives. Once students see the story potential of everyday life events, they may find it easier to uncover topics to write about.

Children may still need support in selecting writing topics that inspire interest and ideas. To start, teachers, adults and peers can talk to young children about books, experiences and subjects that draw their attention. Young writers

Independent writing is as essential to young children's emergent literacy development as daily reading. By making writing part of the school day, teachers create space for children to step into the shoes of real authors and write themselves.

may become motivated to write about topics they know when they discover the potential and shared curiosity around them. Children's imaginations and writing ideas can grow from rich experiences and sources such as field trips, curriculum units, school events, literature, play episodes, and community sites. Sometimes, prompts can serve as springboards for children's writing. Guiding youngsters through visualization exercises may awaken their minds to a cast of characters or settings that can lead to story writing or stir thoughts and emotions that may inspire works of poetry. Ritual props, artifacts, thematic toys (puppets), books, photographs, cultural goods, and other personal objects can also provide children with potential writing topics. Young people can use tools such as disposable cameras and art supplies to create photographs that may inspire writing. At times, teachers and other language partners might provide sentence starters or topic lists to rouse reluctant writers. Over all, though, children should be motivated to select writing topics and develop ideas themselves.

After deciding on a topic, young writers are ready to choose a form they are comfortable with (narrative, poem, report, letter, procedure). The format may depend upon the audience and purpose. Encourage students to select an intended audience (other peers, younger or older students, family members, community members, or teachers) and consider the reasons for writing (e.g., to entertain, inform, instruct, explain, raise an issue, or teach a lesson). Once these decisions are made, students can begin to plan their writing.

Finding the Inspiration to Write—Exploring Sources of Children's Writing Ideas

Travel journal page

Page from a pattern book based on class field trip and literature book (*Picture Book* by Mem Fox)

Planning and Brainstorming—After discovering an interest, and deciding on form, audience, and purpose, children can organize their thoughts and decisions by mapping out their work. When students commit to a writing project, they need time to brainstorm and record ideas in preparation for writing, publishing, and sharing. Young people can use graphic organizers, charts, story grammars, sketches, outlines, and other tools to group ideas and plan their writing effectively. Using visual organizers provides children with a place to gather, compose, and record ideas before writing.

At this stage of the writing process, young children begin to practice the ways professional authors work. Stepping into an author's shoes challenges students to think, plan, and compose ideas using the same tools to safeguard and develop their ideas. As thoughts come to mind, writers can jot them down and return to them later. The maps, outlines, or sketches become the sources of innovation where story ideas and published works originate. These plans provide teachers with records of student assessment that show early writing and story development. After mapping out their writing in this way, children can build on their ideas by producing a first draft.

Writing a Draft—Young writers can bring their ideas to life by drafting a rough copy of their work. As children take their plans to fruition, they attend to the form of writing, as well as to sentence structure, text features, and voice. At this stage, students work to develop ideas by focusing on writing sentences, interesting leads, supportive details, fluency, language choices, and endings. Once youngsters have composed their first drafts, they can revisit the rough copy and begin revising their work.

Revising and Rewriting—During the revision stage, young children can improve on their writing by taking up the first draft and reworking the content, flow of ideas, and language usage. Students can begin by reading the original copy aloud several times while attending to different components. As children turn an ear

When the Queen finaly arrived at the palis six doormen let her in. When she entered the room the princess was sound asleep. So the Queen whispered to the royel servants.

"I found a miracle! Now this is how you're supost to use it." The queen began. "The princess must drink the liquid every day. Put it in the bath-tub and let her soak in it too."

So that is what they did.

Page from a chapter book inspired by a storytelling episode

Name of Invention: The Sunscrean Mashin.
Date it was Invented: April 14 2005
Purpose (what it is used for): It is use for puting on Sunscrean

How It Works:
You have to go in a pachel room and on the cealing there is a shower head and it is ful with sunscrean. you have to pres a butin and from the shawerhead is Sun -screan. It goes rite over your head

Illustration/Drawing (Label Parts)

Page from a book on explanations based on practical life experiences and everyday purposes

to their writing, they may focus more on voice, clarity, meaning, language flow, sentence variety, text organization, word choices, and genre features. Teachers can model the revision process using an overhead projector, chart paper, or chalkboard to show how using different strategies (such as adding new ideas or crossing out text) can improve a writing sample. Later, students can strengthen their writing by polishing up the areas that still need work. Through peer conferences, young writers can revise their work further with suggestions from others. As children make changes to their writing, they rewrite their rough copy and produce successive drafts before editing their work.

Proofreading, Editing, and Conferencing—As young children practice the work of professional authors, they develop greater attention to the aspects of their writing. In working to produce a published piece to share with others, writers focus on the mechanics of writing as part of the process. At this stage, authors begin proofreading and editing their work for grammar, punctuation, spelling, capitalization, and other language conventions. Beginning writers often find this task overwhelming. To make it manageable, encourage students to read back their own writing and begin self-editing by focusing on one aspect at a time. Young authors can brush up on their language skills by conferencing with others. Several writing conferences can be held with peers and adult language partners. Each conference might focus on a specific language convention. During this stage as well, mini-lessons on grammar, spelling, and punctuation can be taught through guided writing and large-group instruction.

Spelling accuracy is one of the most difficult strategies that young children face in their writing and editing. Students can learn effective spelling techniques with practice, instruction, and useful resources. At first, emerging writers should be encouraged to use invented spelling as they find their voice and begin expressing themselves through print. Youngsters cleverly use invented spellings at the early stages of their writing development. When children approximate spelling, they start to form sound-letter relationships and develop phonetic knowledge. Once students move beyond these approximations, they progress towards conventional spelling with guidance and support. The strategies, learning activities, and resources described here and in the following section (Playing with Words) give children effective tools to spell words with increasing accuracy.

As children develop strategies to spell words correctly, they may draw upon the resources, lessons, and models gained from the language experiences described here. However, students should be taught not to rely on these reference tools alone when writing. These techniques are ways to help students refine their writing. Attention to these strategies should not be so great that students are distracted from the process of writing. It is important not to place greater value on perfect spelling than on children's voice, expression, and ideas. The best way for young readers and writers to improve their spelling is through purposeful and meaningful daily reading and writing activities.

Once children have proofread and edited their work for spelling, grammar, punctuation, and other language conventions, changes can be made to their drafted copies. Through proofreading, editing, and conferencing, students can work with others to produce coherent and polished texts that others can read with fluency and ease. At this stage, teachers can meet with students in formal conferences to check their final work before publishing. The goal is to ensure that students' writing has reached a level of quality that they feel proud of and want to share with others.

Helping Children Spell Correctly—Strategies, Activities, and Resources

Phonemic Awareness and Phonics Activities

To spell correctly, students need practice and support in developing phonemic awareness and phonetic understandings (see Chapter 3). Sound out strategies can be improved in word building and language play activities during which children can learn, isolate, blend, and substitute phonemes.

Word Wall

Visual displays of words children know or need to know for reading and writing are highly accessible tools to develop word knowledge and spelling accuracy. Alphabetic listings of words that are commonly misspelled or not phonetically spelled (such a high-frequency and sight words) offers students an immediate reference they can turn to as they read and write. Picture clues or symbols can be added to the growing list of words featured on a classroom word wall.

High Frequency/Sight Words

The challenge of spelling high-frequency words that have irregular patterns or spellings that are not phonetically standard may demand that young children just learn them. Many high-frequency words (the, to, one) simply must be learned by sight. Through guided reading and explicit instruction, students can be taught to correctly spell common sight words and basic vocabulary they will encounter in their reading and writing. Word walls and other spelling strategies below (such as making words with magnetic letters) can be effective aids in learning sight words.

Sorting Words and Making Word Lists

Children may encounter patterns in words as they practice building word walls and sight word lists. Students can build on patterns they discover by sorting words and compiling further lists that show different relationships. Word lists can be compiled and classified based on common features such as:

- known letter (words with "s" or "c", for example)
- the same starting or ending sounds
- silent letters
- double consonants
- compound words

- root words
- rhyming words
- word families
- words with the same number of syllables
- other classifications (such as plurals and contractions)

Theme Dictionaries and Alphabet Books

As children explore themes, topics and interest areas through current events, research, and curriculum studies, they may encounter unfamiliar related words and subject-specific vocabulary. To help students learn these words and their spelling, invite the class to compile a list of words they encounter in books, lessons, and activities that deal with these subjects or interest topics. This vocabulary list can be used to produce alphabet books and theme-based dictionaries on different areas of study.

Personal Dictionaries or Word Banks

Children make progress in vocabulary and spelling development by taking ownership of the words they learn. The genres and topics that inspire children's interest and enthusiasm in reading and writing are a rich source of word knowledge. As youngsters encounter new vocabulary in books and texts, they may commit new terms to memory. Learning to spell unfamiliar words can be made easy when students develop personal word banks or dictionaries. When children choose the key words to include in these resources, they begin to recognize, use, and correctly spell the words they have selected because these terms are more meaningful to them.

Spelling Lists and Weekly Tests

At times, students can benefit from the practice of learning words on a spelling list developed by the teacher or class. Lists can be based on common sight words children are still learning, topics in other curriculum areas, or words used in reading or writing. In my experience, the best way to use spelling lists is to ensure that the words students are expected to learn are linked to texts and subjects they are studying, reading, and writing about. When preparing for a weekly test, students may review words regularly, practice them in exercises (such as sentence building or putting words in alphabetical order), and learn to recognize and spell them with greater ease. To help children find meaning in these words, encourage them to select three to five words from the assigned spelling list and use them in context by creating a personal experience story to share with others. review words regularly, practice them in exercises (such as sentence building or putting words in alphabetical order), and learn to recognize and spell them with greater ease. To help children find meaning in these words, encourage them to select three to five words from the assigned spelling list and use them in context by creating a personal experience story to share with others.

Spelling Rules, Reminders, and Tips

At times, it is useful to provide young children with helpful tips and reminders to help them learn words and spell them correctly. Teachers can guide students in discovering important spelling rules or teach these conventions explicitly. Children can keep a record of helpful hints in a writer's notebook or on a desktop for daily reference. The tips, reminders, and rules become reliable tools to help students spell correctly and use in their own writing.

Print Resources

Students can use poetry collections, picture books, short story anthologies, and other works of children's literature as reference tools to check the spelling of new or unknown words. They can use other print resources for this purpose as well, including dictionaries (picture, regular, and dual-track/bilingual), thesauri, and posters and displays.

Playing with Words—Learning to spell words correctly does not have to take place only through instruction or in work-oriented activities. Children can explore the meaning and spelling of words during play as well. Here are additional strategies and learning activities that remind us of the strong connection between play and literacy.

Play-oriented Spelling Strategies and Learning Activities

Word Play

Delightful word play activities can help children learn to spell. Through the echo of alliterative verses and playful puns in riddles, jokes, and tongue twisters, youngsters develop the phonological awareness they need to hear the sounds in words they later try to spell. Students can make up riddles, puns, jokes, or tongue twisters for words they are learning. As children play with language in amusing ways, they study words and spelling patterns closely to discover homonyms, homophones (hair, hare), and other words and phrases that are used humorously.

Rhythm and Music Activities

Clapping games, songs, and music and rhythm activities provide authentic and enjoyable opportunities for children to learn about spelling. The alliteration, repetition, and word patterns in songs and playground verses contribute to children's spelling development. As children tap out syllables in words, call out letters in jump-rope rhymes, and play with rhyming words they practice spelling strategies through the joy of music and play.

Alphabet Play

Young children can develop the ability to spell words through alphabet and letter play. Encourage students to use letters (magnetic, felt, tile, block) to construct combinations of three-, four-, and other-letter words on the board or play surface. As youngsters build words, they practice alphabet knowledge, sound-letter relationships, and spelling techniques before putting pen to paper..

Memory Tricks

Children may develop their own effective techniques to learn how to spell. Students can discuss special memory tricks they use to spell words correctly. Young people

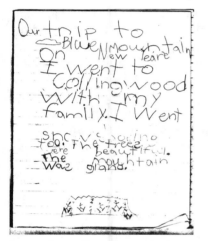

Personal experience story using weekly list words

Page from a medieval picture dictionary

Samples of Children's Published Work

Picture book page from child's story *Once Upon A Mattress Cover*

Page from child's joke book

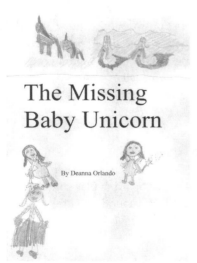

Cover of child's picture book entitled *The Missing Baby Unicorn*

may draw on visual strategies or mnemonic devices as useful aids. Developing rhymes or phrases, recalling personal experiences, making vivid associations, or using other mental techniques can help children learn to spell.

Sketches and Word Puzzles
Children can use visual strategies to learn to spell correctly. Youngsters can produce sketches, picture clues, or symbols to represent whole or parts of words. Teachers and students also can design a rebus, visual riddle, or other puzzle (e.g., Elkonin sound boxes) to assist with spelling.

Word Games
Board games such as *Scrabble* or *Boggle* or other word games (e.g., Hangman) challenge young people to use words and learn to spell them correctly in the context of fun language activities. Word searches, crosswords, and other puzzle games also help children to become better spellers.

Publishing and Sharing—As writers move towards publication, they take up the final draft and use it to design layouts, illustrations, graphics and other visual formats for their printed copy. Children can draw on various tools to produce their publications. A range of art materials and techniques can be used to create illustrations, covers and other pages for their completed work. Students can produce graphics and layouts using computer applications (e.g., word processing programs, graphic design workshops) as well. Even young children enjoy the art of designing typefaces, fonts, lettering and spacing for computer-generated copies. Others may put printing skills to practice by handwriting their final work. Once students have published their writing using a style and format they are comfortable with, they can take their work public in a writer's fair or other classroom event where they can present and share their texts with others. Celebrating the success of young children as authors allows their writing, interest and confidence to grow as they find joy and rewards in working through the process.

* * *

Teachers and parents can nurture children's writing development in many ways. From an early age, youngsters learn to make markings on paper within a supportive environment where there are many engaging and natural opportunities in write every day. The routines, practices, strategies, resources and experiences at home and in the classroom may provide the open invitations, space and motivation children need to begin their journey. Becoming a writer often starts in the ordinary, everyday life activities and play episodes where youngsters' imaginations and meaningful interactions with others provide the inspiration and focus for wanting to pick up the pen. The artwork and drawings that young children produce in the early years lead the way to conventional writing too. Besides these, there are many moments in children's lives that present rich opportunities to gain literacy knowledge and language expertise. Youngsters form these essential understandings and skills through the family literacy practices, home literacy experiences, art ventures, nature events, and media encounters they face as they grow. Over the years, children may trade toys, books, and pencils for paintbrushes, magnifying glasses, computers, or musical instruments to discover other pathways to literacy.

7

Other Pathways to Literacy

"There is no single road to becoming literate…" (Y.M. Goodman, 1997, p. 56). Literacy learning happens in the play engagements, oral language practices, word play activities, environmental print encounters, reading events, and writing experiences of a child's early years. These episodes are the essential cornerstones to building a strong literacy foundation.

Children come into literacy in many other ways. Life is a playground filled with learning potential. Everything children encounter—"nature and the social context, the house and the street, language and custom, the world of history and the world of daily news in the form of rumor, of broadcast and newspaper, music and technical science, play and dream - everything together"—become a source of knowing (Martin Buber, 1965, p. 106). Life encounters form a rich backdrop for children's language learning and literacy growth. In a report published in 2000, the Alliance for Childhood outlined the essentials for youngsters to have a healthy life and reach their full human potential. Among their recommendations, children need: time for unstructured play (especially make-believe play); nature encounters and outdoor activity; experiences in the arts from music, drama, puppetry, and dance; read-aloud events, conversation, poetry, and storytelling; along with hands on learning experiences (Alliance for Childhood, 2000, p. 47). The cornerstones to early literacy outlined in this book draw on these childhood essentials and other life events that are building blocks to literacy learning.

Home Literacy Practices and Family Literacy Experiences

The process of language learning begins long before children enter school. Both the family and home environment provide the opening setting where children's early language encounters and emergent literacy experiences first take place (Leichter, 1984). From birth, youngsters start engaging in literacy events within the patterns of family life. Reading and writing are naturally embedded in the daily lives of children at home (Taylor, 1983). For many, the path to literacy begins with storybook reading experiences. As Yetta Goodman explains: "There has been an undue emphasis on the idea that literacy learning occurs when children are read to by their parents"(p. 56). In reality, there is a great deal of literacy found in homes and communities that go beyond traditional "book reading" (Cook, 2005, p. 421).

Children experience a rich diversity of literacies throughout their young lives. From an early age, they take part in family rituals, cultural practices, and social events that help them grow into readers and writers. Many complex factors may influence the family literacy events that youngsters take part in, such as race, ethnicity, religion, and socio-economic background (Rowsell, 2006). Children today share family arrangements, interests, traditions, and pastimes that change between households. As we follow the lives of young children at home and in their communities, we see many literacy practices, including reading aloud from religious books, storytelling, library visits, and attending faith services, cultural events, family literacy programs (e.g., adult and toddler/preschooler classes), and other community happenings (e.g., museum visits, movie outings, play performances). These occasions form the "out of school" literacy practices that shape children's lives and also contribute to language learning (Cook, 2005).

Home literacy practices and family literacy experiences play an important role in early literacy development. As children grow up in a literate society, they have chances to observe and participate in family events in which literacy is part of daily routines such as shopping, cooking, paying bills, and other everyday practices (Teale, 1986; Purcell-Gates, 1996). From an early age, youngsters may come to see how reading, writing, oral language, and other forms of literacy are used for practical and social purposes such as work, religious practice, interpersonal communication, school-related activities, and other common functions (Teale, 1986, Purcell-Gates, 1996). In the pattern of daily living, children discover ways their families use and encounter print for different reasons (writing cards/notes and lists, filling out forms, scanning labels, reading the newspaper). In the process, youngsters come upon a variety of texts in the forms of entertainment that literacy provides, such as reading books aloud, telling stories, playing games, watching television, and other related family activities (Teale, 1986). When they participate in family literacy events, children encounter a range of literacy materials and print, visual, and linguistic resources (religious books, folk literature, manuals, magazines, toy catalogues, television, film, video games, stories) that prepare them for literacy. Youngsters find resourceful ways that family members use literacy knowledge and skills to carry out their daily activities (Compton-Lilly, 2004). Children come away from these experiences inventing their own literacies, sources of knowing, and ways of making meaning (Rowsell, 2006).

Understanding the home literacy background and family literacy experiences of our students may help teachers build on the foundations of what children already know and integrate the practices by they children learn. To do so, we need to draw on the rich literacy resources and store of knowledge that students carry with them. The "out-of-school" experiences that are part of children's literacy lives at home and in the community are fundamental to language learning. In recognizing and valuing the diversities of literacies that children bring into the classroom, we can start to provide the kind of text encounters, language events, and overall learning activities that link children's home lives with their school experiences (Cook, 2005).

Teachers can build on the emergent literacy knowledge that children gain in family and home literacy practices by drawing on the strengths and resources of households and cultures in their community (Rowsell, 2006). After all, children bring with them "funds of knowledge" (Moll et. al., 1992) in various areas of expertise (reading, storytelling) that can enrich our programs. Teachers can elicit these funds of knowledge in many ways when planning lessons and designing curriculum. They may start by expanding their definitions of text to include the rich print, verbal, and linguistic resources that are part of a child's world (Auerbach, 2003; Cook, 2005). By incorporating a wide variety of texts (films, artifacts, video, media) and literacy practices from students' daily lives and family rituals into the classroom, we can make use of cultural resources in ways that make learning meaningful and possible for all children.

Teachers need to draw on the rich literacy resources and store of knowledge that students carry with them. The "out-of-school" experiences that are part of children's literacy lives at home and in the community are fundamental to language learning.

Nature and Outdoor Activities

In *Family Literacy Experiences* (Pembroke, 2006), Jennifer Rowsell examines ways of bringing family literacy experiences from home into the classroom by using various forms of texts to build literacy based on the cultural resources that surround children every day.

Children love to spend time outdoors playing and discovering the world around them. Playgrounds, gardens, parks, and yards provide wonderful settings for learning. Children's encounters with nature begin with wandering, exploring, and actively moving outdoors—chasing butterflies, building with sticks or snow, climbing trees, planting seeds, watching birds, pondering the shapes of clouds, and gathering items around them. As youngsters play outside, they learn to examine life more closely, marveling at what they see happening in the natural world. I recall my own children stopping to observe a group of working ants carrying a load or to follow the flight of an insect. These occurrences heighten children's senses, build their observation tools, and enhance their ways of knowing. Time spent in nature can lead to a broader form of intelligence that strengthens growing minds and deepens the human experience.

Childhood experiences with nature provide rich and authentic contexts for language learning and literacy building. As youngsters collect rocks, leaves, flowers, seashells, and other interesting objects in the world around them, they may start to explore their properties (size, shape, texture, color) and use sensory language to describe the features they note (Burke, 2010). Building nature collections and taking up hobbies outdoors can motivate children to seek information on interesting topics (rocks and minerals, butterflies, bird-watching) from non-fiction resources (reference books, magazines, internet sites). As youngsters discover facts (names, types, features, uses), they may start to make connections between items they have collected and the content they have read. Children's observations of nature may prompt questions and curiosity that can direct them towards further inquiry and research (about migration patterns, life cycles, animal breeds).

Nature has a way of moving children into reading and writing. Apart from inquiry-based research, youngsters may come across print as they engage in a range of outdoor activities. Planting gardens requires youngsters to read seed packs and discover related texts in gardening books and magazines. As youngsters come upon play spaces, they may encounter signs, posters, billboards, ads, and storefronts that introduce them to environmental print. Children may take up tools to write and make marks on paper while playing outdoors too. Youngsters enjoy creating chalk drawings, bark and leaf rubbings, and taking part in other activities during which they can use different literacy materials outdoors. Nature provides an inspiring setting for journal and narrative writing. Research that has been inspired from nature collections can lead to book publications too.

Children's encounters with nature can lead to other discovery and play events that contribute to emergent literacy. As youngsters closely explore the world around them, they may come across shapes in their environment that resemble letters of the alphabet. Parents and teachers can take children outdoors to play language and word games. Playground games, rhymes, verses, and songs allow youngsters to learn about language in a charming and engaging way as they interact closely with others. Nature can provide the creative setting for children's imaginative and narrative play too. The outdoor environment may give youngsters more space and options for pretend play and storytelling. Through these experiences, children may construct tales to reenact and share based on what nature holds. My own children devised an outdoor play episode in which they stepped into the role of marine biologists and cared for sea creatures and marine life.

Today, society is faced with more changes and obstacles that are transforming the nature of outdoor play. With the rise of urban development, rapid increase in technology, demands of daily living and increased concerns for children's safety, youngsters have limited time and space to play outdoors and enjoy the experiences that nature provides. Making time for play-based learning and discovery of nature through field trips, classroom activity centres, and playground lessons can provide the space and security for children to enjoy outdoor learning and environmental experiences throughout the school day. After all, time spent in nature inspires learning, curiosity, questions, and discoveries of the world around us. Perhaps the greatest gift that these events allow us all is the universal human need to feel connected to the natural world we live in.

Art as Literacy

Children are young artists who enjoy painting, sculpting, drawing, and making music. Youngsters use art as a form of meaning-making that reveals their understanding of the world (Albers, 1997). Learning through the arts allows children to develop literacy. "If we consider literacy holistically we realize that it grows out of non-verbal contexts out of play, out of sociality, and out of physical activities that include the arts" (Moffet, 1994, p. 239). By broadening our view of texts and print-based concepts of meaning making, we can begin to move past conventional forms of written language to embrace works of art, music, and drama as pathways to literacy (Harste, Woodward, and Burke, 1984; Albers, 1997).

Early childhood art experiences form the groundwork for literacy building. From the time that youngsters first pick up a crayon or paintbrush, they learn to use symbols to make marks on paper. These early forms of childhood art become "the very foundation upon which all later reading, writing and drawing are built" (Striker, 2001, p. 2). The scribbles and drawings produced in children's first masterpieces often signify the beginning of writing. In the act of drawing and scribbling, youngsters put early writing skills (fine motor abilities, arm and hand movements) to practice (Striker, 2001). Children start off filling the page with squiggles and shapes they have invented. Soon these shapes and symbols turn into letters they know. Children's early markings on paper are closely related to forms of the alphabet. In fact, all of the world's alphabets are derived from the scribbles, lines, and shapes that youngsters experiment with (Kellogg and O'Dell, 1967; Striker, 2001). As children learn to use lines and shapes to represent their drawings and writing, they begin to produce and recognize symbols needed for literacy. Scribbling and drawing introduces children to the symbol recognition and formation required in later reading and writing (Striker, 2001). Producing art contributes to children's language development by naturally leading them toward symbol systems they will encounter in print. Once youngsters can distinguish between drawing and writing, the marks they produce on paper begin to show signs of convention, such as print concepts (e.g., directionality) and other writing features. Engaging in art activities, like early scribbling and drawing, lays the foundation for literacy by preparing children with knowledge and skills that will make it easier to read and write later on.

Early art experiences form the basis for learning about life. Producing artwork gives children occasions for problem solving, creative thinking, and self-expression as they make new discoveries, explore materials, and cope with emotions. Children's engagements in the arts provide important insights into literacy

Producing different works of art enables young people to construct meaning using a process method and genre approach that draws on specific elements, forms, and concepts that mirror print-based literacy.

(Albers, 1997). As youngsters produce drawings, paintings, sculptures and other creative works, they take part in a process of art and meaning making that closely resembles print literacy (Albers, 1997). Children learn to use art tools, media, and techniques to construct meaning in artwork that reflects their personal experiences and interpretations of life. To turn out drawings, sculptures, paintings and other works of art, young people need to generate and draft ideas, discuss plans with others, form, critique, revise, edit, and reflect on their work. The process of art making is similar to that in print-based literacy that uses the writing process and authoring cycle to develop written texts (Harste, Short and Burke, 1988; Albers, 1997). As children engage in a variety of art experiences, they begin to experiment with elements, principles, tools, and concepts that are specific to the forms they are producing. Examining and making different styles of art allows young people to grow in their understanding of form (e.g., painting) and genre (still life, landscape, abstract, portrait) as it relates to art. The process of making art enables children to try out various genres, styles and techniques that may parallel the work done in writing. Producing different works of art enables young people to construct meaning using a process method and genre approach that draws on specific elements, forms and concepts that mirror print-based literacy.

The process of art making is important to children's literacy development in many ways. Becoming inspired to learn and produce works of art can lead children towards art books and collections they may enjoy reading out of interest. By providing youngsters with literature about famous art, artists, and art making, young readers can gather information and ideas from different genres (non-fiction and instructional texts like *Usborne The Children's Book of Art, The Usborne Art Treasury, The Usborne Complete Book of Art Ideas*). As children uncover artwork and projects in a variety of resources, they may discover styles, techniques, and methods that can shape their understanding and appreciation of art.

Literacy grows from the study and reflection of art (Albers, 1997). Artwork provides meaningful topics for discussion (D. Thompson, 2002). Through the examination of different works of art that young people or professional artists have made, children can begin to talk about and critique artwork in ways that help them make meaning, express their growing understandings, and note effective techniques. As youngsters study and reflect on artwork, they begin to interpret, discuss, and write about art in expressive ways. Moving towards the study of art can turn lessons in art making and reflection into rich language experiences where children can "read" art as "texts" together. Interpreting art through discussion and reflection can expand children's visual knowledge, vocabularies, and perspectives as they come to view the world through different aesthetic works.

Art production allows young people a means of expression and form of communication in itself. While young people can gain insights and communication skills by studying art closely, the process of art making can bridge the gap between spoken words and the page. Like print-based literacy, many children use oral language to map out drawings, paintings, and other works of art (e.g., dramatic works). As youngsters produce various art forms, they often narrate their actions step-by-step as they create works. Many children use talk to label and dictate what they draw, paint, or sculpt (C. Thompson, 2002). The process of planning and "storying" while making art also supports literacy learning.

Children's experiences in the arts move beyond the frames of drawing, painting, and sculpting to include print making, drama, music, children's literature, and other creative forms (puppetry, dance, poetry). Many art engagements provide occasions for literacy learning and language development in the formative years. Music is a natural way that children learn to communicate. Through the joyful sounds and rhythms of nursery rhymes, chants, clapping games, action songs, marches, dances, and other musical activities, youngsters develop skills that are essential for literacy.

Children's musical encounters in the early years contribute in many ways to their reading and writing abilities. Through tapping, singing, rapping, and other musical activities, youngsters are introduced to the sounds, patterns, rhythms, and cadences of written language that build phonological awareness and phonic knowledge (Palmer and Bayley, 2005). Marching, dances, action songs, and finger rhymes help children develop the motor skills, hand-eye coordination, and muscular control needed for handwriting and understanding print concepts like directionality (Palmer and Bayley, 2005). Music provides children with a language experience that enables them to play with words as they innovate on texts they know by adding new verses or creating different variations of familiar songs in text reconstructions. Through music, youngsters encounter various genres and text features that are specific to this art form (verse, chorus). The experience of reading and making music also allows children to grow in literacy as they encounter musical notations and lyrics on song sheets and picture books based on popular children's tunes (books like *Baby Beluga, Wheels on the Bus* by Raffi). Youngsters can respond to literature by turning stories into action songs or reenacting scenes set to music. Children may even become inspired to pick up the pen to construct their own songs and experiment with musical notation. The process of composing music parallels the steps of the writing process, giving children genuine writing practice as they generate ideas, draft lyrics, edit and revise words, and share their songs with others. Using instruments and vocals to play with language can make literacy learning fun too. Introducing props (finger puppets) and adding movement to songs, nursery rhymes, poetry and children's verses can transform a musical or language experience into a drama performance.

As children explore the art of drama, they may come to produce role-plays, mimes, games, improvisations, tableaux, and other dramatizations based on literature, life, and play events. In planning out these performances, young people may move fluidly through the roles of acting out and talking about the drama in a form of metacommunication that is central to literacy development, as discussed previously. Like socio-dramatic play, experiences in drama also serve literacy in many ways. Many of the techniques and strategies used in drama including role-playing, improvisation, scripting plays, interviewing, and writing-in-role involve children in the construction of narrative that leads to a stronger understanding of literary genres, word knowledge, and effective language use both orally and in print. Apart from music and drama, literacy through the arts can be enriched through poetry experiences where writing is explored as an art form rather than a literary skill (D. Thompson, 2002).

Awakening children to the arts may establish many pathways to literacy. Art is a source of literacy learning both at home and at school. By engaging children in a variety of art experiences, teachers and parents can create endless opportunities to promote literacy and language development in the formative years. Children are natural artists who are capable of using creative tools to learn. Whether using a crayon to make scribbles on a page, moving a paintbrush across a canvas, following the lyrics on song sheet, or writing a script for a drama performance, children put literacy to work in the art experiences they take part in naturally each day. Youngsters are adept at using the tools, strategies, and techniques they gain from life events to make meaning. While children's experiences in the arts allow them to build the essential skills needed for literacy, youngsters can develop their tool-using capacities in other ways too.

Computers, Technology, and Media Literacy

Children's lives today are full of technologies of every kind (Alliance for Childhood, 2000). From an early age, youngsters learn to master remote controls, electronic games, computer programs, interactive media, and other portable digital devices. Technology is now the dominant feature of our rapidly changing world. High-tech devices are continually being updated or replaced with more advanced tools. Since the time of our own childhoods, many devices have even grown obsolete. Long before today's children enter the workforce, technology will revolutionize itself into new formats we can only imagine. Computers, media tools, and screen-based technologies will remain a significant part of children's lives into the future (Burke, 2010). The challenge comes in preparing young people to use rapidly changing technology in ways that fit into the 21st century. The goal of technology, computer, and media literacy is to educate children to use these tools in creative and critical ways to enhance their lives (Alliance for Childhood, 2000).

Traditional ways of thinking may have us believe that part of the problem with computers and other forms of technology is the amount of use and type of interaction that takes place. After all, many children spend countless hours watching television or interacting with computer screens in passive forms of play or viewing. Some participate actively in violent and aggressive video games that may be harmful. Many popular games and films deal with ethical and moral issues that are inappropriate for young children. As children work their way through endless levels of pointless games, they may develop rigid and narrow ways of thinking.

These realities hinder our views on computer use, leading many cautious parents and teachers to limit children's interactions to educational games and conventional learning software that resemble old-fashioned worksheets with simple animation added in (Burke, 2010). Despite their explicit goals and use for skill reinforcement, these programs may take the power of invention out of the creative hands of children. By watching youngsters innovatively use technology, we may start to understand the potential it holds for learning.

From the time that children start to pick up pencils and books, many also learn to use computers and other screen devices almost effortlessly. More parents and teachers are beginning to embrace the use of technology as a tool for living, one that will inevitably be part of children's lives in the future. Young people are already using computers, technology, and media as a source of play, communication, and entertainment. Nevertheless, computer games, on-line programs, and interactive media also may present children with valuable learning experiences in which they can actively participate. Although the educational outcomes may seem implicit in some uses, children's mastery of these digital games, sites, and devices may reveal growing sophistication and expertise. Young people are discovering resourceful ways of using computer technology and media to enhance their cognitive development (Burke, 2010). Playing games and watching television can help children learn facts, information, and skills such as problem solving and inventive thinking. To promote positive social, emotional, and intellectual outcomes, software games, websites (on-line games), films, and television programs should be carefully chosen and used in moderation (Burke, 2010). As parents and teachers, we must look for balance in the use of technology in children's world. At the same time, we must also accept that the advanced number of software programs, game systems, interactive websites, DVDs, and other digital media are quickly becoming the new texts of childhood. By taking these realities into account, we can start to provide children with experiences where they can use a full range of technologies as resources for learning and literacy building.

As with print materials, computer games, interactive software, and media programs serve as tools for literacy. When playing on-line games, youngsters enter an immersive environment that requires them to use basic literacy skills. As children navigate these virtual worlds to complete related on-line tasks, they learn to follow directions through digital reading. In searching the internet for play or learning resources, youngsters scan information on screen and use other reading strategies to carry out their investigations. The world of on-line communication has opened up possibilities for children to write all the time by corresponding with others through e-mail, texting, and social networking. Young people are inventing their own genre forms and conventions (unconventional grammar, spelling, and punctuation) to communicate and make meaning. Children's comfort with technology allows them to produce different forms of digital media (personal websites, blogs) with self-direction and ease. Watching on-line video clips, downloading music, and creating multimedia presentations give children advanced opportunities to use technology as a new form of literacy. More and more classrooms are using technology resources, such as interactive whiteboards, to effectively teach literacy, print concepts, and other topics too. These are just some of the positive ways that technology can be integrated at home and at school to promote literacy.

For today's children, nothing is more authentic than computers and television (Burke, 2010). As we work towards finding balance in children's lives, we need to look for ways of incorporating these "out-of-school" texts into their school experiences. We must find value in family literacy practices such as television and movie viewing. Films and television present children with visual narratives for them to "read" as texts (Marhsall and Werndley, 2002; Rowsell, 2006). These media formats are built on a narrative framework that can enhance children's understanding of story. As young people watch movies and television programs, they may note narrative features, organizational structures, visual-image effects, or genres that may be specific to film and television, thereby expanding their notion of text. When children study film alongside literature, they may start to make comparisons between the cinematic elements in a movie and the narrative aspects in the book. As young people compare and contrast genres and programs, they begin to develop critical listening and viewing skills that can deepen their text experience. Watching movies and television programs can lead to critical literacy work that calls children to interpret visual images, study character portrayals, draw inferences, and examine issues more closely. These viewing events can lead to literacy experiences in which children can recall mass-produced texts in oral recounts and critical discussions. The possibilities for media literacy are endless.

The world of interactive media, computers, and technology has the power to change all our lives. Allowing children time, space and materials to use these advanced tools will inevitably help them grow in literacy. Young people are already entering school with an intricate set of knowledge and skills that emerge from using media and technology. As educators, we need to find ways of integrating a wide range of interactive texts and multifaceted tool-capacities that students bring with them into classroom learning experiences. In working to encompass the technologies and literacies that children experience outside of school, we begin moving towards a new form of curricula that expands our notion of text and our understanding of how youngsters learn to read and write.

Today, teachers and parents are challenged to rethink the paths to literacy we have conventionally known (Kress, 1997). Children come into literacy in ways that go beyond traditional reading and writing. While many early childhood experiences, like those explored in this book, lay the strong foundations for literacy, youngsters are discovering building blocks of their own. Children, we have seen, are sophisticated language users who find multimodal ways (visual, audio, written, movement) of making meaning in their daily lives. Children's interactions with print have grown to include various kinds of text from books, magazines, film, video, television, computer games and cultural resources (religious texts, folk literature). Young people encounter print and visual media everywhere, allowing literacy to take place in any context. From these understandings, a field of New Literacy Studies has emerged to move us forward in our thinking and teaching (Kress, 1997; Rowsell, 2006). In order to impart children with the knowledge and skills they will need to enter an innovative workforce in the 21st century, we must embrace the growing technologies and new literacies that exist in our rapidly changing world.

Life affords children with many pathways to literacy. Reading, writing, talking, playing, drawing, print and nature encounters, home literacy practices, and technology, all work together to establish a strong literacy foundation in childhood. As teachers and parents, we can build on the understandings we know to provide children with more rich occasions to grow in literacy. The prospects are inspiring and never-ending. Grasping the possibilities puts our own imaginations to work.

Appendix

Reading is an interactive process in which the reader uses a variety of strategies and problem-solving techniques to make meaning of texts. Understanding the cueing systems is key to supporting children's literacy development.

Language Cueing Systems

System	Description
Semantic —Knowledge of the World and Life Experiences	Semantic cues come from a reader's prior knowledge, personal experiences, and conceptual background about the topic or subject material in a text. This knowledge is gained through everyday life experiences and prior learning that provide the conceptual framework and context for readers to attach meaning to the words in print. To understand a text, readers must have some pre-existing knowledge of the experiences and concepts in the selection in order to integrate new facts and information into their personal experience base. Without this frame of reference, texts based on unfamiliar events or "out of reach" life experiences will be more difficult to comprehend.
Syntactic —Knowledge of Words and Language	Syntactic cues consist of the information provided by the grammar structures and syntax of the English language. This information comes from the vocabulary, sentences, grammatical structures, language patterns, and word functions that are part of both spoken and written language. Understanding word order, sentence construction, and word function are useful to readers as they draw on their knowledge of grammatical features and common sentence patterns to predict upcoming words in texts. When readers encounter an unknown word, they may use syntactic cues to approximate the type of word needed to make meaning. Children must be able to use syntactic cueing strategies to read proficiently and fully comprehend texts.
Graphophonic —Knowledge of Letters and Sounds	Graphophonic cues provide information based on the relationship between sounds or words and the written symbols of language or conventions of print. These visual arrays of cues are drawn from letters of the alphabet and the sounds of individual letters and combinations of letters that we hear in words. Because English does not have a complete one-to-one correspondence between letters and sounds, between sounds and symbols, or between spoken and written forms of language, children who are learning to read benefit from activities that focus on aspects of letter-sound relationships in order to apply this knowledge to reading actual texts.
Pragmatic —Knowledge of Text	Pragmatic cues refer to the characteristics of different types of texts and their appearance on a page. Print materials include a variety of genres and styles that are organized in specific ways or forms (e.g., menus, lists, novels, poems). The language, function, style, syntax, and other text features of narrative and expository texts are different. Knowing the print characteristics of different types of texts helps readers identify the genre and determine the processes they will use to read the material. The ability to distinguish between different genres (picture book, magazine article, and recipe, for example) helps readers organize their thinking around a text and use this information to understand a variety of print forms..